APOLOGETICS TO THE GLORY OF GOD

AN INTRODUCTION

▼

JOHN M. FRAME

P&R PUBLISHING
P.O. BOX 817 • PHILLIPSBURG • NEW JERSEY 08865

Quotations from the English Bible are taken from the HOLY BIBLE, NEW INTERNATIONAL VERSION. Copyright © 1973, 1978, 1984 International Bible Society. Used by permission of Zondervan Bible Publishers.

Printed in the United States of America

Library of Congress Cataloging-in-Publication Data

Frame, John M., 1939-
    Apologetics to the glory of God : an introduction / John M. Frame.
        p.   cm.
    Includes bibliographical references and indexes.
    ISBN 0-87552-243-2
    1. Apologetics—20th century. I. Title.
BT1102.F74 1994
239—dc20   93-47929

To all my students,
from whom I have learned much

Contents

Preface

As the title indicates, this book is an "introduction" rather than a comprehensive system of apologetics. However, it is intended for people who can do college-level reading and are serious about resolving issues of some difficulty.

Those who want or need a more comprehensive, philosophical background for considering the issues of apologetics should peruse my *Doctrine of the Knowledge of God*. That is a somewhat larger study, presenting the general theory of knowledge which underlies this introduction to apologetics. Many of the points made in this book are discussed there at greater length. The epistemology developed in that book is applied in the present volume to specific apologetic issues. This book will, I trust, be more suitable as a textbook in apologetics.

In good conscience I can describe this volume as "Reformed" apologetics and as belonging to that special kind of Reformed apologetics developed by Cornelius Van Til. I do not necessarily agree with every sentence Van Til wrote; indeed, some Van Tillians will describe this work as "revisionist." But I believe that Van Til's approach is still the best foundation for Christian apologetics at the present time. However, although I will refer to Van Til from time to time, it will not be my goal in this book to explain Van Til or to show the precise relationships between his ideas and mine. That will come later, God willing. I am preparing another book, which will attempt to comprehensively analyze and evaluate Van Til's work. (I am praying that it will be published in or before 1995, the one hundredth anniversary of his birth.) That book will show more adequately than I can here why I continue to follow, and occasionally depart from, the Van Tillian model.

Why another introduction to apologetics? Well, Van Til's work is still valuable, but it has always been in need of translation into more easily understood language. I think also that it needs some revision, as I have indicated, lest its weaknesses obscure its tremendously important insights. And, apart from the writings of Van Til, few if any introductions to apologetics go to Scripture itself to ask in some detail concerning the norms for apologetics. I hope this book will fill that gap.

One weakness in Van Til's own writings is the lack of specific arguments. Van Til always said that there was an "absolutely certain argument" for Christianity, but he rarely produced an example, except in the barest outline form. I am somewhat less inclined to make the claim of an "absolutely certain argument," for reasons that appear within. But this book does include some specific examples of reasoning which the reader is free to criticize or emulate.

Although this book is a bit heavy on theoretical matters, I realize that the Reformed apologist has a responsibility to speak in ordinary language. Chapter 9 is one step in that direction, although in the final analysis others may be better suited than I to do this kind of popularization. At any rate, if the reader is unsure about his aptitude for or interest in the theoretical portion of this book, he might still find chapter 9 helpful, and I would suggest that he read that chapter first.

Besides Van Til, I am indebted to a great many other people who have, in one way or another, contributed to these thoughts and their publication here. I would like to give special thanks to McIlwain Memorial Presbyterian Church of Pensacola, Florida, for inviting me to lecture at their Pensacola Theological Institute in August, 1990. The institute audiences gave me some good feedback and encouragement, motivating me to develop the material (here greatly expanded) for publication.

I am also indebted to a number of friends who read the first draft of this book and gave me much encouragement and many suggestions. Jim Scott did a fine job in editing the manuscript for publication. Special thanks go to Derke Bergsma, Bill Edgar, Thom Notaro, Scott Oliphint, Jim Jordan, and R. C. Sproul, who contributed many helpful ideas concerning both the broad structure of the book and many of its details. I could not accept all of their suggestions (indeed, some of them contradicted others!), but I have taken all of them seriously, and that process of self-critical thought has been invaluable. I trust that this book will, in turn, stimulate others to respond to the apologetic challenge for the love of God and the fulfillment of Jesus' Great Commission.

Frank, introduces himself as a Reformed apologite. falling into the same count as Van T.I. Frame pointing out a lack of specifity in Til's model promising specific examples in this text.

ONE

▼

Apologetics: The Basics

In 1 Peter 3:15–16, the apostle exhorts his readers:

> But in your hearts set apart Christ as Lord. Always be prepared to give an answer to everyone who asks you to give the reason for the hope that you have. But do this with gentleness and respect, keeping a clear conscience, so that those who speak maliciously against your good behavior in Christ may be ashamed of their slander.

Definitions

Christian apologetics (which has nothing to do with "apologizing") seeks to serve God and the church by helping believers to carry out the mandate of 1 Peter 3:15–16. We may define it as *the discipline that teaches Christians how to give a reason for their hope.*[1]

---

[1] In *The Doctrine of the Knowledge of God* (Phillipsburg, N.J.: Presbyterian and Reformed, 1987)—henceforth cited as *DKG*—which relates apologetics to other forms of human knowledge, I define apologetics as "the application of Scripture to unbelief" (p. 87). That shows that apologetics is part of Christian theology, which I define in general as "the application of Scrip-

I believe that we can distinguish three aspects of apologetics, which we will discuss in detail in later chapters:

1. *Apologetics as proof:* presenting a rational basis for faith or "proving Christianity to be true." Jesus and the apostles often offered evidence to people who had difficulty believing that the gospel was true. Note John 14:11; 20:24–31; 1 Corinthians 15:1–11. Believers themselves sometimes doubt, and at that point apologetics becomes useful for them even apart from its role in dialogue with unbelievers. That is to say, apologetics confronts unbelief in the believer as well as in the unbeliever.

2. *Apologetics as defense:* answering the objections of unbelief. Paul describes his mission as "defending and confirming the gospel" (Phil. 1:7; cf. v. 16). "Confirming" may refer to number 1 above, but "defending" is more specifically focused on giving answers to objections. Much of Paul's writing in the New Testament is apologetic in this sense. Think of how many times he responds to imaginary (or real) objectors in his letter to the Romans. Think of how often Jesus deals with the objections of religious leaders in the gospel of John.

3. *Apologetics as offense:* attacking the foolishness (Ps. 14:1; 1 Cor. 1:18–2:16) of unbelieving thought. In view of the importance of number 2, it is not surprising that some will define apologetics as "the defense of the faith."[2] But that definition can be misleading. God calls his people, not only to answer the objections of unbelievers, but also to go on the attack against falsehood. Paul says, "We demolish arguments and every pretension that sets itself up against the knowledge

---

ture." The definition given in the present volume arises from 1 Peter 3:15–16 and focuses on the person of the apologist rather than upon the discipline of apologetics in the abstract, but in my view it is logically equivalent to the definition in *DKG*. The "reason for our hope" is precisely the certitude of God's Word, as we shall see. (Notice, by the way, how a word may have more than one useful definition.)

[2]Van Til's major exposition of his apologetics is entitled *The Defense of the Faith* (Philadelphia: Presbyterian and Reformed, 1955; 2d ed., 1963). But his apologetics is certainly less "defensive" and more "offensive" than most others.

of God, and we take captive every thought to make it obedient to Christ" (2 Cor. 10:5). Non-Christian thinking is "foolishness," according to Scripture (1 Cor. 1:18–2:16; 3:18–23), and one function of apologetics is to expose that foolishness for what it is.

These three types of apologetics are perspectivally related.[3] That is to say, each one, done fully and rightly, includes the other two, so that each is a way of looking at (i.e., a perspective upon) the whole apologetic enterprise. To give a full account of the rationale of belief (no. 1), one must vindicate that rationale against the objections (no. 2) and alternatives (no. 3) advanced by unbelievers. Similarly, a full account of number 2 will include numbers 1 and 3, and a full account of number 3 will involve numbers 1 and 2.[4] So in a way the three forms of apologetics are equivalent. But it is good for us nevertheless to distinguish these perspectives, for they certainly represent genuinely different emphases which complement and strengthen one another. For example, an argument for the existence of God (perspective no. 1) which takes no account of unbelievers' objections to such arguments (no. 2) or to the ways in which unbelievers satisfy themselves with alternative worldviews (no. 3) will to that extent be a weakened argument. So it is often useful in apologetics to ask whether an argument of type 1 can be improved by some supplemental argumentation of type 2, 3, or both.[5]

Presuppositions

Our theme verse, 1 Peter 3:15, begins by telling us, "In your hearts set apart Christ as Lord." The apologist must be a be-

---

[3]There are many such relationships in Scripture; see *DKG* for more examples.

[4]So Van Til might well have argued that by "defense of the faith" he intended to include positive evidence for Christianity and attacks on the inadequacies of unbelief.

[5]For students of my three perspectives in *DKG*, constructive apologetics is normative, offensive apologetics is situational, and defensive apologetics is existential. You figure it out!

liever in Christ, committed to the lordship of Christ (cf. Rom. 10:9; 1 Cor. 12:3; Phil. 2:11).[6]

Some theologians present apologetics as if it were almost an exception to this commitment. They tell us that when we argue with unbelievers, we should not argue on the basis of criteria or standards derived from the Bible. To argue that way, they say, would be biased. We should rather present to the unbeliever an unbiased argument, one that makes no religious assumptions pro or con, one that is neutral. We should, on this view, use criteria and standards that the unbeliever himself can accept. So logic, facts, experience, reason, and such become the sources of truth. Divine revelation, especially Scripture, is systematically excluded.[7]

This argument may appear to be simple common sense: since God and Scripture are precisely the matters in question, we obviously must not make assumptions about them in our argument. That would be circular thinking. It would also put an end to evangelism, for if we demand that the unbeliever assume God's existence and the authority of Scripture in order to enter the debate, he will never consent. Communication between believer and unbeliever will be impossible. Therefore, we must avoid making any such demands and seek to argue on a neutral basis. We may even boast to the unbeliever that our argument presupposes only the criteria that he himself readily accepts (whether logic, fact, consistency, or whatever).

This sort of apologetic is sometimes called the traditional or classical method,[8] because it claims many advocates down

---

[6]*DKG* includes quite a bit of reflection on the centrality of Jesus' lordship in Scripture, Christian theology, and the Christian life. In the light of this central and pervasive biblical teaching, recent assertions that one can be a believer without trusting Jesus as Lord must be rejected as not only wrong but wrongheaded. On the other hand, this teaching must not be confused with perfectionism. The sincere confession that Jesus is Lord marks the beginning, indeed the essence, of the Christian's testimony, but the young Christian only gradually and progressively comes to understand and act upon the full implications of Jesus' lordship.

[7]On the role of natural revelation, see the section so titled later in this chapter.

[8]One recent book that attacks Van Til's presuppositionalism and advocates

through church history, particularly the second-century Apologists (Justin Martyr, Athenagoras, Theophilus, and Aristides), the great thirteenth-century thinker Thomas Aquinas
and his many followers down to the present day, Joseph But-
ler (d. 1752) and his followers, and indeed the great majority
of apologists in our own time.[9]

In saying that traditional apologists espouse "neutrality,"
I am not arguing that they seek to put their Christian com-

---

the traditional approach is *Classical Apologetics,* by R. C. Sproul, John Gerstner, and Arthur Lindsley (Grand Rapids: Zondervan, 1984). On the other
side would be my *DKG* or any book of Van Til's, such as *The Defense of
the Faith.* See my review of the Sproul-Gerstner-Lindsley volume in the
Westminster Theological Journal 47, 2 (Fall 1985): 279–99. I've included it
as appendix A at the end of this book.

[9]My friend R. C. Sproul, in correspondence, insists that the classical tradition, notably Aquinas and Sproul(!), does not claim "neutrality," but rather
appeals to God's general revelation—his revelation in nature, history, and
conscience. (See the discussion of Romans 1 later in this chapter and the
discussion of natural revelation.) However, in this connection Aquinas distinguished not between natural and special revelation but rather between reason and faith—that is, between reasoning unaided by revelation and reasoning aided by it. Further, he (unlike Sproul, interestingly) had very little
practical awareness of the effects of sin upon human reasoning, so that he
was able to use the views and arguments of the pagan philosopher Aristotle
uncritically, with a few notable exceptions. Unlike Calvin, Aquinas did not
believe that one needs the "spectacles of Scripture" to rightly interpret God's
revelation in nature. In my view, Aquinas saw Aristotle's reasoning as neither pro- nor anti-Christian, but neutral. As for Sproul himself, I have nothing critical to say about his exposition of the effects of sin on unbelieving
reasoning in Rom. 1. He clearly denies the neutrality of unbelieving thought
(see *Classical Apologetics,* 39–63). Thus, he recognizes that the apologetic encounter between believer and unbeliever is not between two parties who are
seeking to think neutrally, but between an unbeliever who is biased against
the truth and a believer who is seeking to correct that bias and is therefore,
inevitably, biased in the opposite direction. But I don't find this discussion
consistent with the treatment of autonomy on pp. 231–40. To encourage the
unbeliever to think autonomously is to encourage him to think without the
correction of revelation—that is, to think "neutrally" (which is actually to
think disobediently, replacing God's standards with the unbeliever's own).
(For more detail on this point, see my review of *Classical Apologetics,* noted
earlier.) My guess is that the three authors of this book were not entirely
agreed among themselves. Making comparisons with books and articles these
gentlemen have written independently, I would guess that the treatment of
Romans 1 is the work of Sproul and pp. 231–40 is the work of Gerstner. I

mitment aside in doing apologetics. Indeed, many of them believe that their type of apologetic is warranted by Scripture and is thus very much a "setting apart of Christ as Lord." They do, however, tell the unbeliever to think neutrally during the apologetic encounter, and they do seek to develop a neutral argument, one that has no distinctively biblical presuppositions.

I am far from wishing to declare this tradition worthless. But on the precise point at issue, the question of neutrality, I do believe that its position is unbiblical. Peter's reasoning, in our theme verse, is very different. For Peter, apologetics is certainly not an exception to our overall commitment to Jesus' lordship. On the contrary, the apologetic situation is one in which we are especially to "set apart Christ as Lord," to speak and live in a way that exalts his lordship and encourages others to do so as well. In the larger context, Peter is telling his readers to do what is right, despite the opposition of unbelievers (vv. 13–14). He tells us not to fear them. Surely it was not his view that in apologetics we should set forth something less than the truth, out of fear that the truth itself might be rejected.

Peter tells us, on the contrary, that the lordship of Jesus (and hence the truth of his word, for how can we call him "Lord" and not do what he says [Luke 6:46]?) is our ultimate presupposition.[10] An ultimate presupposition is a basic heart-commitment, an ultimate trust. We trust Jesus Christ as a matter of eternal life or death. We trust his wisdom beyond all other wisdom. We trust his promises above all others. He calls

---

am happy to welcome R. C. Sproul as an honorary presuppositionalist, but I do hope he will keep talking to his colleagues about this matter.

[10]See *DKG*, 1–49, esp. p. 45. "Lord" in Scripture refers to the head of a covenant relationship. In that relationship, the Lord dictates to his covenant servants the way they are to live and promises them blessings for obedience and curses for disobedience. He also tells them of the blessings that he has already given to them—his "unmerited favor," or grace, which is to motivate their obedience. Without words of grace, law, and promise, there is no lordship. To recognize the Lord is to believe and obey his words above the words of anyone else. And to obey the Lord's words in that way is to accept them as one's ultimate presupposition.

us to give him all our loyalty and not allow any other loyalty to compete with him (Deut. 6:4ff.; Matt. 6:24; 12:30; John 14:6; Acts 4:12). We obey his law, even when it conflicts with lesser laws (Acts 5:29). Since we believe him more certainly than we believe anything else, he (and hence his Word) is the very *criterion*, the ultimate *standard* of truth. What higher standard could there possibly be? What standard is more authoritative? What standard is more clearly known to us (see Rom. 1:19–21)? What authority ultimately validates all other authorities?

The lordship of Christ is not only ultimate and unquestionable, not only above and beyond all other authorities, but also over all areas of human life. In 1 Corinthians 10:31 we read, "Whether you eat or drink or whatever you do, do it all for the glory of God" (cf. Rom. 14:23; 2 Cor. 10:5; Col. 3:17, 23; 2 Tim. 3:16–17). Our Lord's demand upon us is comprehensive. In all that we do, we must seek to please him. No area of human life is neutral.[11]

Surely this principle includes the area of thinking and knowing. The fear of the Lord is the very beginning of knowledge, says the author of Proverbs (1:7; cf. Ps. 111:10; Prov. 9:10). Those who are not brought to fear God by the new birth cannot even see the kingdom of God (John 3:3).

The point is not that unbelievers are simply ignorant of the truth. Rather, God has revealed himself to each person with unmistakable clarity, both in creation (Ps. 19; Rom.

---

[11]This was the insight of the great Dutch thinker Abraham Kuyper. He saw that the lordship of Christ requires radically different Christian forms of culture. Christians should be producing distinctively Christian art, science, philosophy, psychology, historical and biblical scholarship, and political and economic systems. And Christians should educate their children in distinctively Christian ways (note the God-saturated education urged in Deut. 6:6ff. after the challenge to love God exclusively). For many of us, such considerations mandate home schooling or Christian schools for our children, for how can we otherwise compete with up to seven hours a day of public-school secularism mandated by law? In any case, Christians may not take the easy road, uncritically following the thinking of the unbelieving world. Consider Kuyper's famous remark: Of all the territory in the creation, Jesus says, "It is mine."

1:18–21) and in man's own nature (Gen. 1:26ff.). In one sense, the unbeliever knows God (Rom. 1:21). At some level of his consciousness or unconsciousness, that knowledge remains.[12] But in spite of that knowledge, the unbeliever intentionally distorts the truth, exchanging it for a lie (Rom. 1:18–32; 1 Cor. 1:18–2:16 [note especially 2:14]; 2 Cor. 4:4). Thus, the non-Christian is "deceived" (Titus 3:3). He knows God (Rom. 1:21) and does not know him at the same time (1 Cor. 1:21; 2:14).[13] Plainly, these facts underscore the point that God's revelation must govern our apologetic approach. The unbeliever cannot (because he will not) come to faith apart from the biblical gospel of salvation. We would not know about the unbeliever's condition apart from Scripture. And we cannot address it apologetically unless we are ready to listen to Scripture's own principles of apologetics.

---

[12]Some have tried to stress the past (aorist) form of "know" in Rom. 1:21 to prove that the knowledge in view is past, not continuing into the present. Paul's purpose in this passage, however, is part of his larger purpose in 1:1–3:21, which is to show that all have sinned and therefore that none can be justified through the works of the law (3:19–21). In chap. 1 he shows us that even without access to the written law, Gentiles are guilty of sin before God (chap. 2 deals with the Jews). How can they be held responsible without access to the written law? Because of the knowledge of God that they have gained from creation. If that knowledge were relegated to the past, we would have to conclude that the Gentiles in the present are not responsible for their actions, contrary to 3:9. The past form is used (participially) because the past tense is dominant in the context. That is appropriate, because Paul intends to embark on a "history of suppressing the truth" in vv. 21–32. But he clearly does not regard the events of vv. 21–32 merely as past history. He clearly is using this history to describe the present condition of Gentiles before God. Therefore, the aorist *gnontes* should not be pressed to indicate past time exclusively. As the suppression continues, so does the knowledge that renders the suppression culpable.

[13]Obviously, there is some complexity here that requires further explanation. There are different kinds of knowledge in view, for the Christian's knowledge of God (which the unbeliever lacks) is very different from the unbeliever's own knowledge of God (Rom. 1:21, 32). Further, there is psychological complexity: the unbeliever knows things at one level of his consciousness that he seeks to banish from other levels. To put it as simply as I can, he knows God, he knows what God requires, but he does not want that knowledge to influence his decisions, except negatively: knowledge of God's will tells him how to disobey God. See *DKG*, 1–61.

But this means not only that the *apologist* must "set apart Jesus as Lord," but also that his *argument* must presuppose that lordship. Our argument must be an exhibit of that knowledge, that wisdom, which is based on the "fear of the Lord," not an exhibition of unbelieving foolishness. Therefore, apologetic argument is no more neutral than any other human activity. In apologetic argument, as in everything else we do, we must presuppose the truth of God's Word. We either accept God's authority or we do not, and not to do so is sin. It doesn't matter that we sometimes find ourselves conversing with non-Christians. Then too—perhaps especially then (for then we are bearing witness)—we must be faithful to our Lord's revelation.

To tell the unbeliever that we can reason with him on a neutral basis, however that claim might help to attract his attention, is a lie. Indeed, it is a lie of the most serious kind, for it falsifies the very heart of the gospel—that Jesus Christ is *Lord*. For one thing, there is no neutrality. Our witness is either God's wisdom or the world's foolishness. There is nothing in between. For another thing, even if neutrality were possible, that route would be forbidden to us.

Circular Argument?

Does this mean that we are called to embrace circular argument? Only in one sense. We are not called to use arguments like "The Bible is true; therefore, the Bible is true." It is quite legitimate, as we shall see, to argue on the basis of evidence, such as the testimony of five hundred witnesses to the Resurrection (1 Cor. 15:6). Eyewitness accounts may be used argumentatively as follows: "If Jesus' post-Resurrection appearances are well attested, then the Resurrection is a fact. His post-Resurrection appearances are well attested; therefore, the Resurrection is a fact." This is not a circular argument on any reasonable definition of circularity. And yet a certain circularity becomes evident when someone asks, "What are your ultimate criteria for good attestation?" or "What broad view of human

9

knowledge permits you to reason from eyewitness testimony to
a miraculous fact?" The empiricist philosophy of David Hume,
to use only one example, does not allow for that kind of argument. The fact is that the Christian here is presupposing a Christian epistemology—a view of knowledge, testimony, witness, appearance, and fact that is subject to Scripture. In other words,
he is using scriptural standards to prove scriptural conclusions.[14]

Does that procedure deserve to be condemned as "circular"? Everyone else reasons the same way. Every philosophy
must use its own standards in proving its conclusions; otherwise, it is simply inconsistent. Those who believe that human
reason is the ultimate authority (rationalists) must presuppose
the authority of reason in their arguments for rationalism.
Those who believe in the ultimacy of sense experience must
presuppose it in arguing for their philosophy (empiricism).
And skeptics must be skeptical of their own skepticism (a fact
that is, of course, the Achilles' heel of skepticism). The point
is that when one is arguing for an ultimate criterion, whether
Scripture, the Koran, human reason, sensation, or whatever,
one must use criteria compatible with that conclusion. If that
is circularity, then everybody is guilty of circularity.[15]

Does this fact eliminate the possibility of communication
between believer and unbeliever? It might seem so. The Christian argues on biblical criteria that the Resurrection is a fact.
The non-Christian replies that he cannot accept those criteria and that he will not accept the Resurrection unless we
prove it by, say, the standards of Hume's empiricism. We re-

---

[14]This epistemology is uniquely biblical in the sense that an unbeliever cannot consistently accept it. Indeed, the revelation of God in creation and in
Scripture is central to it. Any theory of knowledge must specify the ultimate standard or criterion for determining truth and falsity. The Christian's
ultimate standard is God's word in Scripture; the unbeliever's ultimate standard must be located elsewhere. See *DKG*, in which this epistemology is
worked out in some detail.

[15]Granted these clarifications, I don't care very much whether the Christian apologist accepts or rejects the term *circular* to describe his argument.
There are obvious dangers of misunderstanding in using it, dangers that I
sought to brave in *DKG*. But I am more inclined now to say to my critics,
"Granted your definition of circularity, I don't believe in it."

ply that we cannot accept Hume's presuppositions. The unbeliever says he cannot accept ours. Does that end the conversation?

Certainly not, for several reasons.

In the first place, as I have said, Scripture tells us that God has revealed himself clearly to the unbeliever, even to such an extent that the unbeliever knows God (Rom. 1:21). Although he represses that knowledge (vv. 21ff.), there is at some level of his consciousness a memory of that revelation. It is against this memory that he sins, and it is because of that memory that he is held responsible for those sins. At that level, he knows that empiricism is wrong and that Scripture's standards are right. We direct our apologetic witness not to his empiricist epistemology or whatever, but to his memory of God's revelation and to the epistemology implicit in that revelation. To do that, to accomplish such meaningful communication, we not only may but must use Christian criteria, rather than those of unbelieving epistemology. So when the unbeliever says "I can't accept your presuppositions," we reply: "Well, let's talk some more, and maybe they will become more attractive to you (just as you hope yours will become more attractive to me) as we expound our ideas in greater depth. In the meantime, let's just keep using our respective presuppositions and move along to some matters we haven't discussed."

In the second place, our witness to the unbeliever never comes alone. If God chooses to use our witness for his purposes, then he always adds a supernatural element to that witness—the Holy Spirit, working in and with the word (Rom. 15:18–19; 1 Cor. 2:4–5, 12ff.; 2 Cor. 3:15–18; 1 Thess. 1:5 [cf. 2:13]; 2 Thess. 2:13–14). If we have doubts about our own ability to communicate, for whatever reason, we need not doubt the ability of the Holy Spirit. And if our witness is fundamentally his tool, then our strategy must be dictated by his Word, not by our supposedly common-sense suppositions.

In the third place, this is in fact what we do in similar cases that are not normally considered religious. Imagine

11

someone living in a dreamworld—perhaps a paranoid, who believes that everyone is out to kill him. We'll call him Oscar. Let's say that Oscar presupposes this horror, so that every bit of evidence to the contrary is twisted and made to fit the conclusion. Every kind deed, for example, becomes in Oscar's view evidence of a nefarious plot to catch him off guard and plunge a knife into his ribs. Oscar is doing what unbelievers do, according to Romans 1:21ff.—exchanging the truth for a lie. How can we help him? What shall we say to him? What presuppositions, what criteria, what standards would we employ? Certainly not his, for to do that would lead us to embrace his paranoia. Certainly not "neutral" criteria, for there are none. One must either accept his presupposition or reject it. Of course, the answer is that we reason with him according to the truth as we perceive it, even though that truth conflicts with his deepest presuppositions. On some occasions, he might answer, "Well, we seem to be reasoning on different assumptions, so we really cannot get anywhere." But on other occasions, our true reasoning might penetrate his defenses. For Oscar is, after all, a human being. At some level, we assume, he knows that everyone is not out to kill him. At some level, he is capable of hearing and being changed. Paranoids do sometimes, after all, revert to sanity. We speak the truth to him in the hope that that will happen, and in the knowledge that if words are to help at all in this situation, they must convey the truth, not further error, to bring healing.

I take it, then, that a "presuppositional"[16] approach to apologetics is warranted not only in Scripture, but also in common sense!

---

[16]I do not particularly like the term *presuppositional* as a description of Van Til's apologetics or my own, although it is often used in this way. Presuppositions are often contrasted with evidences, so that to call a system presuppositional tends to convey the message that that system recognizes the importance of presuppositions but despises evidences. Gordon Clark used the term of himself, and rightly so, because he had a very skeptical view of what could be known through human sense experience, and thus a skeptical view of what is usually called "evidence." He believed that the term *knowledge* should be reserved only for what we learn from Scripture. Van

In the fourth place, Christian apologetics can take many forms. If the unbeliever objects to the "circularity" of the Christian's evidential arguments, the Christian can simply change to another kind of argument, such as an "offensive" apologetic against the unbeliever's own worldview or epistemology. That apologetic will also be circular in the precise sense noted above, but less obviously so. It could be presented Socratically, as a series of questions: How do *you* account for the universality of logical laws?, How do *you* arrive at the judgment that human life is worth living?, etc. Or, perhaps, as the prophet Nathan did with King David, when David would not otherwise repent of his sin (2 Sam. 11, 12), we can tell the unbeliever a parable. Maybe we can tell the one about the rich fool (Luke 12:6–21). Those who believe that presuppositionalism eliminates communication between believer and unbeliever underestimate God's power to reach the unbelieving heart. They also underestimate the variety and richness of a biblical apologetic, the creativity that God has given to us as his spokesmen, and the many forms that biblical apologetic can take.

Til, however, did not have such a skeptical view of sense experience, did not believe that knowledge was restricted to the Bible in that way, and was not inclined to reject the use of evidence. Thus, the term *presuppositional,* used in that sense, is not an adequate description of Van Til's position or mine. Others, such as (I believe) John Gerstner, misunderstand Van Til's use of the term. They stress the *pre* in *presupposition* and thus take it that a presupposition is something that one believes *before* (temporally) one believes anything else. This is wrong. The *pre* should be understood mainly as an indicator of eminence (e.g., *pre*eminence), not temporal priority. (However, there is a sense in which the Christian presupposition—i.e., the knowledge of the truth that even unbelievers have while dishonoring it—is temporally prior: it is present from the beginning of life.) Still others equate *presupposition* with *hypothesis* or assume it to be an arbitrary, groundless supposition. (On Van Til's view, presuppositions are grounded in divine revelation and are categorical, not hypothetical.) With such confusions abroad, I am reluctant to use the term at all! Still, I don't want to quibble over words, and the term has become a standard label for all of those who understand that there is no religious neutrality in thought and knowledge. So I will occasionally use that label of myself and Van Til, by way of accommodation, and also to emphasize what we share with Clark and others: the rejection of neutrality.

In the fifth place, I have, in *Doctrine of the Knowledge of God* and elsewhere, distinguished between "narrowly circular" and "broadly circular" arguments. An example of the former would be, "The Bible is the Word of God because it is the Word of God." That may itself be a way of saying "The Bible is the Word of God because it says it is." There is a profound truth vividly displayed in this narrow argument, namely, that there is no authority higher than Scripture by which Scripture may be judged, and that in the final analysis we must believe Scripture on its own say-so. Nevertheless, the narrow argument has some obvious disadvantages. In particular, an unbeliever will likely dismiss it out of hand, unless a great deal of explanation is given. We may overcome those disadvantages to some extent by moving to a broader circular argument. That broader argument says, "The Bible is the Word of God because of various evidences," and then it specifies those evidences. Now the argument is still circular in a sense, because the apologist chooses, evaluates, and formulates these evidences in ways controlled by Scripture. But this argument tends to hold the unbeliever's attention longer and to be more persuasive. "Circularity," in the sense that I have conceded it, can be as broad as the whole universe; for every fact witnesses to the truth of God.

God's Responsibility and Ours

The relation of divine sovereignty to human responsibility is one of the great mysteries of the Christian faith. It is plain from Scripture in any case that both are real and that both are important. Calvinistic theology is known for its emphasis on divine sovereignty—for its view that God "works out everything in conformity with the purpose of his will" (Eph. 1:11). But in Calvinism there is at least an equal emphasis upon human responsibility.

An equal emphasis? Many would not be willing to say that about Calvinism. But consider the Calvinistic emphasis on the authority of God's law—a more positive view of the

It should be pointed out God does not depend on us but graciously chooses → Man instrumentally.

law than in any other tradition of evangelical theology. To the Calvinist, human beings have duties before God. Adam failed to fulfill his duty and plunged the human race into sin and misery. But Jesus fulfilled his duty and brought eternal salvation to his people. Although God is sovereign, human obedience is of the utmost importance. God will fill and subdue the earth, but only through human effort (Gen. 1:28–30). He will gather his elect from all nations into his church, but only through faithful human preaching (Matt. 28:18–20; Acts 1:8; Rom. 10:13–15). Salvation comes to people solely by God's sovereign grace, without any human effort; yet we are to receive that salvation by grace and "work [it] out" with "fear and trembling" (Phil. 2:12)—not in spite of, but because of, the fact that "it is God who works in you to will and to act according to his good purpose" (v. 13). You see that typically—God's sovereignty does not exclude, but engages, human responsibility.[17] Indeed, it is God's sovereignty that grants human responsibility, that gives freedom and significance to human choices and actions, that ordains an important human role within God's plan for history.

It is important for us to maintain this balance between divine sovereignty and human obedience in apologetics. We have already seen that apologetics cannot be successful apart from a supernatural element, namely, the testimony of the Holy Spirit. In that sense, apologetics is a sovereign work of

---

[17]These points have many important applications apart from apologetics, such as: (1) Christians often object that some kinds of scientific or technological progress amount to "playing God." Thus, they develop generalized objections to birth control, genetic research, ecology, space exploration, or whatever—even to medical care in general. At some points, to be sure, God has set limits (e.g., to fetal-tissue experimentation), but the lordship of God in these areas does not preclude a responsible human role—quite the contrary. (2) Some Christians insist that since God sovereignly builds his church, we ought not to make human plans and study human techniques of church growth. Granted that some growth schemes are not pleasing to God, the fact remains that there is room for human responsibility here too. Denying this is like saying "God converts and sanctifies people, so preaching is unnecessary, or at least we can ignore the techniques of effective preaching."

God. It is he who persuades the unbelieving mind and heart. But there is also a place for the human apologist. He has the same place as the preacher mentioned in Romans 10:14. Indeed, he *is* the preacher.

Apologetics and preaching are not two different things. Both are attempts to reach unbelievers for Christ. Preaching is apologetic because it aims at persuasion. Apologetics is preaching because it presents the gospel, aiming at conversion and sanctification. However, the two activities do have different perspectives or emphases. Apologetics emphasizes the aspect of rational persuasion, while preaching emphasizes the seeking of godly change in people's lives. But if rational persuasion is a persuasion of the heart, then it is the same thing as godly change. God is the persuader-converter, but he works through our testimony. Other terms are also roughly synonymous (or perspectivally related): witnessing, teaching, evangelizing, arguing,[18] etc.

Another way of putting it is this: the Spirit is the one who converts, but he normally works through the word. Faith wrought by the Spirit is trust in a message, a promise of God.[19] As the earth was made by Spirit and word together

---

[18]I will occasionally use the term *argument* in this book, although it is sometimes misunderstood. By it I do not mean a hostile encounter, as the term is sometimes used in ordinary language. Nor do I mean an arid, purposeless discussion of abstract or theoretical issues—the concept that some people connect with the word. Rather, I use it in the logical sense: an argument is simply a group of premises which, the arguer claims, imply a conclusion. So understood, the term is roughly synonymous with *reasoning,* which, e.g., Paul did, according to Acts 17:2; 18:4, 19; 24:25. People sometimes advise Christian witnesses not to argue. That advice may be good if we take *argument* in the sense of a hostile confrontation (but see the section on "Dangers," later in this chapter). It may also be good if *argument* refers to a mere debate over abstract issues unrelated to sin and salvation. But in the logical sense, argument is quite unavoidable. Every sermon, every Bible study, and every witness to Christ seeks to warrant a conclusion (faith, repentance, obedience) and thus has an argumentative aspect.

[19]We are, of course, speaking of faith as exercised by adult human beings of normal intelligence. The Spirit also works in the hearts of infants (2 Sam. 12:23; Luke 1:41–44; 18:16; Acts 2:39)—and presumably also in the hearts of people who are without the gifts of speech or even thought. That is very mysterious. Some theologians would describe the Spirit's work in such cases

(Gen. 1:2–3; Ps. 33:6 ["breath" = Spirit]), so God re-creates sinful human beings by his word and Spirit (John 3:3ff.; Rom. 1:16ff.; James 1:18; 1 Peter 1:23). As we have seen, the Spirit's work is necessary, but he works by illumining and persuading us to believe God's words (1 Cor. 2:4; 1 Thess. 1:5). Thus, as I indicated above, the Spirit is necessary, but the preacher-apologist is also necessary. The work of the preacher-apologist is to present the word. And his job is not just to read the word, but to preach it—that is, to expound it, to apply it to his hearers, to display its beauty, its truth, its rationality. The preacher-apologist seeks to combat the unbeliever's false impressions and present to him the word as it really is. It is to this testimony that the Spirit also bears witness.

This discussion will suffice to answer those who oppose the work of apologetics out of fear that it is an attempt to "play God." There need not be any such competition between God's work and ours, as long as we recognize both God's ultimate sovereignty and his determination to use human agents to accomplish his purpose. Apologetics, rightly understood, is not playing God; it is merely practicing a divinely ordained human vocation.

Our discussion of divine sovereignty and human responsibility will also help us to answer those who insist that the Bible needs no defense. Charles Spurgeon is sometimes quoted (from somewhere!) as saying, "Defend the Bible? I would as soon defend a lion." Well, it is certainly true that Scripture, attended by the Spirit, is powerful (Rom. 1:16; Heb. 4:12–13). And it does defend itself, giving reasons for what it says. Think of all the "therefores" in Scripture, such as in Romans 8:1 and 12:1. Scripture does not merely tell us to believe and do certain things; it tells us to do them for certain reasons. This is Scripture defending itself, indicating its own rationale. But, of course, when we as human preachers expound Scripture, we too must expound that rationale. Thus,

---

as regeneration without faith; others would describe it as a regeneration producing faith in "seed form," that is, a disposition to hear and obey a word of God which as yet the person is unable to understand.

we defend Scripture by using Scripture's own defenses. Indeed, Scripture not only defends itself but goes on the attack against sin and unbelief! Still, remarkably enough, Scripture itself calls us to be its defenders (Phil. 1:7, 16, 27; 2 Tim. 4:2; 1 Peter 3:15). To defend the Bible is ultimately simply to present it as it is—to present its truth, beauty, and goodness, its application to present-day hearers, and, of course, its rationale. When that message is preached so that people understand, the Bible defends itself. But the Bible will not defend itself to those who have never heard its message. Spreading that message is a human task, the task of human defenders. Listen to the apostle Paul: "Preach the Word; be prepared in season and out of season; correct, rebuke and encourage—with great patience and careful instruction" (2 Tim. 4:2).

Sola Scriptura

"The Bible needs no defense" can also be used somewhat differently: as a way of invoking the Protestant principle *sola Scriptura*, the sufficiency of Scripture. Some fear that apologetics (which over the years has been notorious for injecting nonbiblical philosophical notions into Christian theology) may be seeking to subject Scripture to the judgment of something beyond Scripture. That is, of course, a great danger for the "traditional" apologetic, and it may happen unintentionally even when an apologist seeks to be "presuppositional." But when apologetics is consistently presuppositional—i.e., when it frankly recognizes that its own methods are subject to biblical norms—then it will avoid this danger.

Sola Scriptura, after all, does not require the exclusion of all extrabiblical data, even from theology. It simply requires that in theology and in all other disciplines, the highest authority, the supreme standard, be Scripture and Scripture alone. As the Westminster Confession (1.6) puts it, it is as "the whole counsel of God" that Scripture may not be added to. There can be no objection to mentioning extrabiblical data in apologetics, as long as those data are not presented as "counsel of God" on the same level as Scripture. Human thought, even theology, requires the use of extrabiblical data, for we are always dealing with the contemporary world in which God has placed us. Obviously, physics, sociology, geology, psychology, medicine, and so forth must respond to data beyond the Scriptures. Theology must do the same, because it is not a mere *reading* of Scripture, but an *application* of Scripture to human need.[20] Theology, therefore, always faces the danger of elevating the theologian's own conception of human need to a position of equal authority to, or even greater authority than, the Scriptures. But through prayer and meditation on God's Word, that danger can be avoided.

Therefore, to defend the Bible according to its own standards, even when we use extrabiblical data in the process, is not to add anything to Scripture as our supreme standard. It is simply to expose, as we saw above, the rationality of Scripture itself.

It is sometimes hard to rid ourselves of the notion that when we argue the truth of Scripture based on facts outside of Scripture, we are elevating those facts (ultimately our own fact gathering) to a position of greater authority than Scripture. It seems that we are measuring Scripture by those facts—that we are judging Scripture on the basis of their (presumably higher) authority. Van Til himself seemed to fear this, though not consistently.[21] But this is not necessarily the case.

---

[20]See *DKG*, 76–88, 93–98.

[21]For example, in *Defense of the Faith*, 252, he criticizes arguments that "started from human experience with causation and purpose and by analogy argued to the idea of a cause of and a purpose with the world as a whole." He objects that "if you start with the ideas of cause and purpose as intelligible to man without God when these concepts apply to relations within the universe, then you cannot consistently say that you need God for the idea of cause or purpose when these concepts apply to the universe as a whole." True enough. But arguments about cause and purpose do not necessarily assume that "cause and purpose are intelligible to man without God," even as they "apply to relations within the universe." In fact, an apologist may very well advance such an argument because of his conviction that cause and purpose are not at all intelligible without God. Indeed, if

When I say, "There is design in the world; therefore, God exists," I may in fact be getting the premise from Scripture itself! (Surely Scripture teaches that there is design in the world!) In addressing the unbeliever, I may be addressing the knowledge that, according to Romans 1:18ff., he has obtained from creation. Indeed, when I say that, I may very well be expressing the certainty of my heart that design is unintelligible apart from the biblical God, and therefore that the very existence of design implies his reality. It is not that my concept of design is something by which I judge the Bible; rather, the Bible tells me what must be true if design is to exist.

What about using extrabiblical historical or scientific data to confirm biblical teachings? Surely, some might say, to do that implies that we have more confidence in this data than we do in the Bible, that we consider this data to have more credibility. And again, my reply is negative. I have far more confidence in the truth of the biblical history than I have in the reliability of, e.g., Josephus.[22] But he does occasionally confirm biblical statements, and I think it is perfectly legitimate to mention that fact in apologetic discussions. The point is not that Josephus is more authoritative than, say, Luke. It is rather that even the non-Christian Josephus at points recognized the facts that Scripture records. And modern skeptics, who are often willing to believe even the least reliable non-Christian historians in preference to God's Word, must take note that even first-century non-Christian historians

Thomas Aquinas's causal argument is sound, it makes, in effect, that precise claim. His causal argument implies that if God doesn't exist, there is no *complete* causal explanation for anything, and therefore there is nothing that can rightly be called "cause." (Thomas himself may or may not have thought along those lines; I am deducing what is implicit in his argument. But whether he did or not is a question of his personal piety, not a question about the value of his argument.) Thomas is usually considered (by Van Til and others) to represent the antithesis of Van Til's presuppositional method, but in this case the antithesis is not obvious. I intend to explore more examples of this sort in my forthcoming book on Van Til.

[22]Josephus is a well-known Jewish historian who lived approximately from A.D. 37 to A.D. 100 and thus was a younger contemporary of the apostles.

wrote as one would expect them to, granted the truth of Scripture.

Again, this sort of argument does not add anything to Scripture in a way that would compromise the *sola Scriptura* principle. It adds nothing to our stock of supremely authoritative truth. That is in the Bible and nowhere else. Further, in one sense, arguments like the causal argument or the Josephus argument, even though they involve extrabiblical data, aim simply at communicating the Scripture "as it really is." After all, to see Scripture rightly, it helps to see it in its various *contexts:* the context of its contemporary culture (with writers like Josephus), the context of the overall universe (including cause and purpose). To see Scripture rightly is to see how it fits and illumines those contexts. In that sense a proper causal or historical argument does not go beyond Scripture. It simply shows the applicability of scriptural truth to some area of the world, and thus it displays the Bible in its full meaning.[23]

I conclude that we may use extrabiblical data in apologetics, but not as independent criteria to which Scripture must measure up. How ridiculous it would be to imagine that God's Word must be considered false if it fails to agree with Josephus or Eusebius or Papias—or with some anthropologist's theories about "early man"! Precisely the opposite is the case. We should simply present Scripture as it is, that is, as sometimes agreeing with other writings and sometimes not. That is what we would expect if God's word were to enter a world of finitude and sin. And that very fact can, by God's grace, be persuasive. Our job is to present the Bible as it is, and to do so we must often refer to it in various contexts.

---

[23]Note that *DKG*, 76–100, equates "meaning" with "application." Scripture is written for people who live in the world. It is written for people with eyes and ears, people who will read it in the context of the rest of their lives. It expects us to apply its teaching to what is happening around us. Indeed, it says, to properly understand Scripture *is* to apply it to these situations (Matt. 16:3; 22:29; Luke 24:25; John 5:39–40; Rom. 15:4; 2 Tim. 3:16–17; 2 Peter 1:19–21; John 20:31).

Sola Scriptura and **Natural Revelation**

To relate Scripture to its contexts is to relate it to natural revelation. Natural revelation is the revelation of God in everything he has made (Pss. 19:1ff.; 104:1ff.; Rom. 1:18ff.), including human beings, who are his image (Gen. 1:27; 9:6; James 3:9). Every human being is surrounded by God's revelation, even within himself. This includes, of course, the unbeliever. As I stated earlier, the unbeliever knows God clearly (Rom. 1:21) but seeks to repress that knowledge in various ways.

Natural revelation reveals the eternal power and nature of God (Rom. 1:20). It also reveals his moral standards (Rom. 1:32) and his wrath against sin (same verse; cf. v. 18). However, it does not reveal God's plan of salvation, which comes specifically through the preaching of Christ (Rom. 10:17; cf. vv. 13–15). We have that preaching of Christ in definitive form in the Scriptures, and on the authority of Scripture we continue to preach the gospel to the world.

Why do we need two forms of revelation? For one thing, direct divine speech shortens the "learning curve." Even unfallen Adam needed to hear God's direct speech that supplemented and interpreted God's revelation in nature. He didn't need to figure everything out for himself; in many cases that may have taken a long time or indeed been impossible for the finite mind. So, as God's faithful covenant servant, Adam accepted this help gratefully. He accepted God's interpretation of the world until he made the tragic decision to accept Satan's interpretation instead.

But after the Fall, at least two other reasons for special divine speech entered the picture. One was man's need of a saving promise, a promise that could never be deduced from natural revelation alone. The other reason was to correct our sinful misinterpretations of natural revelation. Romans 1:21–32 shows what people do with natural revelation when left with no other word of God. They repress it, disobey it, exchange it for a lie, disvalue it, and honor those who rebel against it.

22

Thus, God has given us Scripture, or "special revelation,"[24] both to supplement natural revelation (by adding to
it the message of salvation) and to correct our misuses of natural revelation. As Calvin said, the Christian should look at
nature with the "spectacles of Scripture." If even unfallen
Adam needed to interpret the world according to God's verbal utterance, how much more do we!

The point is not that Scripture is more divine or more
authoritative than natural revelation. Natural revelation is every bit the word of God and absolutely authoritative. The difference is that Scripture is a verbal divine utterance that God
gives us to supplement and correct our view of his world. We
must humbly accept that assistance. In doing so, we do not
make Scripture more authoritative than natural revelation;
rather, we allow the Word (with its ever-present Spirit) to correct our *interpretations* of natural revelation.[25]

To allow Scripture this corrective work, we must accept
the principle that our settled belief[26] as to Scripture's teaching must take precedence over what we would believe from
natural revelation alone.[27] God gave Scripture as the covenant

[24]"Special revelation" in Reformed theology includes special utterances of
God's voice (as in Ex. 19–20); the words of Jesus, prophets, and apostles;
and the written word that records and preserves the oral forms of God's
speech. My own view is that the distinction between general and special
revelation is not adequate to characterize all the forms of revelation described in Scripture and that additional categories are needed. I hope to develop that scheme in a later book, *Doctrine of the Word of God*. But the traditional twofold distinction will have to do for now.

[25]Granted, our interpretations of Scripture also need to be corrected at
times. But the proper order is: Scripture itself corrects our interpretations
both of Scripture and of nature. Can natural revelation (e.g., knowledge of
ancient languages) sometimes correct our understanding of Scripture? Yes,
but only insofar as such correction appears on reflection to be justified by
the scriptural text itself. So Scripture has a primacy over all else. See *DKG*,
part 2, "The Justification of Knowledge."

[26]The adjective "settled" is important; I am of course not advocating dogmatic adherence to ideas based on half-baked exegesis and rejection of, say,
scientific theories on the basis of such sloppy theologizing.

[27]This is not, of course, to say that our settled beliefs concerning the teaching of Scripture are infallible. See *DKG*, 134–36, on the subject of certainty.
But I repeat: those settled beliefs must take precedence over our beliefs,

constitution of the people of God, and if it is to serve us in that way, it must take precedence over all other sources of knowledge. It is wrong, for example, to suggest (as many do) that the "two books of nature and Scripture" should be read side by side, carrying equal weight in every respect. That sort of argument has been used to justify relatively uncritical Christian acceptance of evolution, secular psychology, and so on. In such arguments, Scripture is not permitted to do its corrective work, to protect God's people from the wisdom of the world (see 1 Cor. 2:6–16). Hence, *sola Scriptura.*

Nevertheless, natural revelation, rightly understood through the "spectacles of Scripture," is of tremendous value to the Christian and, specifically, to the apologist. As we look at nature with God's help, we see that the heavens really do "declare the glory of God" (Ps. 19:1). We see some of the very interesting ways in which human beings image God.[28] We see how it is that God furnishes the rational structure of the world and of the human mind, so that the two structures are adapted to one another. We see through science the astonishing wisdom of God's plan (see Ps. 104). We see through history and the arts what evils result when people abandon God and what blessings (and persecutions, Mark 10:30!) follow those who are faithful to him.

Traditional apologists have not always understood nature to be revelation of God. Aquinas did not distinguish between natural and special revelation, but between reasoning with and reasoning without the assistance of revelation. It is easy to understand how such views can be characterized as "autonomous" or "neutralist." Other traditionalists, however, have made much of the concept of natural revelation, even describing their method as one that presents natural revelation (somehow apart from special) to the unbeliever.

---

settled or not, from other sources. Otherwise, we do not allow Scripture to be a true corrective to our understanding of natural revelation.

[28]Meredith G. Kline's *Images of the Spirit* (Grand Rapids: Baker, 1980) and James B. Jordan's *Through New Eyes* (Brentwood, Tenn.: Wolgemuth and Hyatt, 1988) have some remarkable insights in this area.

Certainly there can be no objection to presenting natural revelation to the unbeliever. We must, however, be careful that our statements about natural revelation are in line with scriptural teaching—that we are looking at nature through the "spectacles of Scripture." Showing natural revelation to the unbeliever is not an invitation to him to reason neutrally or autonomously or to ignore the Scriptures. Therefore, in a sense, natural and special revelation must never be separated in an apologetic encounter.[29]

The use of extrascriptural evidence, therefore, may be seen as part of a godly use of Scripture itself. It is an obedient response to Scripture's own view of the world. In Scripture's teaching, nature points to God; so, the obedient Christian apologist will show the unbeliever the various ways in which nature reveals God, without claiming neutrality and without allowing the use of non-Christian criteria of truth. Thus, while he appeals to natural revelation, he inevitably appeals to Scripture at the same time. Indeed, the very purpose of Scripture (as I emphasized in *Doctrine of the Knowledge of God*) is application, the use of Scripture to illumine situations and persons outside itself. "Viewing creation in the light of Scripture" and "applying Scripture to creation" are the same activity, seen from different perspectives.[30]

---

[29]Some have asked, "If nature and Scripture may never be understood apart from one another, then how can you say that the unbeliever, who sharply separates (even opposes) nature and Scripture, knows God?" But my claim is not that nature by itself gives no true knowledge. That claim would be contradicted by Rom. 1:19–20. Rather, my claim is that only an obedient response to the biblical message can provide the needed supplement and corrective to the unbeliever's use of natural revelation, so that his knowledge of God (Rom. 1:21) becomes a knowledge in love (1 Cor. 8:1–3; 1 John 2:5; 4:8), a saving knowledge. Obviously, what the apologist seeks to communicate is not a knowledge (however correct) buried in the mind beneath layers of rationalization, darkness, foolishness, and lies (Rom. 1:18, 21–23), but a knowledge affirmed with confidence and delight, a knowledge that transforms the life, turning hatred into love.

[30]In *DKG*, the former was called the situational perspective; and the latter, the normative perspective.

Granted this approach, there need be no competition between presuppositions and evidences. Our scriptural presupposition authorizes the use of evidence, and the evidence is nothing more than the application of Scripture to our situation. The use of evidence is not contrary to *sola Scriptura*, but a fulfillment of that principle.

Values

What is the use, the purpose, the value of apologetics? Since apologetics and preaching are perspectivally related, the benefits of the two are the same. As preaching leads to the conversion of the lost and the edification of the saints, so does apologetics.

The specific work of giving an intellectual rationale has its usefulness within these broader contexts. For the believer, apologetics gives reassurance to faith as it displays the rationality of Scripture itself. That rationality also gives to the believer an intellectual foundation, a basis for faith and a basis for making wise decisions in life. Apologetics is not itself that foundation, but it displays and describes the foundation presented in Scripture, as well as the way we should, according to Scripture, build upon that foundation.

For the unbeliever, God may use apologetic reasoning to sweep aside rationalizations, arguments by which the subject resists conversion. Apologetics may also provide evidence conducive to a change in conviction. We are not saying that the unbeliever lacks evidence. He is surrounded by evidence in creation (Ps. 19:1ff.; Rom. 1:18ff.) and in himself (Gen. 1:26ff.) for the existence of God, and there is plenty of evidence in Scripture for the truth of other Christian doctrines. But an apologist can formulate that evidence, and do so in provocative ways, drawing the unbeliever's attention to it. And he can apply it to the unbeliever's particular objections.

For those who never come to faith, apologetics may still be doing God's work. Like preaching, again, it adds to their condemnation. Failure to repent and believe, despite faithful presentations of the truth, leads to more severe condemnation (Luke 12:47ff.).

Dangers

[handwritten margin note: Character 1st / How knowledge]

James warns us (3:1), "Not many of you should presume to be teachers, my brothers, because you know that we who teach will be judged more strictly." If we do not teach, our errors affect only ourselves; but if we do, our errors can affect others also. Thus, errors in those who teach are more serious and will be judged more severely. The apologist is, as we have indicated, a teacher; therefore, the scriptural warnings about teachers apply to apologists.

Can we be more specific? In our theme verses, 1 Peter 3:15–16, Peter urges apologists to keep "a clear conscience," so that those who slander them will be "ashamed." It is interesting that Peter does not urge apologists to be intelligent and knowledgeable (although such qualities are certainly helpful), but to lead consistently godly lives. He gives us a practical standard for a discipline we are inclined to regard as theoretical.[31]

The fact is that every apologetic presentation has important practical contexts. Our communication with unbelievers consists not only of what we say, but also of how we live before them. If our life contradicts our doctrine, then our apologetics is hypocritical and loses credibility. But if our life and doctrine are consistent, then those who try to make us look bad will themselves lose credibility. They will, in the end at least, be ashamed.

To be still more specific: apologists are subject to the same sins that everyone else is, but over the years, they have been especially prone to sins in two areas. In terms of Ephesians 4:15, which urges us to speak the truth in love, we may say that apologists have sometimes been guilty of speaking

---

[31]Compare the mostly practical criteria for the teaching office in 1 Tim. 3:1–7; Titus 1:5–9.

falsehoods and sometimes of speaking without love. The first is often condemned in the New Testament polemic against false teaching (2 Tim. 3; 2 Peter 2; etc.). It is remarkable how many heresies are traceable to apologetic motives. Someone will think, "If I am going to present Christianity more persuasively, I will have to show that it is compatible with the intellectual movements of my time. I must present Christianity as 'intellectually respectable.'" Thus, various Christian doctrines are compromised, replaced by the doctrines of popular philosophy. The second-century Apologists (Justin, Aristides, Athenagoras) were for the most part deeply committed Christians, but they compromised the Christian doctrine of creation, accommodating it to the Gnostic philosophical notion of a continuum of being between God and the world. This led to an almost impersonal concept of God (the unknowable being at the top of the scale) and a subordinationist view of the Trinity (Son and Spirit subordinate to God the Father, so that they could interact with the world, as the Father could not). Similar motivations are evident in Clement of Alexandria and Origen, in Thomas Aquinas, and more recently in Schleiermacher's *Speeches to the Learned Despisers of Christianity* and the many modern theologians from Bultmann to Tillich to Pannenberg who want to show "modern man" the intellectual value of Christianity. Very often the apologetic motive has led to doctrinal compromise. That doesn't mean that the apologetic motive is wrong; as we have seen, that motive in itself is scriptural. But the historic pattern and Scripture's explicit admonitions should lead us to be highly cautious. And don't be an apologist unless your first loyalty is to God—not to intellectual respectability, not to truth in the abstract, not to the unbeliever as such, not to some philosophic tradition.

Contributing to such failures are other sins: misdirected love, underestimation of human sin (as if what the unbeliever needs is merely a better argument), ignorance of God's revelation (especially of biblical presuppositionalism), and intellectual pride.

The opposite violation of Ephesians 4:15 is speaking without love.[32] Unfortunately, many contentious or quarrelsome people are attracted to the discipline of apologetics. In their hearts, they are unhappy unless they are in the midst of controversy; and if there is no controversy going on, they will create one, picking fights over matters that could easily be overlooked or resolved peacefully. Scripture speaks often of this spirit and always negatively: Proverbs 13:10; 18:6; 19:13; 26:21; Habakkuk 1:3; Romans 2:8; 1 Corinthians 1:11; 11:16; Philippians 1:16; Titus 3:9. One would do well to meditate on these passages before beginning a career in apologetics!

This sort of contentiousness comes from pride, according to Proverbs 13:10. When one is too proud to "take advice" from others, he insists on his own way until he is forced to desist. Far from being wise, such people are foolish (Prov. 18:6) and under the direction of the Devil himself (James 3:13–16). James goes on to say, "But the wisdom that comes from heaven is first of all pure; then peace-loving, considerate, submissive, full of mercy and good fruit, impartial and sincere. Peacemakers who sow in peace raise a harvest of righteousness" (vv. 17–18). Paul even tells us that "knowledge" without love is not true knowledge: "We know that we all possess knowledge. Knowledge puffs up, but love builds up. The man who thinks he knows something does not yet know as he ought to know. But the man who loves God is known by God" (1 Cor. 8:1–3).

To defend the Christian faith with a quarrelsome spirit is to defend Christianity plus quarrelsomeness—a self-destructive hybrid. True Christianity—the Christianity we are called to defend with word and life—says, "Blessed are the peacemakers, for they will be called sons of God" (Matt. 5:9),[33] and, "If it is possible, as far as it depends on you, live at peace with everyone" (Rom. 12:18).[34]

---

[32]I am aware, of course, that one can commit both violations at once: speaking falsehoods without love!

[33]See my *Evangelical Reunion* (Grand Rapids: Baker, 1991) and Dennis Johnson's sermon on "Peacemakers," added as an appendix.

[34]I grant that many passages of the Bible from the prophets, Jesus, and the

Hear also Peter, again in our theme text, urging the virtues of "gentleness" and "respect." Gentleness is the way of love and peacemaking, a trait quite opposed to the contentious spirit. In circles like my own that emphasize (rightly, in my view) a militant orthodoxy, gentleness is the most neglected of the biblical virtues. Is it possible to be militant and gentle at the same time? Of course. Let the Lord Jesus himself and his apostles show us the way.[35]

"Respect" is the NIV translation of the Greek word *phobos,* "fear." Those translations which use the term "fear" perhaps intend it to be taken as the fear of God (the NASB says "reverence"), or at least the apologist's perception of the spiritual dangers of the situation. "Respect" would mean treating the unbeliever as what he is—a person created in the image of God. It would mean not talking down to him, but listening to him—not belittling him, but taking seriously his questions and ideas. Either idea would be in accord with other scriptural teachings. The bottom line is that we should relate the apologetic encounter to God and his purposes, rather than allow our own emotional evaluation of the unbeliever to dictate our approach to him.

---

apostles do not sound very "peaceful." These men were willing to use very strong, angry language when necessary. On many occasions, however, they showed much patience and gentleness. In my view, strong language is appropriate against people (1) who claim to have some religious teaching authority, and (2) are proclaiming false doctrine on serious matters, leading believers astray, or are dishonoring orthodox doctrine by ungodly lives, and (3) have ignored clear and graciously expressed warnings that their conduct displeased God. The Protestant Reformers used similarly strong language (which can usually be justified on these principles). Most of those today who are seeking to emulate the biblical and Reformation writers in this respect are overdoing it, in my opinion. They should learn to give at least equal attention to peacemaking. See my *Evangelical Reunion,* especially the appendix containing Dennis Johnson's sermon.

[35]Note the preceding footnote in this respect.

TWO

▼

The Message of the Apologist

The apologist's message, ultimately, is nothing less than the whole of Scripture, applied to the needs of his hearers. But in an apologetics text like this one, it is important to provide a brief summary of the content of Scripture to give direction to the apologetic witness. That is not difficult. The teachings of Scripture can be summarized; indeed, there are such summaries in Scripture itself: John 3:16; Romans 6:23; 1 Corinthians 15:1–11; 2 Corinthians 5:17–6:2; Ephesians 2:8–10; Philippians 2:5–11; 1 Timothy 2:5–6; Titus 3:3–8; 1 Peter 3:18.

These texts show us that there are different ways of summarizing the biblical message, each of which carries at least a slightly different emphasis. We may call these emphases "perspectives." For the purposes of the present book, it will be useful to summarize the message of Scripture from two perspectives: first, Christianity as a philosophy, and, second, as good news.

Philosophy

By "Christianity as a philosophy," I mean that Christianity provides a comprehensive view of the world (a worldview).[1] It

---

[1]Such language has its dangers, of course. "Philosophy" sometimes con-

gives us an account, not only of God, but also of the world that God made, the relation of the world to God, and the place of human beings in the world in relation to nature and God. It discusses metaphysics (the theory of the fundamental nature of reality), epistemology (the theory of knowledge), and values (ethics, aesthetics, economics, etc.). As such, it is a viewpoint on *everything*. There are, I believe, distinctive Christian views on history, science, psychology, business, economics, labor, sociology, education, the arts, the problems of philosophy, etc. As we saw earlier, our Lord's authority is comprehensive; whatever we do must be related to Christ (1 Cor. 10:31, etc.).

Christianity therefore competes with Platonism, Aristotelianism, empiricism, rationalism, skepticism, materialism, monism, pluralism, process thought, secular humanism, New Age thought, Marxism, and whatever other philosophies there may be—as well as other religions, such as Judaism, Islam, Hinduism, and Buddhism. One of the more unfortunate repercussions of America's distorted view of "the separation of church and state" is that public school children are able to hear advocacy of every system of thought except those that are arbitrarily labeled "religious."[2] Who is to say that the truth might not be found in, or even limited to, one of these religious positions? Is it even remotely fair, in terms of freedom of thought and speech, to restrict public education to allegedly secular

---

notes an approach to the truth by way of autonomous speculation, and I certainly want the reader to erase any such nuances from his mind when he reads here of Christianity as a philosophy. Further, there has been a historical tendency, unfortunately connected with apologetics, to force Christianity into a structure dictated by an autonomously produced philosophy. That tendency I renounce altogether. The only philosophy I recommend here is the truth of Christianity itself, derived from the Scriptures, by which certain philosophical implications (i.e., implications as to the general features of God and the world) can be derived.

[2]Of course, every system of philosophy is religious, not in the sense that it advocates certain rites of worship, but in the more important sense that (1) it is committed at some point to faith-presuppositions, just as religions are, and (2) it offers a comprehensive worldview and comprehensive solutions for the troubles of human beings.

viewpoints? Is this not brainwashing of the worst kind?[3]

Further, the extreme separationists often seem to be more opposed to the public expression of Christianity in particular than to religion in general. Too often, they have no objection to presentations in schools favoring Eastern mysticism or modern witchcraft—only to Christianity. Inconsistent as it may appear, however, this specifically anti-Christian behavior makes some sense. For, as we shall see, it is Christianity, not Eastern mysticism or witchcraft or Native American chanting, that really stands against the natural drift of the unregenerate mind. Christianity is excluded from the schools although (or perhaps because) it is the only genuine alternative to the conventional wisdom of the modern establishment.

But that "conventional wisdom" has given us enormous increases in divorce, abortion, single-parent families, latchkey children, drugs, gangs, crime rates, AIDS (and related health concerns such as the resurgence of tuberculosis), homelessness, hunger, government deficits, taxation, political corruption, degeneracy of the arts, mediocrity in education, noncompetitive industry, interest groups demanding "rights" of all sorts (rights without corresponding responsibilities and at the expense of everyone else), and pollution of the environment. It has given us the messianic state, which claims all authority and seeks to solve all problems (secular "salvation"), but which generally makes things worse. It has brought about the appalling movement toward "political correctness" on university campuses, which once claimed plausibly to be bastionsof intellectual freedom. It has allowed the language of polite

---

[3]To those who are offended by the advocacy of religion in the classroom, it should be replied that Christians have just as much right to be offended by the teaching of various secular philosophies, which disavow our need for God. Christians ought to express this offense (including their offense at having to pay for this brainwashing with their taxes) more consistently and severely. Why should "offensive" teaching be limited to "religious" expression in some arbitrarily narrow sense? Of course, if a more evenhanded view of these matters were to prevail, we would all have to accept equally the burden of possibly being offended, or we should eliminate public education entirely. Education in which people of all convictions are enrolled, but in which no one is offended, is not worthy of the name.

society to degenerate into the language of blasphemy and mutual contempt. It has created an atmosphere in which popular music ("rap") urges people to kill police.

Under these circumstances, shouldn't we consider some alternatives that are opposed to the conventional wisdom? Or is there indeed, perhaps, only one such alternative? If so, and I shall argue that there is, surely we ought to take that alternative very seriously.

To show that Christianity is *the* alternative, allow me to expound here the content of Christianity as a philosophy—as metaphysics, epistemology, and value theory (focusing on ethics). Christianity as gospel (i.e., as good news) is also important in this connection, perhaps more so. But that will come later. In our time (as opposed to, say, six hundred years ago), people are ignorant of the basic Christian worldview. It will be helpful if they understand that, so that the gospel will make sense to them. So I will present Christianity first as philosophy, then as gospel.

Metaphysics

The four most important things to remember about the Christian worldview are: first, the absolute personality of God; second, the distinction between Creator and creature; third, the sovereignty of God; and fourth, the Trinity.

God, the absolute personality. God is "absolute" in the sense that he is the Creator of all things and thus the ground of all other reality. As such, he has no need of any other being (Acts 17:25) for his own existence. He is self-existent and self-sufficient (*"a se"*). Nothing brought him into being; he always was (Pss. 90:2; 93:2; John 1:1). Nor can anything destroy him; he will always be (Deut. 32:40; Ps. 102:26–27; 1 Tim. 6:16; Heb. 1:10–12; Rev. 10:6). His existence is timeless, for he is the Lord of time itself (Ps. 90, esp. v. 4; Gal. 4:4; Eph. 1:11; 2 Peter 3:8). He knows all times and spaces with equal perfection (Isa. 41:4; 44:7–8). In the words of the Westminster Shorter Catechism, "God is a Spirit, infinite, eternal, and unchangeable, in his being, wisdom, power, holiness, justice, goodness, and truth" (Q/A 4).

This definition emphasizes not only God's absoluteness but also his personality. "Spirit" in Scripture is personal, and God is Spirit (John 4:24). As Spirit, God speaks (Acts 10:19), leads (Rom. 8:14), bears witness (Rom. 8:16–17), helps (Rom. 8:26), prays (same verse), loves (Rom. 15:30), reveals (1 Cor. 2:10), and searches (same verse). Although the Greek word for "Spirit" *(pneuma)* is grammatically neuter, the New Testament sometimes emphasizes the personality of God's Spirit by referring to him with a masculine pronoun (e.g., John 16:13, 14). Also clearly personalistic are the Catechism's references to the attributes of wisdom, power, holiness, justice, goodness, and truth. These qualities are often ascribed to God in Scripture.

The great question confronting modern humanity is this: Granted that the universe contains both persons (like you and me) and impersonal structures (like matter, motion, chance, time, space, and physical laws), which is fundamental? Is the impersonal aspect of the universe grounded in the personal, or is it the other way around? Secular thought generally assumes the latter—that persons are the products of matter, motion, chance, and so on. It holds that to explain a phenomenon in terms of personal intentions (e.g., "This house is here because someone built it to live in") is less than an ultimate explanation, less than fully explanatory. On this view, an ultimate explanation, a fully satisfying explanation, requires the ultimacy of the impersonal (e.g., "The person built the house because the atoms in his brain moved about in certain ways"). But is that a necessary assumption?

Let us think through the consequences of each. If the impersonal is primary, then there is no consciousness, no wisdom, and no will in the ultimate origin of things. What we call reason and value are the unintended, accidental consequences of chance events. (So why should we trust reason, if it is only the accidental result of irrational happenings?) Moral virtue will, in the end, be unrewarded. Friendship, love, and

35

beauty are all of no ultimate consequence, for they are reducible to blind, uncaring process. No one was more clear-eyed and eloquent as to the consequences of this view than Bertrand Russell, who nevertheless upheld it as "the world which science presents for our belief":

> That man is the product of causes which had no prevision of the end they were achieving; that his origin, his growth, his hopes and fears, his loves and his beliefs, are but the outcome of accidental collocations of atoms; that no fire, no heroism, no intensity of thought and feeling, can preserve an individual life beyond the grave; that all the labors of the ages, all the devotion, all the inspiration, all the noonday brightness of human genius, are destined to extinction in the vast death of the solar system, and that the whole temple of man's achievement must inevitably be buried beneath the debris of a universe in ruins. . . . Only within the scaffolding of these truths, only on the firm foundation of unyielding despair, can the soul's habitation henceforth be safely built.[4]

But if the personal is primary, then the world was made according to a rational plan that can be understood by rational minds. Friendship and love are not only profound human experiences, but fundamental ingredients of the whole world order. There is someone who *wants* there to be friendship, who *wants* there to be love. Moral goodness, too, is part of the great design of the universe. If personality is absolute, there is one who cares about what we do, who approves or disapproves our conduct. And that person has some purpose for evil, too, mysterious as that may seem to us (see chaps. 6 and 7 on this subject). Beauty, too, does not just happen for a while; it is the art of a great craftsman. And if indeed the

---

[4]Russell, "A Free Man's Worship," in his *Why I Am Not a Christian*, ed. Paul Edwards (N.Y.: Simon and Schuster, 1957), 104–16, at p. 107.

solar system comes to a "vast death," there is one who can deliver us from that death, if it pleases him to do so. So it may be that some of our thoughts, plans, trust, love, and achievements have eternal consequences after all, consequences that impart to all of these things a great seriousness, but also humor: humor at the ironic comparison of our trivial efforts with "eternal consequences."

What a difference! Instead of a gray world of matter and motion and chance, in which anything could happen, but nothing much (nothing of human interest) ever does, the world would be the artistic creation of the greatest mind imaginable, with a dazzling beauty and fascinating logic. It would be a history with a drama, a human interest, a profound subtlety and allusiveness more illuminating than the greatest novelist could produce. That divine history would have a moral grandeur that would turn all the world's evil to good. Most amazingly: the world would be under the control of a being somehow, wonderfully, akin to ourselves! Could we pray to him? Could we know him as a friend? Or would we have to flee from him as our enemy? What would he expect of us? What incredible experiences might he have in store for us? What new knowledge? What blessings? What curses?[5]

I suspect that many who profess unbelief nevertheless *wish* that something like that were true. It is the work of the apologist not only to argue for the truth, but to portray it as it is, in all its beauty, and not neglecting its dark tones. As we thus describe its attractiveness, but also its challenge, we perform an apologetic service. For very often, before someone confesses the truth, he or she comes to the point of *wishing* it were true. That is all to the good. Wishing does not make anything true or false, and it is slander to claim that Christianity is mere wish fulfillment. But a person with a wish to be fulfilled is often on the road to belief. A consistent unbeliever does not find the biblical worldview appealing; he turns from it.

---

[5]The thrust of this paragraph originates in my memory of a remarkable sermon preached by Francis Schaeffer many years ago.

Absolute personality! A personal absolute! I have not studied every non-Christian religion, and I would not wish to say that only Christianity holds to a personal absolute. There are variants of Hinduism and Buddhism that are sometimes described as "theistic." According to some African animistic religions, there is behind the world of spirits a singular personal being who holds all accountable.[6] But it is certainly the case that the major contender for "absolute-personality theism" in our day is biblical religion.[7]

The major religions of the world, in their most typical (one tends to say "authentic") forms, are either pantheistic (Hinduism, Taoism) or polytheistic (animism, some forms of Hinduism, Shinto, and the traditional religions of Greece, Rome, Egypt, etc.). Pantheism has an absolute, but not a personal absolute. Polytheism has personal gods, but none of these is absolute. Indeed, although most religions tend to emphasize either pantheistic absolutism or personal nonabsolutism, we can usually find both elements beneath the surface. In Greek polytheism, for example, the gods are personal but nonabsolute. However, this polytheism is supplemented by a doctrine of fate, which is a kind of impersonal absolute. Similarly, behind the gods of animism is Mana, the impersonal reality.[8] People seem

---

[6]These sects of course do not challenge the claim of Christianity to be unique, because the differences between them and Christianity outweigh the similarities. If these sects are similar in worshiping an absolute personality, that is not surprising, in view of the teaching of Romans 1:18–20 that God is clearly revealed in creation. That there are so few instances of this confirms the teaching of Romans 1:21ff. about unbelievers' suppression of the truth.
[7]By "biblical religion" I refer to Christianity itself, together with the Christian heresies. Christian heresies are religions influenced by the Bible, but which deny the central biblical gospel. Among the Christian heresies are not only those designated as such in history (Arianism, Gnosticism, Sabellianism, Docetism, Eutychianism, etc.), but also the historic rivals of Christianity, namely, Judaism and Islam. Also among the Christian heresies are the modern cults and denials of the gospel: Jehovah's Witnesses, Mormonism, liberalism, etc.
[8]Buddhism is hard to classify. In its original form, it may have been atheistic; there are problems in interpreting the Buddhist concept of "nothingness." Clearly, though, there is no personal absolute in the mainstream forms of Buddhism.

to have a need or a desire for both personality and absoluteness, but in most religions these two elements are separated and therefore compromise one another, rather than reinforcing one another. Thus, of the major religious movements, only biblical religion calls us with clarity to worship a personal absolute.

Meditate on that fact: the fundamental Christian worldview is virtually unique to biblical religion. Why should that be? One would think that fair-minded people (bereft of evidence,[9] forced to speculate), faced with the question of which was more ultimate, the personal or the impersonal, would be equally divided. But no—they almost always gravitate toward the view that if there is any absolute at all, that absolute must be impersonal. (And if there is no absolute, that is the same as "chance" or "fate" being absolute—an equally impersonalist view.) Modern science is no more an exception today than it was in Russell's time. When scientists seek the causes of things, they almost always assume that the personal elements in the universe can be explained by the impersonal (matter, laws, motion), rather than the other way around. And when scientists seek for absolutes—e.g., the "origin of the universe"—they seek for an "elementary particle," a universal law ("theory of everything"), an initial motion ("the Big Bang"), or a combination of these. Why is this so? Is it not initially at least equally plausible that impersonal matter, motion, and force can be explained by the decisions of a person? We have all observed how persons create and harness impersonal objects and forces to do their bidding. In a factory, human workers produce a tractor (designed and planned by people); a farmer uses that tractor to plow his field. But we have never seen a plowed field produce a farmer, or a tractor produce a work force. The very idea seems ludicrous. Yet to many well-educated scientists, the primacy of the impersonal goes without saying. It is, as it were, their presupposition. They adopt it, not on the basis of evidence (for what evidence could prove the negative proposition that there is no God?), but

---

[9]I do not believe, of course, that we are actually bereft of evidence; but that is the way the situation appears to many people.

by an irrational faith[10] that is opposed to Christianity.[11]

The only even remotely plausible explanation of this situation is that given in the Bible: that though God's existence is clearly revealed to all (Rom. 1:18–20), rebellious mankind seeks to suppress that revelation and thus to operate on the assumption that the God of Scripture does not exist. Is this not the most likely reason for the almost universal, but irrational, preference for impersonalism over personalism?

In this section I have not, of course, proved that biblical personalism is true. I have merely set it forth, over against its antithesis, to show the reader one fundamental aspect of the apologetic task. We are called to stand firmly against the almost universal presupposition that the universe is fundamentally impersonal. We must not allow the unbeliever to suppose what he usually supposes—that *of course* the impersonal is more ultimate. We must challenge him to consider the alternative. And if he says he is certain of his impersonalism, and if he despises anyone who thinks otherwise as superstitious or stupid, we must ask him to give for his view the kind of proof that he demands of us. And once we show him that his impersonalism is the product of irrational faith, we will be in a good position to present the one alternative to that impersonalism, the alternative presented in Scripture.

The Creator-creature relationship. According to Scripture, God is both transcendent and immanent. His transcendence is simply the fact that he is radically different from us. He is the Creator and we are his creatures. He is absolute, as we saw in the last section. We are not. Even his personality is different from ours, for his is original and ours is derivative. God is wholly personal and in no way depends on the impersonal,

---

[10]I do not believe that all faith is irrational, though some would define it that way. In my view, Christian faith is based on divinely revealed evidence. Non-Christian faiths are irrational.

[11]Does it follow, then, that a Christian who is a scientist should avoid discussions of elementary particles and such? No, but he should not regard such discussions as leading to the most ultimate answers. The most ultimate answers are in the Bible.

while we are dependent on impersonal matter (the "dust" [Gen. 2:7]) and forces to keep us alive.

God's immanence is his involvement in all areas of creation. Because he is absolute, he controls all things, interprets all things, and evaluates all things.[12] Because of his omnipotence, his power is exerted everywhere. It is indeed inescapable, and therefore omnipresent. His personality also motivates his immanence. It motivates him to be involved with creation in still other ways. For we are, despite the great differences between ourselves and God, akin to him. We are his "image" (Gen. 1:26–27). According to Scripture, God continually seeks to converse with, to have fellowship with, and to dwell with his people. He spoke to Adam in the Garden of Eden, and when our first parents sinned, he continued to visit mankind, to make covenants, and to adopt families (Noah, Abraham, Israel) to be his own. At various points in history, God has actually (in some mysterious sense, which detracts in no way from his general omnipresence) localized his presence in space and time, dwelling in a particular location (the burning bush, Mount Sinai, the tabernacle, the temple, the person of Jesus, the church as the temple of the Holy Spirit).

God is the planner of, and the main actor in, human history. Ultimately, it is with him that we have to do. From Genesis to Revelation, the ultimate question facing humanity was How shall we respond to God and his word? The same is true today: behind all the challenges and difficulties of this life, our ultimate challenge is whether or not we shall honor God and obey his Word.

It is important that we maintain biblical views of the transcendence and the immanence of God. Transcendence reminds us of the Creator-creature distinction. God is the Creator and we are creatures. We can never become God, losing our creaturehood, nor can God lose his deity.[13] Christian the-

---

[12]See later sections of this chapter for more analysis of these categories.
[13]In the incarnation of Jesus Christ, God did not lose or diminish his deity to become man; rather, he added a human nature to his divine nature.

ologians have sometimes erred in this matter, speaking as if salvation turned men into God.[14]

And non-Christians of all persuasions radically deny the biblical Creator-creature distinction. Atheists deny it, of course, but so do pantheists, who hold that the world itself is divine in character. It is denied in secular humanism, in which the human mind is adored as the ultimate standard for truth and rightness. It is denied in Kantian philosophy, in which the human mind is the author of the forms of its experience. It is denied in existentialism, where man creates his own meaning. It is denied in those forms of naturalistic science that claim in effect that the universe is its own creator. It is denied in Eastern religions and Western New Age thought, which urge people to look to "the God within" and to "create their own reality" by visualization.[15]

Liberal theologians,[16] who refuse to be subject to the Bible and who freely incorporate non-Christian ideas into their theologies, also regularly deny the biblical Creator-creature distinction. They insist on thinking autonomously (i.e., recognizing no absolute standard outside themselves), denying the Creator's authority over them. They regularly

---

[14]I am willing to accept the pleas of my Eastern Orthodox friends that they do not mean this literally. However, their "deification" language is confusing. Others, after all, such as the ancient Gnostics and modern pantheists, have used such language literally.

[15]I grant that this point is harder to make against what I have called the "Christian heresies," those faiths that share substantial elements of the biblical worldview. I do, however, find Creator-creature confusion, e.g., in the remarkable freedom with which these religions allow themselves to manipulate, deny, reinterpret, and supplement the biblical message. Scripture is God's Word and is not open to such manipulation, addition, or subtraction (Deut. 4:2; 12:32; 2 Tim. 3:16–17; Rev. 22:18–19). And occasionally, as in Mormonism, where God was once a man and where people supposedly become gods, the confusion is quite explicit.

[16]Note that by "liberalism" I do not mean only the classical liberalism of Schleiermacher, Ritschl, and their disciples of the nineteenth and early twentieth centuries. As indicated below, I include neo-orthodoxy and also the fashionable theologies of our time: process theology, liberation theology, pluralist theology, theologies of hope, history, and story, and so on. Theology is "liberal" if it finds its ultimate authority somewhere other than in the Scriptures.

The liberal is self-Relational — Authenticity has within self

picture God's transcendence, not as his absoluteness (as defined above), but as his remoteness, his "beyondness." In liberalism (and in so-called neo-orthodoxy) God is "wholly other"—so far beyond us that we cannot (even with the help of revelation) speak or think correctly about him. Thus, the liberal theologian not only evades the authority of Scripture, but also gives to that evasion a theological rationale.

It is equally important to maintain a biblical view of God's immanence. Again, the point is not that God loses his deity or that man becomes God. Non-Christian thinkers, including liberal theologians, often use the rhetoric of immanence to suggest that the world is really divine in some sense, or that God is identical with the historical process (so Hegel, secular theology, and liberation theology). Process theologians use the rhetoric of immanence (e.g., "God is really related") to deny divine sovereignty, eternity, and omniscience in their biblical senses. And Karl Barth, the father of neo-orthodoxy, adds to the notion of God as "wholly other" the contradictory notion that God is "wholly revealed" in Christ.

The "wholly revealed" version of immanence contradicts the biblical doctrine of transcendence; the "wholly other" view of transcendence contradicts the biblical doctrine of immanence. Both of these counterfeits stem from unbelief, from the suppression of truth described in Romans 1:21ff., for both indicate a desire to escape responsibility to God's Word. If God is "wholly other," then of course he cannot speak to us. If he is "wholly revealed," then he is on our level and not entitled to speak with authority.

As Van Til put it, the Christian worldview involves a "two-level" concept of reality. Van Til used to walk into class and draw two circles on the board, one under the other, connected by vertical lines of "communication." The larger, upper circle represented God; the smaller, lower circle represented the creation. All non-Christian thought, he argued, is "one-circle" thought. It either raises man to God's level or lowers God to man's. In any case, it regards God, if it acknowledges him at all, as man's equal, as another part of the "stuff" of the universe. With such notions, Christian apologetics must make no compromise.

The biblical Creator-creature relation, like the biblical doctrine of God's absolute personality, is something beautiful. No longer do we have the intolerable burden of playing God— of trying to be ourselves the ultimate standard of truth and right, with all the attendant anxieties of that position. Rather, we can rest in the bosom of our Creator and learn from him wondrous things of how the world was made and his purposes for us. Then we can integrate our own small and brief experience with his revelation, seeking to apply that revelation to ourselves. And what we cannot understand will never threaten us, for we can accept that as the secret of our loving Father.

The sovereignty of God. In *Doctrine of the Knowledge of God* I wrote at some length about God's lordship, which I understand to mean his control, authority, and presence. I understand the traditional term *sovereignty* to be a synonym of *lordship,* in all three respects.[17] In the present volume I discuss God's presence in the previous section, and I allude to his authority in chapter 1, in the earlier sections of this chapter, and in the subsequent section on epistemology. That leaves the subject of control.

It is important to the Christian worldview that God directs all things, or, as Ephesians 1:11 has it, that "[God] works out everything in conformity with the purpose of his will." The relationship between Jacob and Esau was foreordained before they were born (Rom. 9:10–25). Paul uses this relationship as a figure for the broader relation of Jews to Christians. God works all things together for the good of those who love him (Rom. 8:28).

The doctrine that God foreordains and directs all events is generally regarded as Calvinistic, and I am not embarrassed

---

[17]Granted, it is a bit awkward to describe "presence" as an aspect of "sovereignty," but presence does follow from control and authority if those attributes connote (as they must) universal power and universal interpretation. God's presence is not physical (he does not have a body), but it is precisely a presence of power and authority.

to be called a Calvinist. However, other Christian traditions also accept this doctrine, sometimes in spite of themselves. Take Arminianism, for example. The Arminian makes much of human "free will," insisting that our free decisions, especially those of religious significance, are not foreordained or otherwise determined by God. He seeks thereby to reinforce the doctrine of human responsibility (a doctrine with which, in itself, the Calvinist has no quarrel). But the Arminian also recognizes (1) that God foreknows the future exhaustively, and (2) that he has created the world knowing what the future will bring. For example, before the foundation of the world, God knew that Joe would make the free decision to become a Christian. Somehow, then, before Joe was born, God knew of his free decision. So even at that time, Joe's free decision must have been inevitable. Why was it inevitable? Not because of Joe's free will, for Joe was not yet born. Not because of God's predestination, because the Arminian denies that possibility from the outset. It would seem that the inevitability in question had some source other than either Joe or God.[18] But ultimately, God's predestination remains the key element. For God is the one who (1) foreknows Joe's decision and (2) creates the world in such a way that Joe's decision will be made. The decisive factor is God's foreknowing creation. Creation is what sets the whole universe in motion. Is it too much to say that God's foreknowing creation *causes* Joe to make the decision he makes?

Thus, even Arminianism implicitly concedes the Calvinist point without admitting it. Therefore, some Arminians today have abandoned the premise that God foreknows everything and have moved to a view more akin to that of process theology. But this move is exceedingly dubious scripturally.

The main point is that Christians who honor Scripture as God's word regularly recognize—theological formulations to the contrary notwithstanding—that God rules over all of

---

[18]That is a scary possibility! In rejecting "divine determinism," the Arminian in effect embraces a determinism coming from some mysterious other source—another god? the Devil? world history? impersonal laws? In any case, this idea certainly does not leave much room for free will.

nature and history. The doctrine of divine sovereignty is the possession of the whole church.

This divine rulership is important to apologetics, because it destroys the unbeliever's pretense of autonomy. If God creates and governs all things, then he interprets all things. His plan is the ultimate source of the events of nature and history, and his plan never fails. Therefore, his plan determines what things are, what is true or false, and what is right or wrong. For us to make judgments in these areas, we must consult his revelation (in nature and Scripture), seeking humbly to think God's thoughts after him. We may not claim that our mind, or anything else in creation, is the ultimate standard for being, truth, or right.

The Trinity. Finally, the Christian God is three in one. He is Father, Son, and Holy Spirit. There is only one God (Deut. 6:4ff.; Isa. 44:6). But the Father is God (John 20:17), the Son is God (John 1:1; Rom. 9:5; Col. 2:9; Heb. 1:10ff.), and the Spirit is God (Gen. 1:2; Acts 2; Rom. 8; 1 Thess. 1:5).[19] Somehow they are three, and somehow they are one. The Nicene Creed says that they are one "being" but three "substances," or, differently translated, one "substance" and three "persons." I prefer simply to say "one God, three persons." The technical terms should not be understood in any precise, descriptive sense. The fact is that we do not know precisely how the three are one and the one is three. We do know that since the three are God, they are equal; for there is no superiority or inferiority within God. To be God is to be superior to everything. All three have all the divine attributes. All three are "Lord." All three have the relations to creation that we have earlier ascribed to God. All three are members of the upper circle in Van Til's drawing.

---

[19]There are many hints of the Trinity in the Old Testament: the "Spirit," the "Word," the "angel of the Lord" as a divine being; the prophecies of a divine Messiah, whose coming is the coming of the Lord (Ps. 110:1ff.). One may even find the three persons together in Isa. 63:9–10. The Old Testament God is no "blank unity." But of course this doctrine is not fully revealed until the New Testament, when there are distinct "comings" of the Son and the Spirit.

Even if some question exists about the doctrines we discussed earlier, there is little debate that the doctrine of the Trinity is unique to Christianity. There are interesting triads (threefold distinctions) in other religions, such as the Hindu gods Brahma, Vishnu, and Siva. Many people intuitively grasp that there is something remarkable about the number three. But the Hindu gods are three gods, not one God in three persons, and other alleged parallels between non-Christian religions and the Trinity collapse on examination. Essentially, rivals of Christianity ignore or deny the Trinity. Despite Hegel's triads, there is nothing like it in secular philosophy. There is nothing like it in the other major religions of the world. And even in the Christian heresies there is little of the Trinity. Indeed, in these heresies the doctrine of the Trinity is often the first to be denied.

Why is the Trinity important to apologetics? Well, what happens when unitarianism (the view that God is merely one) is substituted for Trinitarianism? One result is that the God so defined tends to lose definition and the marks of personality. In the early centuries of the Christian era, the Gnostics, the Arians, and the Neoplatonists worshiped a non-Trinitarian God. That God was a pure oneness, with no plurality of any kind. But one what? A unity of what? In answer to those questions, nothing could be said. Anything we say about God would suggest a division, a plurality, at least between subject and predicate. "God is x" creates, they said, a plurality between God and x. So we cannot speak of God at all. To such thinkers, God's nature was, in modern terms, "wholly other." It could not be described in human language, for (among other reasons) the human mind cannot conceive of a blank oneness. The logical conclusion, then, would seem to be not to speak of God at all. But the ancient unitarians would not accept that conclusion. Therefore, in answer to the question One what? they pointed to the creation: God is a perfect unity of those things that are separated in the creation. But if God is defined merely in terms of creation, then he is relative to creation. And, indeed, these early unitarians saw reality as a "chain of being" between the unknowable God and the knowable world (a world that was actually a divine emanation: God in his plurality). God was relative to the world, and the world was relative to God.

Anti-Trinitarianism always has that effect. It leads to a "wholly other" God, rather than a God who is transcendent in the biblical sense. Paradoxically, at the same time, it leads to a God who is relative to the world, rather than the sovereign Lord of Scripture. It leads to a blank "One" rather than the absolute personality of the Bible. It makes the Creator-creature distinction a difference in degree rather than a difference of being. Thus, e.g., Islam's doctrine of predestination often has the ring of an impersonal determinism rather than of the wise and good planning of the biblical Lord. And Islam's Allah can make arbitrary changes in his very nature, in contrast with the abiding, dependably personal character of the God of Scripture. The doctrine of the Trinity reinforces the earlier points we have made about God and the world.

The New Testament has a remarkable answer to the question One what? It answers, "One unity of Father, Son, and Holy Spirit"! It is interesting that when the New Testament most strongly emphasizes the unity of God, it cannot seem to resist naming more than one of the Trinitarian persons. First Corinthians 8:4ff. and Ephesians 4:4–6 are examples of this. Note also the teaching in 1 Corinthians 12:4–6 on the unity of the church as stemming from the one God. John 17:3 and Matthew 28:19ff. are also relevant. Our instinct resists this phenomenon. If I had been writing these texts, I would have wanted to avoid confusing matters by alluding to the Trinity in contexts where I was emphasizing God's oneness. But the biblical writers thought otherwise, because to them the Trinity confirmed, rather than compromised, the oneness of God. God's oneness is, precisely, a oneness of three persons.

Since God is both three and one, he can be described in personalistic terms without being made relative to the world. For example, God is love (1 John 4:8). Love of what? If we immediately answer "love of the world," then we have a problem. For on that account the divine attribute of love depends on the existence of the world. And to say that God's attributes depend on the world is to say that God himself depends on the world. This is the route to the "wholly revealed." Should we say, then, that "love" is merely a metaphor for something mysterious? That is the route to the "wholly other." We can see the logic of Gnosticism, Arianism, and Neoplatonism: If God is a mere one, he is either "wholly other" or relative to the world—or somehow both. But he is not a mere one. He is one in three. His love is initially the love of the Father, Son, and Spirit for one another (John 17). His love, therefore, like his being, is self-existent and self-sufficient. It does not depend on the world (though it surely fills the world), and it need not be swallowed up in religious agnosticism.

The Trinity also means that God's creation can be both one and many. Secular philosophy veers between the extremes of monism (the world is really one; plurality is an illusion)[20] and pluralism (the world is radically disunited; unity is an illusion).[21] Secular philosophy moves from one extreme to the other, because it does not have the resources to define a position between the two extremes, and because it seeks an absolute at one extreme or another—as if there must be an absolute oneness (with no plurality)[22] or else a universe of absolutely unique, unconnected elements, creating an absolute pluralism and destroying any universal oneness.[23] To find such an absolute in either direction is important if the philosopher is to find an adequate standard apart from the God of Scripture. Thus is revealed philosophy's religious quest—to find an absolute, a god, in the world. But the Christian knows there is no absolute unity (devoid of plurality) or absolute plurality (devoid of unity). These exist neither in the world nor in the

---

[20]Examples: Neoplatonism, Spinoza, Hegel.
[21]Examples: Democritus, Epicurus, Leibniz, the early Wittgenstein.
[22]Such as the "Being" of Parmenides, "the One" of Plotinus, and the "God or Nature" of Spinoza.
[23]Examples: Aristotle's *infima species*, the "particulars" of medieval nominalism, and Leibniz's monads.

world's Creator. If either of these existed in the world, it would be a sort of unitarian god, but there is no God but the Trinitarian Lord. Such a unitarian god would be unknowable, for we cannot know a blank oneness or an utter uniqueness. And if that perfect oneness or perfect uniqueness is the metaphysical essence of reality, then nothing can be known at all. But the Christian knows that God is the only absolute, and that that absolute is both one and many. Thus, we are freed from the task of trying to find utter unity or utter disunity within the world. When we search for ultimate criteria or standards, we look, not to some "maximum unity" or "utter uniqueness" within the world, but to the living God, who alone furnishes the ultimate criteria for human thought. Thus, the Trinity also has implications for epistemology.[24]

Epistemology

I have discussed epistemology extensively in *Doctrine of the Knowledge of God* and have outlined my major epistemological concerns in chapter 1 of this volume.[25] Consider also the points made above under "Divine Sovereignty"—that God as Lord interprets everything definitively, so that when we want to know something, we must seek to think his thoughts after him. And note my Trinitarian epistemology in the last section. Since I have already said the most important things on this subject, the present section will be short.

God is not only omnipotent, but also omniscient. As we have seen, he controls all things by his wise plan. Hence, he knows all things (Heb. 4:12–13; 1 John 3:20). All of our knowledge, therefore, originates in him. Thus, "the fear of the LORD is the beginning of knowledge" (Prov. 1:7).

---

[24]This is the best I can do to explain Van Til's claim that "the Trinity solves the 'one and many problem.'" Instinctively, I feel that Van Til is right about this, but the point is terribly difficult to formulate coherently. No doubt my formulation can be improved upon.

[25]Philosophically sophisticated readers might also be interested in my article "Christianity and Contemporary Epistemology," *Westminster Theological Journal* 52, 1 (Spring 1990):131–41.

God is not only the origin of truth, but also the supreme authority for knowledge. Authority is part of his lordship. God has the right to command and be obeyed. He has, therefore, the right to tell us what we must believe.[26]

When sinners try to gain knowledge without the fear of the Lord, that knowledge is distorted (Rom. 1:21–25; 1 Cor. 1:18–2:5). This is not to say that every sentence they utter is false. It is to say that their basic worldview is twisted and unreliable. Their most serious epistemological mistake is, typically, to assert their own autonomy: to make themselves, or something other than the biblical God, the final standard of truth and right.

So rationalistic philosophy declares human reason to be the final standard. Empiricism, recognizing the flights of speculation to which unbridled "reason" is prone, demands that all ideas be ultimately accountable to human sense experience. And skepticism, recognizing that both human reason and sense experience are prone to error, declares (on its own authority!) that truth is unattainable.[27] Kantian and existentialist thought in effect make man the very source of significance in his experience. Liberal theologians are all too eager to go along with these traditions, and the Christian heresies continue to manipulate the biblical message as they see fit.

---

[26]This is the great offense to modern man, indeed to all non-Christian thinkers of all ages—the thought that someone else has the right to tell us what to believe. Philosophy itself may well have developed out of rebellion against the traditional religions, as it sought to find answers to problems determined not by religious traditions but by independent—autonomous— human thought. To tell these intellectuals that their whole movement toward "free thought" (so often praised rhapsodically) was a mistake is to offend them at a very deep level. I will grant to them that it is wrong to allow one's mind to be enslaved to merely human traditions. (In fact, such enslavement continues to be a problem even in the most purportedly "free-thinking" circles. How often we hear from our intellectual mentors that we must question all the certitudes of our forefathers—but must never be "politically incorrect"!) But where God speaks, his words must take precedence over all our cherished conceptions. Accepting such a humble stance is not easy to an intellectual. Once again we see that salvation must be by divine grace!

[27]But is that declaration true?

51

As we saw under "Metaphysics," again it is evident that true Christianity is *the* alternative to the conventional wisdom, to the consensus of philosophers, religionists, liberal theologians, and popular thinkers. Our time is one in which everyone seems to claim autonomy, the right to "do your own thing." God calls that foolishness (1 Cor. 1:18–2:5); he says it comes from the Devil (2 Cor. 4:4).

The apologist must not only refuse to compromise with these distorted epistemologies, but also summon unbelievers to abandon them. For such epistemologies are part of the unbeliever's sinful suppression of the truth. Like the distortions in metaphysics, they represent his desire to escape from responsibility, to avoid hearing the voice of God telling him what to do.

We cannot consistently issue such a challenge if, as has often been done traditionally, we build our own apologetics upon one of those non-Christian epistemological options.

Ethics

Ethics investigates such matters as good and evil, right and wrong. Like Christian metaphysics and epistemology, Christian ethics is distinctive.

God is perfectly good and just (Gen. 18:25; Ps. 145:17). As Lord, he is, as we have seen, the supreme authority over his creatures. Under "Epistemology" we saw that God is the supreme criterion of truth and falsehood. Under "Ethics" we must observe that God is also the supreme standard of what is good and evil, right and wrong. And he has expressed his standards in his words to us (Deut. 4:1ff.; 6:4ff.).

Unbelievers, we are told, know not only of God's existence, but also of his standards, his requirements (Rom. 1:32). Yet they disobey those laws, and, further, seek to evade that responsibility (Rom. 1:26–32).

Again, the history of philosophy illustrates how human thinkers seek to avoid responsibility to God by claiming autonomy. They don't want to obey God's laws, and so they set themselves up as the ultimate judges of what is right. Teleological ethics seeks to base values on sense experience, but it cannot bridge the gap between the "is" of experience and the "ought" of value. Deontological ethics claims a source of duty beyond experience, but that source is ultimately mysterious—to the point where it lacks all usefulness. Subjectivist ethics bases its judgments on mere feeling, but why should one person's feelings command anyone else's attention or behavior?

After the philosophers, the liberal theologians come running in, waving the banner of autonomy. Joseph Fletcher's "situation ethics" comes from their group, leading the flock of more recent ethicists—the Callahans, Childresses, Gustafsons, Kervorkians, Spongs. And the newspaper columnists, the talk show hosts, and the politicians follow suit. Abortions become legitimate for no other reason than that people want to have them. It is a "choice." Thus develops the conventional wisdom—and thus develop the ills of a society governed by that wisdom. If ethical autonomy is really true, then of course we can justify gangs, drugs, sadistic rap music, and all the rest. But if we are responsible to God, we ought to retreat from these social fashions with enormous haste.

Christianity is the alternative. Only Christianity flies right in the face of human claims to autonomy. Only Christianity, therefore, has the answer to lawlessness.

Good News

But Christianity is not just an alternative to the secular philosophies or a set of moral standards better than those of current society. It is *gospel,* good news. In this respect, too, it is unique—a genuine alternative to the conventional ways of thinking. Scripture teaches that human beings, made in God's image, sinned against him (Gen. 3:1ff.). We today bear the guilt of Adam's first sin (Rom. 5:12–19) and the weight of our own sins against God (Rom. 3:10ff.). Our problem, therefore, is not finitude (as we are told by some pantheists, New Age thinkers, and the like), and the solution to the problem is not for us to become God. Nor is our chief problem to be found in our heredity, environment, emotional makeup, poverty, or sicknesses.[28] Rather, the problem is sin: willful transgression of God's law (1 John 3:4). According to Scripture, existing evils of heredity, environment, sickness, and so on are due to the Fall (Gen. 3:17–19; Rom. 8:18–22).

And what is the solution? "For God so loved the world that he gave his one and only Son, that whoever believes in him should not perish but have eternal life" (John 3:16). Jesus died for our sins and was raised for our justification (Rom. 3:20–8:11; 1 Cor. 15:1–11). The scriptural directive is not for us to work harder to achieve God's favor (Rom. 3:20), but to accept God's mercy through Christ as a free gift (Eph. 2:8–10).

No philosophy, no liberal theology, not even any Christian heresy offers any solution to human sin, beyond encouragements to try harder. However persuasive they may be in other respects, these ideologies agree that there is no free gift of divine forgiveness through the sacrifice of Jesus. Empiricism, rationalism, idealism, Judaism, Islam, Mormonism, the Jehovah's Witnesses—all are religions of works righteousness, which is self-righteousness. They offer us only the hollow advice to try harder, or the false and morally destructive claim that God will forgive without demanding anything.

Allow me to draw the application that evangelism is part of apologetics (as the reverse is also true—perspectivally!). The apologist must always be ready to present the gospel. He must not get so tangled up in arguments, proofs, defenses, and critiques that he neglects to give the unbeliever what he needs most.

We see that Christianity, both as philosophy and as good news, is *the* alternative to the conventional wisdom. This uniqueness of Christianity is itself of apologetic significance. Uniqueness does not itself entail truth, but when all the other alternatives march along like Tweedledum and Tweedledee, all claiming implausibly to be able to explain the personal by

---

[28]Jay Adams and others have pointed out the tendency in modern culture to explain moral problems by medical models: mental illness, homosexuality as genetic, etc.

means of the impersonal, all claiming autonomy (and thus denying God's sovereignty), all claiming to find ultimates not in God but in creation, all offering as a solution to our predicament nothing more profound than works righteousness—indeed, without a dime's worth of difference among these conventional ideologies—it certainly makes sense to give a high priority to investigating Christianity and its claims. Indifference to such uniqueness is not wise.

THREE

▼

Apologetics as Proof: Some Methodological Considerations

In the remaining chapters I intend to discuss more fully the three forms of apologetics defined in the first chapter: proof, defense, and offense. In this chapter and the next two, the subject will be "proof," or finding a rational basis for faith.

Faith, Scripture, and Evidence

Faith is not mere rational thought, but it is not irrational either. It is not "belief in the absence of evidence"; rather, it is a trust which rests upon sufficient evidence. This fact is evident in Scripture. Abraham's willingness to sacrifice his son Isaac (Gen. 22) is often presented as an example of a faith which contravenes moral and rational norms. But this analysis often fails to take account of the fact that Abraham had a very firm basis for doing what he did—namely, the command of God. What God says can be neither irrational nor immoral, for his word defines rationality and morality for us. When God tells us to do something, we need no greater rational basis for doing it. So faith does not believe despite the absence of evidence; rather, faith honors God's word as sufficient evidence.

Romans 4:20–21 describes Abraham's faith—always in the New Testament a model of Christian faith—as follows: "Yet he did not waver through unbelief regarding the promise of God, but was strengthened in his faith and gave glory to God, being fully persuaded that God had power to do what he had promised."

Another example: I have often asked students to paraphrase Paul's argument for the Resurrection in 1 Corinthians 15:1–11. They often mention the post-Resurrection appearances, especially to the five hundred eyewitnesses, most of whom were still alive when Paul wrote (v. 6). But they almost always miss the main thrust of the apostle's argument.[1] The main thrust is perfectly clear from the structure and content of the passage: you should believe in the Resurrection because it is part of the apostolic preaching! Note verses 1–2: "Now, brothers, I want to remind you of the gospel I preached to you, which you have received and on which you have taken your stand. By this gospel you are saved, if you hold firmly to the word I preached to you. Otherwise, you have believed in vain." And verse 11: "Whether, then, it was I or they, this is what we preach, and this is what you believed."

Paul is telling the Corinthians that they came to faith through his preaching, which included the preaching of the Resurrection. He warns them not to cast doubt on the Resurrection, for if Christ has not been raised, their faith will be in vain. If the Resurrection is subject to doubt, all the rest of the message will also be subject to doubt, and then "we are to be pitied more than all men" (v. 19; see also vv. 14–18).

The ultimate proof, the ultimate evidence, is the Word of God. Eyewitnesses are important, but they die, and memories of them fade. Only if their testimony is preserved in God's written Word will that testimony have continuing value down through the history of the world.

To trust God's Word as ultimate evidence is not to deny the importance of reasons. God does not always reveal the

---

[1]Perhaps they miss it because they have been influenced by the evidentialist apologetic literature, which focuses almost exclusively on the data just mentioned.

reasons for what he says and does, but as a wise, true, and faithful God, and as the very standard of rationality, he always has a reason—of that we may be confident. Often he does reveal his reasons to us. Abraham knew that God had a reason for commanding him to sacrifice his son, even though that reason was hidden at first. Later, he came to know in some measure what that reason was: to test his faith (Gen. 22:16–18). In the light of the completed canon, we can see more of the reason: God was teaching us to experience something of his own agony in giving up his own Son to death on our behalf.

Scripture often contains its own reasons for the things it says. When Paul tells us in Romans 8:1 that "there is now no condemnation for those who are in Christ Jesus," he adds the word "therefore."[2] "Therefore" indicates a reason. Specifically, Paul is saying that *because of* the saving work of Christ already described, there is no condemnation. We should believe that we are not condemned, and we should believe it on the grounds or reasons offered in chapters 1–7. Here Scripture does not merely proclaim the truth; it also proclaims reasons for believing the truth. And just as its truths are authoritative, so also are its reasons. We have an obligation, not only to believe scriptural truth, but also to believe it *for scriptural reasons.*

"Therefores" abound in Scripture, together with many other indications of authoritative reasoning. When we proclaim Scripture, therefore, we may (and must, if we want to be complete in our exegesis) also proclaim that authoritative reasoning process, the biblical rationale.

Showing biblical reasons for biblical truth is a very important part of apologetics. An unbeliever asks, "Why did Jesus curse the fig tree in Matthew 21:19ff.? That seems like such a cruel and petty thing to do!" The believer should answer by showing from Scripture itself the symbolism of approaching judgment and therefore the point of Jesus' object lesson.

---

[2]You know the old saying: when you see a "therefore" in Scripture, you should always look to see what it's "there for."

This does not mean, however, that direct scriptural proof is the only apologetic evidence that God permits us to use. As we have seen, Scripture itself directs us to consider evidence outside itself.[3] For the first-century believers, at least, the five hundred eyewitnesses of 1 Corinthians 15:6 were a valuable resource, even a supplement to the apostle's word. Certainly Paul's argument in chapter 15 implies that if people have doubts, they can look up the witnesses. Of course, the witnesses' testimony is to be evaluated by way of a biblical view of evidence—not by theories like those of David Hume and Rudolf Bultmann, which reject all supernatural claims from the outset.

Paul argues, as we have seen, that God is clearly revealed in the creation (Rom. 1:18–21). We may infer that there is evidence in creation, God's "general revelation," which, in a way similar to the evidence provided by the witnesses mentioned in 1 Corinthians 15, supplements the evidence of Scripture itself. But that evidence must also be assessed on biblical criteria. As I argued in chapter 1, we may freely use extrabiblical evidence as long as we use it in ways acceptable to Scripture.[4]

The Concept of Proof

Cornelius Van Til says that "there is absolutely certain proof for the existence of God and the truth of Christian theism."[5] He continues:

---

[3]Review at this point the discussion in chap. 1 of *sola Scriptura*. We should remind ourselves also (see the discussions in *DKG*) that it is impossible to make a sharp distinction between arguments based on "Scripture alone" and arguments based on combinations of Scripture and natural revelation. Usually when we cite Scripture, we are citing a version of Scripture, the product of textual criticism and translation principles based in part on natural revelation. Indeed, the very citing of one text rather than another represents a human choice based on factors (audience, need) which cannot be deduced from Scripture alone.

[4]For a discussion of the type of circularity involved in this procedure, see the discussion of circularity in chap. 1.

[5]Van Til, *The Defense of the Faith* (Philadelphia: Presbyterian and Reformed, 1955; 2d. ed., 1963), 103.

The Reformed apologist maintains that there is an absolutely valid argument for the existence of God and for the truth of Christian theism. He cannot do less without virtually admitting that God's revelation to man is not clear. It is fatal for the Reformed apologist to admit that man has done justice to the objective evidence if he comes to any other conclusion than that of the truth of Christian theism.[6]

What do we mean by "proof" in this sort of discussion? The most uncontroversial examples of proof are those in mathematics, where propositions are derived by strictly logical inference from axioms. Axioms are propositions that are considered self-evident or, at least, are assumed for the purposes of the discussion. On this understanding, a proof for God's existence might go somewhat like this:

Premise 1: What Scripture says is always true.
Premise 2: Scripture says that God exists.
Conclusion: Therefore, God exists.

Here, the truthfulness of Scripture would be one axiom, and the teaching of Scripture that God exists would be another. The conclusion then follows by strict logic.

On our previous analysis, this argument is a sound one. The first premise is true because Scripture is God's word and therefore inerrant. The second premise is obvious and uncontroversial. The logical path from premises to conclusion is likewise unimpeachable. In one sense, then, this argument is one form of "absolutely certain proof for the existence of God."

But there is something lacking here. Practically speaking, we would not be likely to use this proof in our witness to non-Christians. Most intelligent unbelievers today would dismiss it simply by denying the biblical authority on which it is based.

---

[6]Ibid., 104.

The circle is too narrow.[7] In one sense, the problem is not with the proof, but with the unbeliever: he ought to accept biblical authority, and therefore he ought to accept our proof. But of course he doesn't.

One way to approach this problem is to revise our concept of proof somewhat by incorporating the unbeliever's response. That is to say, it is not sufficient for a proof to be based on true premises and sound logic; it must also be persuasive. We might say that an argument, in order to be a proof, must be persuasive to every rational person.

I do think that persuasion is an important concept,[8] but I do not agree that it should be incorporated in the concept of proof. That would limit our proofs to those which actually persuade people. But, in fact, Scripture teaches that good proofs do not always persuade, for unbelievers repress the truth. This repression is not always successful; sometimes unbelievers recognize truths, even truths about God.[9] But it is nearly impossible to predict what a given unbeliever will suppress and what he will admit in spite of himself. Ultimately, the only cure for repression is the regenerating work of the Holy Spirit. Therefore, as we construct arguments, we have little idea of what sort of argument will be persuasive to any particular individual or audience. There is *no* argument guaranteed to be persuasive to all people. Not even arguments from Scripture alone are guaranteed in that way, though we know from the above discussion that they are pleasing to God. To have such a guarantee, we would have to be able to predict both the devious process of suppression and the mysterious workings of the Holy Spirit.

One might note that this process of suppression is not rational. Therefore, unbelievers do not fall under the defini-

---

[7]Review the distinction in chap. 1 (and in *DKG*, 131, 303–4) between broad and narrow circularity. The argument in question is narrowly circular because the first premise is so clearly dependent on the conclusion. Of course, all valid deductive syllogisms are circular in the sense that the conclusion is already implicit in the premises. But in this case the circularity is so obvious that it almost begs the unbeliever to challenge the premises.

[8]See *DKG*, 119, 131, 355–58.

[9]The Pharisees described in the New Testament are obvious examples.

tion of "rational person" in the proposed definition of proof. Then that definition is of no apologetic significance. For the whole point of apologetics is to present the truth to unbelievers. The question then becomes: How should we present the truth to nonrational persons? What constitutes a proof in the apologetic situation?

Perhaps we can remedy the situation by defining proof as that which ought to persuade, rather than as something that actually persuades. But this definition brings us back to the narrowly circular proof we originally considered. The unbeliever ought to accept that proof together with the scriptural authority which it presupposes. As a matter of fact, he ought to believe in God without any such argument at all, simply on the basis of God's revelation in creation (Rom. 1:18–21, again). If our task is simply to put the unbeliever into a position where he ought to believe, then we are best advised to do nothing, for he is in that position already.

I think it is right to define proof as that which ought to persuade. But that does not help us to show what is missing in the narrowly circular type of argument, for such arguments fit that definition of proof. At this point we must invoke a godly pragmatism within the overall teaching of Scripture. Broader arguments just seem to work best. Many unbelievers demand that we consider the facts of their experience, which seem to them to refute Christianity. The apologist is not obligated to refuse such requests, for God is revealed in all creation. Even those facts which unbelievers use to oppose Christianity can be seen to have God's mark on them. Even evil is quite unexplainable apart from a Christian theistic worldview (see chaps. 6 and 7). It is therefore useful for the apologist to deal with such demands on their own terms, making a case based on data from both general and special revelation.

The only restrictions on apologetic argument which emerge from our discussion so far are these: (1) The premises and logic of the argument must be consistent with biblical teaching (including biblical epistemology). (2) The premises must be true and the logic valid. (3) The specific subject matter of the argument must take into account the specific situation of the inquirer: his education, his interests, his questions, etc. This third point means that apologetic argument is "person variable."[10] There is no single argument that is guaranteed to persuade every unbeliever or to assuage every doubt in a believer's heart. But since every fact testifies to the reality of God, the apologist has no shortage of resources, but rather a great abundance.

The Need for Proof

In one sense, not everybody needs a theistic proof. Some people, such as W. K. Clifford, have said that it is wrong to believe anything without evidence. But that initially plausible view has been effectively countered in our time by philosophers Alvin Plantinga and Nicholas Wolterstorff.[11] They point out that we believe many things that we cannot necessarily prove. That other persons have minds like mine, for example, is a very difficult proposition to prove to someone disposed to challenge it. Or take my belief that Violet Frame is truly my mother, or my belief that my wife really loves me, or my belief that $2 + 2 = 4$. Such "basic" beliefs (as Plantinga calls them) are easy to accept as being obviously true, especially when alleged proofs for them are complicated and hard to follow.

I would agree with Clifford that we should not believe anything without having evidence in the objective sense. That is, one should not believe anything unless there is objective evidence to support it. Clifford, however, intends to say more, namely, that we should not believe anything without proof—i.e., without being able to formulate an argument based on evidence. (This is having evidence in a subjective sense.) I be-

---

[10] See the discussion of this in *DKG*.
[11] See Plantinga and Wolterstorff, eds., *Faith and Rationality* (Notre Dame: University of Notre Dame Press, 1983). Compare my review of it in *DKG*, 382–400.

lieve that there is more than adequate evidence for the truth of Christianity, but I do not believe that someone must be able to formulate a proof using that evidence in order to justify his belief in Christ.

Evidence has its own persuasive value, quite apart from our verbal formulations of it. When I see someone drive to my door in a Postal Service truck, wearing a uniform, I infer that that person is going to bring me mail. I know that; it is a kind of logical process. I could formulate a syllogism: When people in Postal Service trucks and uniforms drive to my house, it is for the purpose of delivering mail; Mr. P. has driven to my house in a Postal Service truck and uniform; therefore, I can expect him to bring me mail. But why bother with the syllogism? The objective evidence is sufficient; formulating a subjective argument will only waste time.

When we consider the heavens (Ps. 8:3) and observe the incredible vastness of the universe and the magnificence of its order, that experience has a persuasive value equal to, and perhaps beyond, that of any verbal teleological or cosmological argument.

Indeed, Scripture teaches that God's existence is obvious, and many of us would testify that his existence is obvious to us as well. Scripture never argues the existence of God; rather, it states that he is clearly revealed (Rom. 1:18ff.), and it ridicules those who deny him (Ps. 14:1). The "fool" in the psalm who says "There is no God" says it, not out of intellectual error, but out of moral blindness (see the following verses). He has repressed the truth, as have the unbelievers described in Romans 1:21ff. Or, to put the same point differently, he is blinded by Satan (2 Cor. 4:4).

In contrast to such fools, many people grow up with God and receive him gladly. They hear about God in church, in Sunday school, around the family dinner table, and in Christian school. They see their parents making decisions based on the Word of God. They learn Scripture verses and catechism from memory. God is literally the head of their home. They could no easier doubt God's existence than they could doubt the existence of their own father or mother.[12]

Indeed, for people of this sort, trying to prove God's existence would be at best a theoretical exercise, at worst a form of impudence. What shall we think of a child who demands proof that his father really is his father before he agrees to obey? Clearly—in most cases!—he is avoiding responsibility. He ought simply to believe and obey, without "proof."

Scripture never rebukes childlike faith; indeed, Jesus makes such faith a model to be followed by adults (Luke 18:16). One who requires proof may be doing it out of ungodly arrogance, or he may be thereby admitting that he has not lived in a godly environment and has taken counsel from fools. God's norm for us is that we live and raise our children in such a way that proof will be unnecessary.

Still, as we saw in the previous section, there are some who claim that proof is necessary *for them.* As we have seen, Scripture does more than simply rebuke them. It provides much persuasive testimony of God's reality and also points us to sources outside itself where more testimony can be found. Often the most effective thing is for the inquirer simply to read the Bible. God's Word is powerful as the Spirit drives it into the heart. Another valuable piece of advice to an inquirer is simply to be as open as he can be to the creation itself. That, too, clearly reveals God, as we have seen, even when that data is not formulated into an argument. Think of how many, many people have looked at the stars or the wonders of the earth and sea and concluded that someone must have planned and made it all. That conclusion, however vague, is a confession of our God of absolute personality. And in one way, it goes beyond any teleological or cosmological argument. It is as if a teleological argument based on star formation were repeated billions of times— once for each star.

---

[12]Compare Van Til's pamphlet, *Why I Believe in God* (Philadelphia: Committee on Christian Education, Orthodox Presbyterian Church, n.d.).

But, as we have seen, it is possible to go beyond these general recommendations and produce specific arguments for God's existence. A wise man does not really need these; they are for fools. But God is very patient and gracious with fools such as we all once were.

Once we get beyond simply pointing the unbeliever to the creation and the statements of Scripture, proof becomes a fairly complicated matter. Since everything is created and directed by God, nothing may be properly understood apart from him. That means that any fact may become the focal point for an apologetic; the apologist may show how that fact derives its intelligibility from God. There are a wide variety of approaches and methods that we may use, consistent with our overall presuppositional commitment. Since proof is "person variable," we are particularly interested in choosing an argumentative approach that makes contact with the individual or group we are talking to. That decision is not an easy one.

It is interesting in this connection to ask how people actually come to faith in Christ. I have not made a scientific survey of the conversion testimonies of Christians, but I have heard a great many of them in my life, and I can make some rough generalizations. For one thing, few Christians, when asked to list the factors that led them to trust in Christ, list any argument or proof at all. For most, the issue is not intellectual; for them, Christianity was, in an intellectual sense, believable enough. The issue was, rather, that the person was not yet motivated to repent of sin, seek forgiveness, and obey the Christian revelation. That motivation, supernatural in origin, came through various experiences—often merely a very vivid retelling of the gospel of Jesus, especially such a retelling connected by loving, winsome behavior. (As I indicated earlier, behavior is part of communication; our lives are part of our apologetic.)

Then comes a theistic proof, possibly unstated, but representing the following sort of thought process:

Premise 1: If Jesus is Lord and Savior, then he is reliable.
Premise 2: If he is reliable, then God exists.
Premise 3: He is Lord and Savior.
Conclusion: Therefore, God exists.

This is a somewhat narrowly circular argument, but it is very persuasive to many people;[13] it represents the actual thought process that brings many to faith in God. Apologists often routinely assume that an inquirer must consider theistic proofs before he or she considers the specific case for Christianity, but in real life the reverse order is often the case: it is Jesus who assures us that God is real.[14]

Many different orders of argumentation are possible, for three reasons. First, Christianity is a package; its doctrines are interrelated; each, rightly understood, will lead you to the others. Second, at some level everyone knows that the Christian God exists, although each person requires supernatural help to embrace that truth in love. The Spirit works in mysterious ways, and his use of us apologists is not limited to the strategies described in apologetics textbooks. Third, proof is "person variable" and different people respond to different approaches.

For some inquirers, it does seem to be necessary to discuss the existence of God before we discuss Jesus. They simply insist on it, and we have no reason to refuse. When they ask a question, we should be ready to answer it, even if that question is "How can I believe that God exists?" (Recall 1 Peter 3:15–16.) And indeed there are some Christians—not a

---

[13]In practice, of course, it is likely to be much broader, especially since much evidence will be demanded to establish premise 3.

[14]One of my correspondents asks, "Who believes that Jesus is the Son of God without first believing that there is a God who can have a Son?" But we must keep reminding ourselves that unbelievers are not ignorant of God. They know God, but suppress that knowledge (as that particular correspondent is certainly aware!). The theistic proof is only a prod, a stimulus to bring what is suppressed to the surface, if God will so use it. We all have, indeed, many beliefs of which we are only dimly aware, which in some circumstances we might even deny, but which can be brought out through challenges of various sorts. And surely many people are, shall we say, reassured of God's reality by considering Jesus.

great many, but some—who will testify that a proof of God's existence helped them to believe in Christ, or at least that a proof took away one of their excuses for unbelief. The great writer and scholar C. S. Lewis described his quest for God as very much an intellectual journey, and in his case I have no doubt that it was. His writings, in turn, bore much spiritual fruit. Perhaps there are some that we can help today by arguing for the existence of God.

As we do the difficult job of selecting the appropriate strategy for our situation, we want to find an approach that (1) will be intellectually understandable to our inquirers, (2) will arouse and maintain their interest, (3) will perhaps interact with some area in which they admit weakness or uncertainty, pressing it harder, (4) will contain some element of surprise, so that their prepared responses will be nullified and they will be forced to think, (5) will set forth the truth without compromise, and (6) will by its manner communicate the love of Christ.

Transcendental Argument

Van Til understood the need to set forth the truth without compromise to require a specific kind of argumentation, which he called "presuppositional," but which some of his followers have called "transcendental."[15] We saw in chapter 1 the importance of reasoning on the basis of Christian presuppositions. But Van Til took his presuppositionalism one step further, arguing that such reasoning requires the use of a particular type of argument and the rejection of all others.

The term *transcendental* became a major philosophical concept first in the writings of the highly influential thinker Immanuel Kant. Kant believed in a sort of God, but he was not an orthodox Christian; indeed, he advocated the auton-

---

[15]In chap. 1, I indicated some dissatisfaction with the term *presuppositionalism,* and it would certainly be tempting to replace it with *transcendentalism* if the latter term were at all well understood. I don't believe it is, however, and we shall see some confusing ambiguities in it later on.

omy of human thought—its independence from any allegedly authoritative revelation—in the strongest possible terms.

Kant was dismayed by the skeptical implications of the philosophy of David Hume, an equally strong advocate of intellectual autonomy. In Hume's empiricism, all proof (except in mathematics and logic) is reducible to sense experience. But Hume discovered that on that basis one could not prove any propositions concerning physical causes, moral values, God, human freedom, or the human self.

Kant was unwilling to accept these conclusions, for he saw that they would destroy all human knowledge. Therefore, he rejected Hume's pure empiricism (although he granted that we could not know anything beyond our experience) and adopted what he called the "transcendental method." That method does not try to prove that genuine knowledge is possible; rather, it presupposes that it is. Then it asks, What must the world, the mind, and human thought be like if this presupposition is true? The transcendental method then goes ahead to ask what the necessary conditions of human knowledge are.

Hegel and others in the idealist tradition followed Kant in this transcendental method, although they came to very different conclusions. Van Til studied under idealists at Princeton University in the 1920s and emerged advocating a kind of transcendental method that was distinctively Christian. He noted that in Scripture God is the source of all reality, and hence all truth, all knowledge, all rationality, all meaning, all actuality, and all possibility. So, if one asks with Kant what the conditions are which make knowledge possible, the answer must first of all be the existence of the God of Scripture.

To Van Til, this principle was not only a fact, but an argument for the existence of God. Without God there is no meaning (truth, rationality, etc.); therefore, God exists. To Van Til, this was the only legitimate proof of God's existence. He said that all legitimate theistic proof reduces to the "proof from the possibility of predication." God exists, in other words, because without him it would not be possible to rea-

70

son, to think, or even to attach a predicate to a subject ("predication"). A proof with any lesser conclusion, Van Til argued,
makes God something less than he is. We should not use arguments, he said, which prove that God is, e.g., merely a first
cause or an intelligent designer or a moral legislator.

I agree with Van Til that theistic argument should have
a transcendental goal. Certainly our purpose is to prove nothing less than the full biblical teaching about God—that he is
absolute personality, transcendent and immanent, sovereign,
Trinitarian. And indeed, part of that teaching is that God is
the source of all meaning. Certainly we must not argue in a
way that misleads the inquirer to think that God is anything
less than this. But I have some questions.

1. First, I question whether the transcendental argument
can function without the help of subsidiary arguments of a more
traditional kind. Although I agree with Van Til's premise that
without God there is no meaning, I must grant that not everyone would immediately agree with that premise. How, then,
is that premise to be proved? Is it that the meaning-laden character of creation requires a sort of designer? But that is the traditional teleological argument. Is it that the meaning-structure
of reality requires an efficient cause? That is the traditional cosmological argument. Is it that meaning entails values, which in
turn entail a valuer? That is a traditional values argument.

2. Second, I do not agree that the traditional arguments
necessarily conclude with something less than the biblical
God. Take the teleological argument, that the purposefulness
of the natural world implies a designer. Well, certainly the God
of Scripture is more than a mere designer. But the argument
doesn't say that he is merely a designer, only that he is a designer, which he certainly is. Similar things can be said about
the other traditional theistic proofs. It would be wrong to think
of God merely as a first cause, but the cosmological argument
does not entail such a conclusion.

3. It should also be remembered that the traditional arguments often work. They work because (whether the apologist recognizes this or not) they presuppose a Christian

worldview. For example, the causal argument assumes that everything in creation has a cause. That premise is true according to a Christian worldview, but it is not true (at least in the traditional sense) in a worldview like that of Hume or Kant. So understood, the proof is part of an overall Christian understanding of things, and there can be no legitimate objection to it. However, once one defines "cause" as Hume or Kant does, the argument goes nowhere. Now many people can be led to accept the existence of God through the traditional argument because they agree to a Christian concept of cause. This is part of God's revelation that they have not repressed—what Van Til calls "borrowed capital." But once they become more sophisticated and philosophical (i.e., more self-conscious about suppressing the truth) they are likely to raise objections to such proofs on the basis of a more consistently non-Christian frame of reference. At that point, the apologist must be more explicit about differences of presupposition, differences of worldview, differences in concepts like that of causality. Then the argument becomes more explicitly transcendental. But not every inquirer requires this, and for many it actually hinders communication. So one must recognize the "person-variability" of apologetics and deal with each inquirer according to his or her lights. For some, usually unsophisticated inquirers, one or more of the traditional arguments may be sufficient.

4. Van Til's slogan, "Christian theism is a unit," should be understood with such qualifications. I agree that the slogan is true in the sense that one cannot compromise one doctrine without compromising others, and in the sense that accepting one doctrine provides a logical motivation for accepting others. But I do not think that the whole of Christian theism can be established by a single argument, unless that argument is highly complex! I do not think an argument should be criticized because it fails to prove every element of Christian theism. Such an argument may be part of a system of apologetics which as a whole establishes the entire organism of Christian truth.

5. If we grant Van Til's point that a complete theistic argument should prove the whole biblical doctrine of God, then we must prove more than that God is the author of meaning and rationality. Ironically, at this point, Van Til is not sufficiently holistic! For besides proving that God is the author of meaning, we must (or may in some cases) prove that God is personal, sovereign, transcendent, immanent, and Trinitarian, not to mention infinite, eternal, wise, just, loving, omnipotent, omnipresent, etc.[16] Thus, for another reason (in addition to the fact, already discussed, that it cannot function without the help of subsidiary arguments of a more traditional kind), the transcendental argument requires supplementation by other arguments.

6. All this suggests a further reason why there is no single argument that will prove the entire biblical doctrine of God. To generalize: any argument can be questioned by someone who is not disposed to accept the conclusion. Such questions may require further arguments to defend the original arguments, and so forth. Since there is no single argument guaranteed to persuade every rational person, there is no argument that is immune to such additional questioning.

Therefore, Van Til's transcendental argument (like every other argument) is not sufficient, by itself, to prove the existence of the biblical God to everyone's satisfaction. Nor do transcendental considerations exclude arguments that are intended to prove only part of the biblical doctrine of God.

Nevertheless, much that Van Til says about these matters is biblically true and important. There is probably not a distinctively "transcendental argument" which rules out all other kinds of arguments. But certainly the overall goal of apologetics is transcendental. That is, the God we seek to prove is indeed the source of all meaning, the source of possibility, of actuality, and of predication. The biblical God is

---

[16]One may, of course, maintain that "author of meaning" includes all these other attributes. But this fact is not immediately obvious. An inquirer may well ask for additional argument to show this relationship, just as he (despite his innate knowledge of God) asked for initial proof of God's existence.

more than this, but certainly not less. And we should certainly not say anything to an inquirer that suggests we can reason, predicate, assess probabilities, etc., apart from God.

Must we bring this point up explicitly in every apologetic encounter? I would say no.[17] To be sure, part of the lordship of Christ is his lordship over our intellectual life. Surely evangelistic apologetics is never complete without a presentation of Christ as Lord and as Lord of all. From here, we may well go on to stress his lordship over certain specific areas of life. Jesus told the rich young ruler to sell all his goods and follow Jesus (Matt. 19:16–30), in effect declaring his lordship over our wealth and economic life. He displayed his omniscience by telling the Samaritan woman of her multiple marriages and immorality (John 4:7–18), then described a coming change in the very worship of God (vv. 19–25), thus declaring himself Lord over our marital and sexual lives and even over our relationship with God. To the Pharisees, he declared himself Lord of the Sabbath (Mark 2:28). But he didn't specifically describe all the areas of his lordship to every inquirer; he restricted himself to mentioning those areas which were of particular temptation to each individual. Now we should not hesitate to declare the intellectual lordship of Christ (in the manner, e.g., of 1 Cor. 1:18–2:16) to would-be intellectuals, or others who are particularly afflicted with the desire, the prideful ambition, to think autonomously. But I should think that the majority of inquirers would not need to hear this point specifically. "Christ is Lord" covers this field—and many more—implicitly. If someone has a particular problem recognizing Christ's intellectual lordship, then we should make an issue of it; otherwise, not.

Still, modern "apostles to intellectuals" will find many occasions to stress the transcendental direction of apologetics. Autonomy has been routinely assumed in secular thought since the days of Greek philosophy (and its Eastern counter-

---

[17]See point 3, above.

parts).[18] Intellectuals are often proud of their autonomy (sometimes called "neutrality," "unbiased objectivity," etc.), and that pride must be abased. An intellectual will often agree to submit to Christ as Lord in every area except that of the mind. *Sacrificium intellectus,* "sacrifice of the intellect," is a dreaded concept among modern thinkers. "Oh, yes, Jesus is Lord; but we must believe in evolution, because all the best scholars do." "Jesus is Lord, but all the best Bible scholars deny biblical authority and inerrancy." In reply, it is important for us to tell inquirers that Jesus demands all, not some, of our loyalty (Deut. 6:4ff.; Mark 8:34–38). And that includes loving him with the mind—which may well entail holding some unpopular views on scholarly matters (1 Tim. 6:20).

Negative and Positive Arguments

Van Til does not just stress the use of "transcendental" or "presuppositional" arguments. He also insists that if arguments are to be authentically presuppositional, they must be "negative" rather than "positive." A negative or "indirect" argument is sometimes called a *reductio ad absurdum.* An indirect proof or *reductio* in mathematics is a proof in which one assumes a proposition ("for the sake of argument," as Van Til puts it) in order to refute it. One tentatively adopts, say, proposition A and then deduces from it a logical contradiction or some proposition that is obviously false. That shows that A is false. (One must be careful here: the contradiction or falsity in the conclusion may be due, not to the falsity of A, but to some logical fallacy or additional premise used in the course of the argument.)

---

[18]Greek philosophy was itself in part a reaction against the traditional religions, an attempt to gain knowledge entirely apart from religious revelation. Descartes's "fresh start" inaugurating modern philosophy was another housecleaning, seeking to rid philosophy of any dependence upon religious tradition and building up the body of human knowledge afresh from man's own "clear and distinct ideas." The empiricists and Kant pushed the principle of autonomy to even further extremes, and so has the development of secular thinking in all fields since their day. Existentialism and poststructural thought insists in the strongest terms that meaning is a human creation.

In theistic argument, the indirect argument would run like this: "God doesn't exist; therefore, causality (or whatever—ultimately everything) is meaningless." Since we are unwilling to accept the conclusion, we must negate the premise and say that God does exist. Certainly arguments of this form are often useful.[19] But I have a question about them:

Are indirect arguments really distinct from direct arguments? In the final analysis, it doesn't make much difference whether you say "Causality, therefore God" or "Without God, no causality, therefore God." Any indirect argument of this sort can be turned into a direct argument by some creative rephrasing. The indirect form, of course, has some rhetorical advantages, at least.[20] But if the indirect form is sound, the direct form will be too—and vice versa. Indeed, if I say "Without God, no causality," the argument is incomplete, unless I add the positive formulation "But there is causality, therefore God exists," a formulation identical with the direct argument. Thus, the indirect argument becomes nothing more than a prolegomenon to the direct.[21]

Therefore, I think that Van Til's restriction of the apologist to the exclusive use of negative arguments is unreasonable. I also reject the tendency among some Van Tillians to equate negative arguments with transcendental arguments. Positive arguments can be just as transcendental in their thrust as negative ones, and negative arguments

---

[19]Greg Bahnsen utterly bewildered atheist spokesman Gordon Stein in a debate some years ago with his "transcendental argument for the existence of God," developed along these lines. Stein was ready to answer the traditional proofs, but not this one! For a tape of this fascinating exchange, write to Covenant Tape Ministry, 24198 Ash Court, Auburn, CA 95603. Bahnsen teaches on behalf of the Southern California Center for Christian Studies, P.O. Box 18021, Irvine, CA 92713.

[20]See the previous footnote. The indirect form tends to take overconfident unbelievers by surprise.

[21]As for Van Til's objection that a direct argument assumes that we understand something (e.g., causality) apart from God, see my reply in chap. 1, the section on *"Sola Scriptura."* But even if we grant this objection, it would bear equally against the negative argument.

Indirect is only part

are just as likely as positive ones to express a spirit of autonomy.[22]

Van Til had a wonderful eye for spiritual problems in apologetic encounters. He saw the need to rebuke intellectual pride, to reject the spirit of autonomy, to hold fast to the universal lordship of Christ over all structures of meaning. However, Van Til tended to think that these problems were best handled by restricting apologetics to certain formulated methods. Unfortunately, the suggested methods, even apart from their other difficulties, do not necessarily eliminate the spiritual problem, the sinful attitude of the would-be intellectual. Sinful attitudes can be present, no matter what kind of argument we employ. We must indeed be diligent to rebuke these sins. Jesus' lordship must be clearly set forth in word and in deed. But that spiritual result is not guaranteed by a transcendental (actually epistemological) emphasis or a negative argument. To trust such frail reeds is to court disaster. Nothing less than the whole armor of God (Eph. 6:10–18) will allow us to gain victory over Satan's intellectual devices.

Absolute Certainty and Probability

What now becomes of Van Til's claim that there is an "absolutely certain argument" for Christian theism? He seems to think that transcendental arguments, which are negative arguments, are absolutely certain. But I have, I think, cast some doubt upon the clarity of these concepts and the legitimacy of Van Til's attempt to limit apologetics to these types of argument.

"Certainty" is a somewhat problematic concept. I have discussed it in _Doctrine of the Knowledge of God_ in terms of believing psychology and the assurance of salvation.[23] We should begin with the biblical conviction that God wants us to be certain of the truth of Christ (Luke 1:4) and of our own salva-

---

[22]Remember that someone can be relatively orthodox intellectually and still be rebellious against God.
[23]Pp. 134–36.

tion (1 John 5:13). Regenerate knowledge of God is a knowledge which, as we have seen, presupposes God's Word. A presupposition is held with certainty by definition, since it is the very criterion of certainty. Besides this logical fact, the believer is assured by the supernatural factor of God's Spirit, concerning both the truth of the gospel (1 Cor. 2:4–5; 1 Thess. 1:5) and his own relationship to Christ (Rom. 8:16). It is true that believers do sometimes doubt both the truth of God and their own salvation, but they have the resources and the right, both logical and supernatural, to come to full assurance on at least the major points of the gospel message.[24]

This is the certainty which we seek to communicate in apologetics, as in preaching and witnessing.[25] It is the certainty of a person concerning the revelation of God.

But the word *certain* has been attached not only to persons, but also to evidence. "Certain" evidence is evidence warranting certainty of belief. "Probable" evidence warrants a level or degree of belief less than certainty, but possibly of great importance. Scripture speaks of the certainty of the evidence that God has given us for his truth. General revelation is so plain and clear that it obligates belief and obedience—leaving us without excuse (Rom. 1:19–20). John speaks of Jesus' miracles ("signs") warranting belief (John 20:31), and Luke speaks of the "convincing proofs" (Acts 1:3) which Jesus presented to the disciples after the Resurrection. The evidence for Christian theism, therefore, is "absolutely certain." Or, to put it in moral terms, there is no excuse for disbelief. The evidence obligates belief.

We have seen that certainty can apply both to human beings and to evidence. But Van Til also applies it to argument.

---

[24]See the cited section in *DKG* for complications. For example: few Christians have full assurance as to the meaning of "baptism for the dead" in 1 Corinthians 15:29. Since we are unsure as to its meaning, we cannot "presuppose" it in the fullest sense (although we can presuppose that Scripture's statement is true), and for some reason God's Spirit has determined not to give the church assurance concerning any interpretation of this passage.

[25]Recall my earlier point that these differ only in emphasis or perspective.

What might be meant by an "absolutely certain argument?" We are inclined, perhaps, to assimilate the phrase to one of the other two uses: a certain argument is one which either conveys certain evidence (objective certainty) or necessarily creates certainty in the persons who hear it (subjective certainty). As to the second sense: we saw earlier that there is no single argument guaranteed to create certainty in all its hearers. And if we modify our concept to say that the argument "ought" to bring certainty, we must remember that people have an obligation to believe in God—indeed, at some level they do believe in him—from the evidence alone, apart from any argumentative formulation of the evidence. So no argument *creates* an obligation to believe.[26] In the subjective sense, then, there are no certain arguments.

What of the objective sense? We may think of arguments conveying evidence in the way we think of preaching conveying God's Word. As we saw in chapter 1, apologetics is a form of preaching, and of course we may also equate "evidence" with "God's Word," since the evidence is nothing less than God's ("certain") self-revelation. Now the Second Helvetic Confession says that "the preaching of the Word of God is the Word of God." This is a dangerous equation if it leads preachers to presume their own infallibility. But of course the sentence was not so intended. Rather, the point is that when a preacher sets forth the Word of God truly, that Word does not lose its authority from being placed on a preacher's lips. The content of Scripture is always authoritative, whether written on pages, chiseled in stone, recorded on magnetic tape, exemplified in a life (2 Cor. 3:2–3), or spoken through a preacher's mouth. The same can be said of the apologist as he presents evidence through his arguments. Insofar as his argument communicates truly the evidence that God has revealed in nature and Scripture, it may be said to convey the certainty of that evidence. But insofar as the argument ob-

---

[26]Of course, it may *intensify* that obligation somehow. Granted, there is more to be said on this point.

scures, misconstrues, or distorts the evidence, insofar as it fails (whether because of sin or because of some mere inadequacy) to present that evidence as it is, it lacks authority and therefore may not boast absolute certainty.

An argument, therefore, is absolutely certain in the objective sense insofar as it is a clear communication of God's revelation. Now Van Til tended to describe as "absolutely certain" those arguments (and only those) which were presuppositional or transcendental in thrust and negative in form. In view of our earlier discussion of transcendental argument and negative form, I would resist that restriction of the concept. Absolute certainty pertains to all those arguments which convey the truth, whether positive or negative, whether focused on predication or on some other datum.

At one time I was inclined to argue differently for Van Til's "absolute certainty," namely, by appealing to the very circularity (even broad circularity) of the arguments in question. For example, if in using a causal argument, we presuppose the existence of God, does not the argument reduce to "God exists, therefore God exists"—a narrowly circular argument which, since its premise is scriptural and its logic uncontroversial, is, on our above criteria, "absolutely certain"? I once said yes, but now I would reject this approach. As I indicated in chapter 1, the presuppositions of an argument are not among the premises of the argument. Therefore, the circularity in view is not what is normally called circularity in logic textbooks. Also, the precise claim made by this sort of argument is not "You should believe that God exists because God exists." Rather, it is "You should believe that God exists because (to be sure, on a theism-compatible epistemology) causality implies God's existence, and I can show that by reasons a, b, c, d . . ." We are, in other words, offering a more or less complicated argument for God's existence. But when we do this, even assuming a biblical epistemology, there is room for error to enter in and for a possible loss of "absolute certainty."

Now is there any room for arguments which claim only a probability of being true? Van Til thought that if we claim anything less than absolute certainty, we are "virtually admitting that God's revelation to man is not clear."[27] Again, however, it is important for us to distinguish between evidence, argument, and subjective certainty. Van Til's point is strong in the area of evidence. As we noted earlier, the evidence for Christian theism is absolutely compelling; it may not be described as merely probable. As for subjective certainty, again we should note that God has provided the means for it in the large, clearer areas of scriptural truth, but it sometimes escapes us in those or other areas. Our lack of certainty, then, does sometimes lead us, in all honesty, to say "probably."

As for argument, one might describe as "probable" those arguments which, because of their inadequate or incomplete presentation of the evidence, fail to be absolutely certain. The inadequacy may be due to sin or to a lack of understanding. For example, I might consider formulating an argument for God's existence based on the Second Law of Thermodynamics. But since my understanding of that law is quite imperfect, I would not trust myself in that situation to convey adequately the absolute truth of God's evidence. So I would be inclined in that case to use the word *probably* a great deal. I don't believe that Scripture forbids us to explore areas that we don't entirely understand; quite the contrary (Gen. 1:28ff.). Nor do I think that Scripture forbids us to formulate tentative ideas concerning how relatively unknown phenomena relate to God. To do so, and to use the word *probably* in this connection, is not to say that the revealed evidence for God is merely probable; it is rather to say that one portion of the evidence, not well understood by a particular apologist, yields for him an argument which is at best possible or probable.[28] Van Til him-

---

[27]Van Til, *Defense of the Faith*, 104.

[28]In modern philosophy, there are at least three kinds of probability under discussion: "frequency," the occurrences of a phenomenon relative to a statistical sample; "logical," the likelihood of a hypothesis relative to a body of evidence; and "subjective," the degree of belief warranted by the rational odds. Frequency probability can be disregarded in our present context. The logical probability of the truth of Christianity relative to its evidence is "1" or absolute certainty. But in the subjective sense, both the apologist

self recognizes something like this distinction: "We should not tone down the validity of this argument to the probability level. The argument may be poorly stated, and may never be adequately stated. But in itself the argument is absolutely sound."[29]

What is this "argument" that is "absolutely sound," even though the statements of it may all be inadequate? I would prefer to say that the evidence is absolutely sound, and that argument conveys that evidence with more or less adequacy. Insofar as the argument conveys the evidence truly, it also conveys the absolute certainty inherent in the evidence.

Point of Contact

The phrase "point of contact" is rather ambiguous. Some readers may assume that it simply refers to some common interest which the apologist may share with an inquirer for the sake of friendship and conversation, an interest that may eventually lead to an opportunity to present the gospel. But in theology (chiefly with Barth and Van Til) the phrase has a somewhat more technical meaning.

The issue provoking the use of this phrase is this: Granted that the unbeliever is totally depraved, what is there in him, if anything, that is capable of receiving God's grace? The Arminian answers, "Man's reason and free will." Karl Barth answers, "Nothing at all." In Barth's view, God's grace creates its own "point of contact." This position coheres with Barth's view that the reception of grace has no intellectual element. Grace brings us no "propositional revelation" which the unbeliever by grace comes to understand and trust. It is rather a "bolt out of the blue," which makes no contact at all with the thinking or will of the unbeliever.

---

and his hearers are often left with uncertainties because of inadequacies in the formulation of the argument and in our reception of it. And where there is suspicion of at least some legitimacy to uncertain reasoning, we may speak of some degree of probability. (Thanks to Scott Oliphint for reminding me of these distinctions.)

[29]*Defense of the Faith*, 197.

Image of God = Pl. of Contact.

Orthodox Calvinists,[30] however, recall that God made man in his image—an image that is marred by sin, but not destroyed. Van Til argues that part of that image is knowledge of God, which, though repressed (Rom. 1), still exists at some level of his thinking. That is the point of contact to which the apologist appeals. He does not appeal merely to the unbeliever's reason and will, for his will is bound by sin and his reason seeks to distort, not affirm, the truth. We do not ask the unbeliever to evaluate Christianity through his reason, for he seeks to operate his reason autonomously and thus is deep in error from the outset. Rather, says Van Til, we appeal to the knowledge of God which he has (Rom. 1:21) but suppresses.

That suppression, as we have noted, is never complete. The unbeliever would like to snuff out his knowledge of the true God, but he cannot. Indeed, it is this knowledge, however he may distort it, which enables him to go on living in God's world.[31] Thus, the unbeliever, contrary to his own assumptions, often says things which agree with the truth as the Christian sees it. The effect of sin upon reasoning does not mean that the Christian and the non-Christian disagree over everything, although if both were consistent with their presuppositions that would be the case. Defining the possible extent of that agreement is difficult. The Pharisees acknowledged so much of God's truth that Jesus actually commended their teaching (Matt. 23:3), while deploring their works (Matt. 23:3–39). Thus, as we appeal to the unbeliever's native knowledge of God, we may find him agreeing with us, at least part of the time.[32]

So, how can we tell whether an apologist is using a correct or an incorrect point of contact? When someone argues "Causality, therefore God," is he appealing to the unbeliever's pretense of autonomous knowledge, or is he speaking to the

---

[30]Barth opposes historic orthodoxy on this and many other matters.

[31]I recall Van Til's illustration of the little girl slapping her daddy's cheeks while being held on his lap. Without his support, she could not continue her assault.

[32]See *DKG*, 49–61.

unbeliever's repressed knowledge of the truth? It is not easy to tell, without knowing much more of that apologist's work. If he tells us, of course, then we know, assuming that he is trustworthy. If we know something of his views of epistemology, we can at least make a good guess. Can we tell by what he says to the unbeliever? Well, yes, if he tells the unbeliever what his point of contact is. But he may never do that.

Incidentally, is it necessary in an apologetic encounter to tell the unbeliever what our point of contact is? Certainly the point may be made if it comes up naturally, and I would not recommend intentional concealment; but I cannot think of any reason why it must be part of any apologetic encounter. We can surely appeal to the unbeliever's repressed knowledge even when we do not say that is what we are doing.

In the absence of such explicit statement, it is hard to tell what an apologist is appealing to. Was C. S. Lewis appealing to and therefore compromising with unbelieving autonomy in the argument of his *Mere Christianity?* Or was he appealing to the unbeliever's repressed knowledge of God? Probably he was not doing either self-consciously, for he was not aware, so far as I know, of that particular issue.

Perhaps the major issue in evaluating an apologetic is simply whether it is true. If it is true, then whatever the apologist may think about the point-of-contact problem, his argument will nevertheless address the unbeliever in the right place. If what the apologist says is true, it will address the unbeliever's repressed knowledge of God, whether or not the apologist specifically intends to do that. And if the unbeliever seeks, as sometimes he will, to integrate that truth with his unbelieving worldview, he will find that it is not so easily domesticated. A truth, any truth, will introduce awkwardness, if not contradiction, into an unbelieving system. That will happen no matter what the apologist's views and intentions concerning the point of contact may be.

The apologist's intentions concerning the point of contact are, therefore, not particularly relevant to the external description or evaluation of his apologetics. However, these intentions are relevant to its internal description and evaluation. For the question of the point of contact boils down to this: are we accepting and thus addressing the unbeliever's distorted worldview, or are we accepting and thus addressing the undistorted revelation which he holds within himself despite his distorted worldview?

Here again, Van Til has identified a spiritual issue which is not easily defined by methods or other externals. Van Til may have thought that using a positive or a "merely probable" argument was a sure sign that the apologist was not aiming at the right point of contact. However, we cannot so easily assess others in this connection. What we can assess is ourselves—our motives, our loyalties. Are we so impressed by unbelieving "wisdom" that we seek to gain the approval of unbelieving intellectuals based on their own criteria? That danger, as we saw in chapter 1, has been very real in the history of apologetics. We can guard against it by reminding ourselves that our job is to rebuke unbelieving criteria, not affirm them. Our appeal is not to those criteria, but to that knowledge of God which the unbeliever has "deep down," as Van Til liked to say. The point-of-contact issue, therefore, is a spiritual one, one by which we examine our motives, not one by which we can quickly assess the intentions of our fellow apologists.

Some Conclusions: A Presuppositionalism of the Heart

On this account of transcendental direction, negative argumentation, certainty, and point of contact, there is less distance between Van Til's apologetics and the traditional apologetics than most partisans on either side (including Van Til himself) have been willing to grant. I am not at all saddened by this implication. This way of thinking opens to the presuppositional apologist many, and perhaps all, of those arguments generally associated with the traditional apologetics in the past. We should no longer be embarrassed, for example, to argue for the existence of God on the basis of cause, purpose, and values. These can be elements in an overall argument which has a transcendental purpose (indeed, which has more than a merely transcendental purpose).

I would also conclude that the word *probability* deserves to be rehabilitated in Reformed apologetics. We dare not concede that the evidence for God's existence or the justification for believing in God's existence is merely probable. To do that would be, as Van Til says, to deny the objective clarity of revelation. But to be honest we ought to admit that many of our arguments are only probable,[33] if only because there is so much room for error in their formulation.

Certainly, however, I have not removed all the differences between Van Til and his critics. The issue of neutrality (discussed in chap. 1) is still a high barrier between the two schools of thought, and on that matter Van Til is definitely right. Legitimate apologetic argument presupposes the truth of Scripture, and it renounces the idea of human intellectual independence or autonomy. Its aim, as Van Til says, is not to teach some kind of bare theism, but to confirm the full riches of biblical doctrine, including the teaching that God is the source of all meaningful predication.

There is also a residual Van Tillian point that needs to be made concerning proof. Van Til says, "If, therefore, he [the Christian] appeals to the unbeliever on the ground that nature itself reveals God, he should do this in such a manner as to make it appear in the end that he is interpreting nature in the light of Scripture."[34]

We have seen that Van Til is wrong to disavow direct arguments on the ground that they presuppose an autonomous understanding of the premises. A direct argument can, as easily as an indirect one, spring from the conviction that nothing is intelligible except through God. In the above quotation,

---

[33]We must remember, of course, the distinctions made earlier in our discussion of how fallible arguments can convey infallible truth infallibly.

[34]Cornelius Van Til, *An Introduction to Systematic Theology* (Philadelphia: Presbyterian and Reformed, 1974), 197.

Van Til seems almost to recognize that possibility.[35] Yet he adds a warning—and an important one. There is always the danger of communicating to the unbeliever—through body language, a cocksure tone of voice, or omissions of significant points—that one has adopted an autonomous stance. In the above quote, Van Til urges us to find some way—whether in the argument itself or in the behavior/language accompanying the argument—to communicate that our stance is not a neutral one. Van Til would most like for us to communicate that by using indirect rather than direct arguments.[36] We have seen that that is an illegitimate requirement. But there are other ways to communicate our Christian "bias." Our whole attitude as apologists, our personal piety, our way of speaking—all of these can show the unbeliever that we are committed to the God of Scripture and not to the advancement of our own intellectual status or to the "search for truth" in the abstract or to victory in a battle of wits. All of this is part of the process of communication, and it affects the content of what we actually do communicate. It was not easy for Van Til to talk about such subtleties, but these things, not some rigid restrictions on apologetic form, represent God's way of dealing with what is essentially a spiritual problem.

It may no longer be possible to distinguish presuppositional apologetics from traditional apologetics merely by externals—by the form of argument, the explicit claim of certainty or probability, etc. Perhaps presuppositionalism is more of an attitude of the heart, a spiritual condition, than an easily describable, empirical phenomenon. To call it "spiritual" is certainly not to say that it is unimportant—quite the contrary. Our biggest need in apologetics (as in all other areas of

---

[35]The words "nature itself reveals God" suggest a direct argument more naturally than they suggest an indirect one.

[36]Again I would say that Van Til has a tendency to confuse issues of piety (What is my deepest loyalty, my presupposition?) with issues of method (What comes first in my argument? Should I prove the conclusion directly or disprove its opposite?). Certainly our piety must govern our method, but we must be careful before we, in effect, impute evil motives to apologists who simply prefer to do things in a different order.

life) has always been spiritual at the core. And our "presup-positionalism of the heart" is not something vague and inde-finable. The presuppositionalism we are talking about is (1) a clear-headed understanding of where our loyalties lie and how those loyalties affect our epistemology, (2) a determination above all to present the full teaching of Scripture in our apolo-getic without compromise, in its full winsomeness and its full offensiveness, (3) especially a determination to present God as fully sovereign, as the source of all meaning, intelligibility, and rationality, as the ultimate authority for all human thought, and (4) an understanding of the unbeliever's knowl-edge of God and rebellion against God, particularly (though not exclusively) as it affects his thinking. And if there are some apologists who maintain these understandings and attitudes without wanting to be called Van Tillians or presupposition-alists, I am happy to join hands with them.

FOUR

▼

Apologetics as Proof: The Existence of God

I shall now present an example of a way to prove God's existence, taking into account the preceding introductory points. It will be rather different from the ways to God described in the preceding section. In a way, it will resemble the more traditional sorts of apologetic. Yet the ultimate conclusion is quite Van Tillian: nothing is intelligible unless God exists, and God must be nothing less than the Trinitarian, sovereign, transcendent, and immanent absolute personality of the Scriptures.[1]

This argument will not be appropriate for every witnessing situation—no argument is. As we have seen, apologetics is "person variable." Nonetheless, many educated adults from traditional Western culture should be able to follow its main thrust and appreciate its logical force. These are the people I

---

[1]As indicated in the last chapter, I do not believe that any single argument can prove all of this. My argument is really a group of arguments, and no one of them by itself proves the entire conclusion. It would be unreasonable to expect every argument to prove the whole system at once. However, every argument should contribute to the establishing of this conclusion and to nothing contrary to it. For there is no other God that we are interested in proving.

am most used to dealing with. I leave to other apologists the important work of developing approaches more suited to those of other cultural and socioeconomic groups.

My argument is not absolutely certain.[2] Many readers will find problems in it. Certainly it is far from being a complete argument; at many points it could be improved by providing additional logical steps and clarifying some concepts.[3] Yet it should have some persuasive value—granting that persuasiveness is very difficult to measure in apologetics.[4] I think it is logically sound and in keeping with scriptural norms. I believe that it draws the reader's attention to some data which God has created to testify of him. And the testimony of that revelation *is* absolutely certain. It will convince anyone who looks at it rightly.[5]

This proof should help the reader to see in what sense the evidence for God is "obvious." Romans 1:20 tells us that God's existence is "clearly seen" in creation; but, alas, we so often look and fail to see. My moral argument begins with moral values which, to be sure, cannot be literally seen, but which, nevertheless, all of us do and must acknowledge if we are to make rational judgments. Moral values, then, are pervasive; they enter into all our reasoning and all our decisions. They are inescapable and unavoidable—and they point to God. In that sense, the argument presents a God who is "obvious."

---

[2]Except, of course, in the sense of chap. 3: that it conveys some of the evidence which God has revealed in Scripture and the world.

[3]This book is written in more of a theological than a philosophical vein. My intended readers are Christian workers and laymen with some higher education. Philosophers rightly demand more precision and detailed argument than are found here, and I am capable of meeting that demand up to a point. But I feel that to go through an elaborate philosophical demonstration would inhibit communication with my main intended audience.

[4]The point, of course, is that we never know for sure what will lead an unbeliever, humanly speaking, to abandon his suppression of the truth and therefore be persuaded; or, in other words, we never know precisely what kind of argument the Holy Spirit will choose to use in a particular case.

[5]And looking at it rightly, of course, for us fallen creatures, requires divine grace.

This argument should also help us to see how all intelligibility and meaning, and indeed all predication, depend on God. I intend to show that all such predication, etc., depends on moral values and that those in turn depend upon God. This proof has, therefore, the force of a transcendental argument, though it is formulated in positive rather than negative form for the most part.

I will be arguing, in effect, "Moral values, therefore God." Let me immediately insist that we cannot understand moral values apart from God and then deduce his existence from them, as if the true God depended on values which have meaning apart from him. Quite the contrary. The syllogism will not work unless the moral values themselves are construed theistically. And if someone calls that "circular," I simply invoke my previous discussion on that matter.

This approach cannot, therefore, be characterized as "blockhouse methodology."[6] Indeed, Scripture itself tells us that God is the author of authentic moral standards—that they reflect his nature (Lev. 19:1; Matt. 5:48; 1 Peter 1:16).

I will seek to gain agreement on each premise before passing on to the next one. In my mind, I am not here appealing to the unbeliever's would-be autonomous knowledge, but to his true knowledge of God and creation, which he has by revelation, yet represses. Granted, it is hard to tell from the external course of the argument which of these procedures is which; we noted at the end of chapter 3 that it is difficult to distinguish presuppositional from traditional methods by externals alone.

The conclusion of the argument will not be some bare theism acceptable to many religions and philosophies, but the distinctive God of Scripture. And the argument proceeds by way of the standards and methods of a biblical epistemology.

This argument is not the means by which I came to faith, and it is not the ground of my present trust in Christ.

---

[6]This is Van Til's phrase describing those who begin with a foundation of autonomous reasoning and then attempt to establish Christianity as a second story, built on that foundation.

Yet it should put some truths of Scripture into focus for some people.

Atheism and Agnosticism

My moral argument integrates beliefs and moral values in a way that will be more fully explained in later sections.[7] Our values determine our beliefs in the same way that they determine our other behavior.

People sometimes have in their minds conflicting beliefs, however offensive that may be to logic. In such cases, we are often inclined to ask, e.g., "What does Susan *really* believe?" One test is to observe behavior. One's dominant belief will most often or most profoundly govern one's behavior. As Scripture says, "By their fruit you will recognize them" (Matt. 7:20).

There are many who claim to be neither theists nor atheists, but agnostic. They claim they do not know whether or not God exists. Of course, Scripture denies that anyone can be agnostic: God is clearly revealed to all (Rom. 1:18–20), so that all know him (v. 21), although they repress the truth (vv. 21ff.). In one sense, everyone is a theist, for everyone knows God. But in another sense, unbelievers are atheists, for they seek to erase, to deny, this knowledge and to live on atheistic presuppositions. In this model, no one is an agnostic.

There is no agnosticism by the scriptural "behavior test." If someone were genuinely agnostic, he or she would be frantically trying to find ways of hedging bets: at least giving lip service to God, who after all might one day judge him or her. But, as a matter of fact, most professing agnostics do not hedge their bets in that way. Rather, they totally ignore God's Word in their decision-making. They never go to church, never seek God's will, never pray. In other words, they behave exactly like atheists, not as if they were in some halfway position between atheism and theism.

---

[7]It is also explained in *DKG*, 62–64, 73–75, and elsewhere.

There are some exceptions. I do want to leave the door open for cases in which the Holy Spirit is leading someone toward Christ who has not yet finalized the intellectual issues. People in that position might be described as genuine agnostics. But their openness to the Word of God does not allow them to remain agnostic forever (John 7:17). There may also be some agnostics who do in fact hedge their bets. One of my correspondents claims to have been that kind of agnostic before he became an explicit Christian. Whether such hedging is the hypocritical pose of an unbeliever or the first baby steps of a believer is not usually clear to human observers (and perhaps not even clear to the person taking those steps), although it is clear to God. This phenomenon does not disprove the ultimate antithesis, that everyone is either for God or against him. But if an argument (like that below) is successful in dealing with atheism, it will be successful with agnosticism as well—even sincere agnosticism.

We should always remember, however, that there is no halfway house between being God's friend and being his enemy. "Choose for yourselves this day whom you will serve," said Joshua (Josh. 24:15). "No one can serve two masters," said Jesus (Matt. 6:24). And, "He who is not with me is against me" (Matt. 12:30).

Therefore, the argument which follows is directed to atheists. Others, however, are welcome to read on.

The Moral Argument

Excellent.

Traditional theistic arguments have sometimes focused on causality, sometimes on purpose and/or design, and sometimes on ontology (the nature of being in general). More recently, various arguments have emerged that focus on moral values. My argument is of the latter sort; at least that is how it begins. As it develops, it incorporates the more traditional categories.

Moral values, after all, are rather strange. We cannot see them, hear them, or feel them, but we cannot doubt that they exist. A witness to a bank robbery can see the thief walk into the bank, pull out his gun, speak to the teller, take the money, and walk out. But the witness does not see what is perhaps the most important fact—the moral evil of the robber's action. Yet that evil is unquestionably there, just as moral good is unquestionably present when a motorist stops to help someone whose car has broken down on a dangerous stretch of highway.

What are moral values, and how can we come to know them? Some have argued that although right and wrong cannot be directly seen or heard, they do arise from experience. "Right" behavior tends to be rewarded, but "wrong" behavior tends to lead to bad consequences. Thus, we form the concepts of right and wrong on the basis of consequences. However, these consequences are not at all uniform in our experience. As the psalmists often complained, the wicked sometimes prosper and the righteous sometimes die penniless. And even if the consequences were uniform, that uniformity would be of dubious moral relevance. As David Hume pointed out, "x brings good consequences" does not logically imply that "x is morally good." Statements about facts (without presupposed principles of moral evaluation) cannot entail any conclusions about morality. Valueless facts do not imply values. "Is" does not imply "ought."[8]

Some would say that these values are merely individual subjective feelings. On this view, I call the thief's action "evil" or "wrong" because I am emotionally repulsed by robbery. Well, it's easy enough to describe other people's ethical standards as subjective or emotional. But few of us, if any, would be willing to describe our own standards that way. When we call an action "evil" or "wrong" (rather than, say, merely "repellent"), we normally intend to say something objective. Robbery is not wrong because we dislike it; rather, we dislike it because it is wrong. Our evaluation of robbery, in other words, is not just our own subjective taste; it is a judgment which we

---

[8]Otherwise, if we could show that wickedness on the whole brought prosperity, then we could draw the conclusion that we ought to be wicked; then wickedness wouldn't be wicked, but good.

are obliged to make and which, moreover, we believe everyone else is also obliged to make. Those who make the wrong
judgment are not merely creatures with odd emotions; they
have violated a basic principle that binds human beings.
Those who approve of robbery and murder are not merely
mistaken, not merely odd in their emotional makeup; they
are wicked. They are violating a norm[9] which is just as real
as the law of gravity.[10]

Is it possible that moral values are, if not individual subjective feelings, merely the subjective feelings shared in a given
culture and passed down from generation to generation? Well,
again, as a matter of fact we do not generally regard moral
values as mere cultural tastes (like the Polish taste for piro-
gies). When we hear of cannibalism in a far-off tribe, our response is not "Well, that's their particular taste (!)" but rather,
"That is wicked." So, if these values are culturally subjective,
we must try very hard to change our reactions to things.[11]

So, as a matter of fact, we act and think as if these values were objective, rather than merely subjective. Theoreti-
cally, of course, it is possible that we are wrong in thinking
this way. But if we deny objective values, we should be aware

[9]A norm is a divine law or standard, in this case one which tells us what
values are indeed objective and should therefore be honored. One of my
correspondents insists that all values are subjective, but that norms are objective. I take that to be a matter of definition. My friend can define these
terms as he likes; I don't think my definitions violate any linguistic invari-
ables. But in substance we are agreed: our subjective concepts of what is
right and wrong must be brought into line with the objective revelation of
God, however we describe it.

[10]Of course, the difference between moral norms and physical laws like the
law of gravity is that one can violate moral laws, but not physical ones. On
the other hand, maybe the difference is not so great, for one cannot violate
moral laws with impunity. It is just as true that "the wages of sin is death"
(Rom. 6:23) as that "what goes up must come down." With moral laws, of
course, we often have to wait a while for the consequences to take effect,
but some physical laws are that way too: e.g., we are still experiencing effects of the sun's formation.

[11]For further discussion of non-Christian ideas concerning the source of
morality, see my *Perspectives on the Word of God* (Phillipsburg, N.J.: Presbyterian and Reformed, 1990), 39–50.

of the price we must pay. For denying objective values is something far more drastic than merely denying conventional, parochial standards of behavior. It is to deny rationality itself.

For what is truth, after all? It is many things, but among them, it is certainly an ethical value. The truth is what we ought to believe and what we ought to speak with one another. And those "oughts" are oughts of ethical value. If they were merely subjective, we would be free to believe and maintain whatever we liked, unconstrained by evidence, logic, or revelation. If ethical values were merely subjective, we could make no ethical case against someone who refused to consider facts and who consequently lived in a dreamworld of his own making.

The assertion that ethical values are merely subjective is self-contradictory, like all statements of subjectivism or skepticism. For the subjectivist is telling us that we have an objective moral obligation to agree with subjectivism, while telling us that no one has an objective moral obligation to do anything. Subjectivists regularly make this error. Jean-Paul Sartre, for example, argued vehemently against objective values; but he also demanded that we admire those who "live authentically" by affirming their own freedom and creating their own meaning. If "authentic existence" is not an objective value, why should we admire it or, indeed, care about it at all? And if it is, then Sartre has refuted himself.

Before we consider the origin of moral values, let us note one more point: ethical values are hierarchically structured. "We should seek to make our children feel good" is one ethical value, but for most of us it is secondary to the value "We should seek to teach our children self-discipline." In many cases, there is a conflict between these two values; a good parent will in such cases follow the second maxim, granting it more authority than the first. Conceivably, however, there are maxims even more important and authoritative than the one about self-discipline. For example: "We should teach our children to be kind to others." Eventually, as you climb this ladder, you reach a maxim which is higher than any others in the context. For Christians, in the context of child rearing, that maxim would be, "We should teach our children to love God with all their heart and love their neighbor as themselves" (see Matt. 22:37–40). And in the broadest context, the highest maxim is that we should all love God and neighbor perfectly.

Hierarchies do change with time, for our ethical values change. Even our highest commitments change from time to time.[12] But at any single moment, there is one principle which takes precedence over all the others, one which prevails over all the others in governing our behavior. That highest value is not only objective but also absolute, for it takes precedence over all others and serves as a criterion for the truth of others.

To Christians, that absolute would be God's will as expressed in Scripture. To Muslims, it would be the will of Allah, expressed in the Bible and especially in the Koran. To some it would be the Golden Rule. To some it would be the principle to be kind. To others it would be the maxim "Live and let live." To others, "Do no harm." People can argue with one another as to which of these should be regarded as the highest ethical principle, the absolute norm. But all of us do acknowledge one; otherwise, we would make no moral judgments at all.

Now, where does the authority of the absolute moral principle come from? Notice that I am not asking where the conviction itself comes from, as if this were a causal argument. That is not the point—at least not yet. The question concerns the authority of that principle: why should we give to it the enormous respect which indeed we do give to it?

Ultimately, only two kinds of answer are possible: the source of absolute moral authority is either personal or impersonal. Consider first the latter possibility.[13] That would mean that there is some impersonal structure or law in the

---

[12]Of course, once a person is born anew by the Spirit of God, God's grace preserves his fundamental commitment. This is the doctrine of perseverance (see John 10:28ff.; Rom. 8:29ff.). But even in the Christian life there are ups and downs—times in which we are more, and other times in which we are less, governed by what is on the whole our ultimate presupposition.
[13]Note here elements of a Van Tillian *reductio*.

universe which sets forth ethical precepts and rightly demands allegiance to them. But what kind of impersonal being could possibly do that? Certainly if the laws of the universe reduce to chance, nothing of ethical significance could emerge from it. What of ethical significance can we learn from the random collisions of subatomic particles?[14] What loyalty do we owe to pure chance?

Of course, most antisupernaturalists find ethical value not in pure chance, but in some sort of impersonal structure in the universe. Perhaps it is conceived on the model of physical law: just as what goes up "must" come down, so in the moral sphere one "must" love one's neighbor. But as I indicated earlier in a note, there are significant differences between physical and moral laws. And the main question here is, How can an impersonal structure create *obligation?* (Again, we have a major "is/ought" problem.) Or: on what basis does an impersonal structure demand loyalty or obedience?

One thinks of the fatalism of ancient Greek religion, in which, essentially, fate calls the tune for history. When the tragic hero learns of his fate, he may fight it, but in time he will be crushed by that all-controlling destiny. Here, impersonal fate is stronger than anything else. It cannot be resisted. But does that fact imply that we ought to submit to it? Is one nobler if he submits or if he fights? Some Greek thinkers, at least, seemed to think that one who fights fate is noble, even if fate eventually crushes him. Is that not also our own instinct? The fact is that an impersonal principle like fate is insufficient to create an "ought," to rightly demand loyalty and obedience.

Where, then, does the "ought" come from? What is there that is capable of imposing an absolute obligation upon human beings? For the answer, we must leave the realm of impersonal principles and turn to the realm of persons. Obligations and loyalties arise in the context of interpersonal relationships. In terms of Reformed theology, we may put it this

---

[14]Remember what we said earlier about the is/ought relation.

way: obligations, loyalties, and therefore morality are covenantal in character.

When I receive a bill from a man who has repaired my roof, I feel an obligation to pay it. It is not just that that person (plus the police!) is, like the Greek fate, strong enough to crush me. In the personal arena, there is always another factor: I recognize in the roof repairman a person like myself. And I have the sense about him that he deserves to be paid. Or, to put it differently: when we agreed that he would fix my roof, I promised to pay him. That promise created an obligation, and I would have little respect for myself if I did not keep that promise.

We learn morality, typically, in the family—another deeply personal, covenantal environment. Parents rightly demand the obedience of their children, not only because they are bigger and can spank, but also because they presumably have greater wisdom and experience, greater compassion and goodness, and deep responsibility and love for their children. Beyond all of that, they bear authority simply because they are parents, even when, so far as we can tell, they do not deserve that authority. Other adults may be wiser and more compassionate than one's parents, but the word of the parent still counts for more—unless it contravenes a still higher moral authority.

Our obligations to repairmen and even to parents are not absolute. If the repairman's bill is ten times his estimate, a higher moral arbiter, the court, may have to be involved. If parents tell a son to murder somebody, it is best that he resort to higher moral authorities, perhaps to his absolute or ultimate moral authority. But where does *that* authority come from?

If my reasoning so far has been correct, then that authority can come only from what we called in chapter 2 a "personal absolute" or an "absolute personality." If obligations arise from personal relationships, then absolute obligations must arise from our relationship with an absolute person. If we obey our parents because they are wiser and more experienced than we, because they are responsible for us, and because they care for and love us, then we obey the absolute person because he is *supremely* wise, experienced, responsible, good, and loving. And if our parents deserve honor even above and beyond what their good qualities deserve, simply because they are parents, then the absolute person *supremely* deserves our honor, simply because he is the ultimate personal authority.

Moral standards, therefore, presuppose absolute moral standards, which in turn presuppose the existence of an absolute personality. In other words, they presuppose the existence of God. But what God? Well, consider again the argument of chapter 2. Of all the major religious traditions, it is only biblical religion that affirms a God who is both personal and absolute. We have also seen that the idea of absolute personality is closely linked to the ideas of a Creator-creature distinction, divine sovereignty, and the Trinity. Compromise these and you compromise the personality of God. This precise pattern of thought is found only in the Bible and in traditions which are heavily influenced by the Bible. Is it then too much to say that morality presupposes the God of the Bible? I think not.

Other divine attributes, too, are evident from the logic of the moral argument. The fact that God himself thinks, knows, plans, and speaks is evident from the very meaning of personhood. God's justice is implicit in the fact that he is the very source, the very definition, of moral standards. He himself can never be charged with injustice (see chap. 6). And he is truth, for he is the very criterion of truth and can therefore never be charged with falsehood. (Recall from earlier in this chapter how truth is itself a moral concept.) We may never doubt his word.

If God is truly absolute, then he is without beginning or end. The reason is that just as we cannot rationally understand the present without taking his absolute standards into account, so we cannot conceive of any past or any future without him. A past without God would be chaos, from which order could never emerge; the same would be true for a future without God. Indeed, God is *a se* (self-sufficient and self-existent); no circumstances are conceivable without him, and so it is impossible for him not to exist.[15]

And since he is absolute, he must be one (though with the Trinitarian complexity we have noted). For there can be only one final, ultimate standard for morals and knowledge.[16]

And there are no limitations on his knowledge, power, or presence; that is, he is omniscient, omnipotent, and omnipresent. Why? Because if something existed, but God did not know it, that something would exist apart from God's intelligent planning, creation, and providence. That something, therefore, would be intelligible apart from God. In that case, God would not be the origin of the world, but only of part of it. But we have seen that that is impossible. The world has only one origin, and that is personal. Therefore, God is omniscient. Similarly, if something could be done,[17] but God could not do it, then its "doability" would be measured by something other than God. Therefore, he is omnipotent. And if he is omniscient and omnipotent, he must be omnipresent. Since God does not have a body, his power can be at work (by his knowledge, of course) in all particular locations only if he is in some sense present everywhere.

The argument is transcendental. Rather than offering straightforward empirical evidence for God, it asks the deeper question: what must be the case if evidential argument and knowledge (and hence objective moral standards) are to be possible?

The argument, of course, does not prevent anyone from choosing unbelief. One can do that in the face of any argu-

---

[15]Put positively, he exists necessarily.

[16]If there are two, and they sometimes disagree, then either only one of them is God (if one of them is right all the time), or there is no ultimate standard at all (if neither is right all the time). If there are two, and they always agree, then the fact of that agreement, together with its grounds or reasons, is our actual standard: a singularity, not a duality. If the reason is a unity underlying a Trinitarian type of complexity, which is the most likely reason, then that especially confirms the Christian position.

[17]By limiting my discussion to what "can be done," I am ruling out logical impossibilities like the making of round squares. Omnipotence does not mean the ability to do illogical things.

ment, no matter how strong the argument may be. Human beings, tragically, are able to act irrationally. Further, the argument itself leaves open the theoretical possibility that we could be wrong in claiming an objective knowledge of morality. One could therefore reason that we are wrong about this and therefore about God. Of course, that reasoning would also lead to a denial of objective truth and thus to an end of reasoning itself. So the choice is this: either accept the God of the Bible or deny objective morality, objective truth, the rationality of man, and the rational knowability of the universe. Some might maintain that they don't care much about this. They might say that they can go on living happily enough without having a rational basis for thinking and acting. For these people, other forms of gospel communication may be needed. But let no one say that Christianity lacks a rational basis or that non-Christian "conventional wisdom" is more rational than Christianity.

The choice is between God and chaos, God and nothing, God and insanity. To most of us, those are not choices at all. Believing in an irrational universe is not believing at all. It is, as we have seen, self-contradictory. But if someone has resolved to live without logic, without reason, and without standards, we cannot prevent him. He will, of course, accept logic and rationality when he makes his real-life decisions, and so he will not live according to his theoretical irrationalism. In many apologetic situations, it is useful to point this out.[18] But for a tough-minded irrationalist, logical inconsistency is not a problem. Still, at some level he knows he is wrong. God still speaks, around and in the unbeliever.

The Epistemological Argument

Epistemological arguments traditionally start with the phenomenon of human rationality and ask how that can be. How is it possible that the human mind correlates so well with the

---

[18]Perhaps the most persuasive element of Francis Schaeffer's apologetic was his emphasis that irrationalists (or relativists or subjectivists) cannot live con-

structure of the world that people can make sense of the world? There must be a rational structure in the world which mirrors (or is mirrored by) the rational structure of the human mind.

If the world developed by pure chance, it would be highly unlikely that human experience would mirror the reality of the world in the way we usually assume it does. Why should we assume that chance has equipped me with eyes and a brain so that I can actually see what I'm doing? Isn't it equally possible that when I think I'm a seminary professor typing at my desk in California, I am really a cockroach running around the New York City subway?

The theory of evolution, of course, tries to show (usually on a nontheistic basis) the likelihood of human rationality developing into a reliable interpreter of the world. But even if evolution were true (and there are some pretty impressive scientific and philosophical witnesses against it these days), why would pure chance have given rise to evolution itself—a system so meticulously and rationally (!) calculated to maximize the preservation of species?

Certainly, again, the hypothesis of absolute personality explains the data far better than the hypothesis of ultimate impersonality. An absolute personality can make a rational universe, because he himself is rational and his plan for creation and providence is therefore rational. And the absolute personality is able to make man in his image and to equip him to understand the universe as much as he needs to. Why should one prefer the hypothesis of ultimate impersonality, when that creates such an enormous gap between the nature of the creator (nonrational) and the nature of the universe including human beings (rational)?

The case becomes even stronger when we recall what was said in the last section: truth is an ethical value. The rational quest, like the ethical quest, is covenantal. It essentially

sistently with their beliefs. Indeed, when one tries to live as if there were no rational order (arbitrarily stepping in front of moving cars, etc.), one is not likely to live very long! That message had a strong impact on many minds.

amounts to discovering the will of an absolute person. Ethics discovers his will for our actions; epistemology discovers his will for our beliefs.[19]

Even logic itself is value based. If I confess that "all men are mortal" and that "Socrates is a man," what is it that requires me to confess that "Socrates is mortal"? The laws of physics certainly do not stop anyone from making errors in logic. Is it that being logical leads to success and happiness? But it doesn't, always. Is there some abstract, impersonal principle of rationality that imposes such a conclusion upon me? But why should I be required to act in accord with such a principle? Why should I not rather rebel against it, as a logical Prometheus? Is logic an evolutionary development to ensure the preservation of the human species? But even assuming that evolution were true (and it is no more than an unproved theory), it is not clear that being logical always or even usually preserves life; after all, cockroaches have inhabited the world much longer than man. Furthermore, if evolution seeks to ensure the preservation of species, then it would seem to have personal characteristics or to be the tool of a person. If it is entirely impersonal, with no personal causes, then it has no power to make logic normative. And if logic is not normative, we have no obligation to it. On that basis, even "preservation of the species" is only a concept; no one has an actual obligation to carry it out.

No, the power of logic is normative and ethical. It tells us what we ought to confess as a conclusion, granting our confession of premises.[20] And if it is ethical, it is covenantal; like moral values, it rests on the dependable word of a trustworthy person, a Lord, our absolute divine personality. Thus, when unbelievers use logic to raise objections against Christianity, they are using something which, manipulate it how they may, points in the opposite direction.

---

[19]For more on the correlation between epistemology and ethics, see *DKG*, 62–64, 73–75, 108, 149, 248.

[20]It is, of course, a bit more complicated than this. See *DKG*, 247–51.

Metaphysical Arguments

Most of the arguments traditionally used in apologetics begin with some fundamental reality in the universe and try to show that that reality presupposes, implies, or somehow requires God.[21] These are called "metaphysical" arguments, and the most common ones start from purpose, cause, and being itself. Let us consider them in turn.

Purpose: The Teleological Argument *for God*

The teleological argument is perhaps the strongest argument of all when it is considered informally, but it has always been one of the weakest when theologians and philosophers have tried to state it formally. Even Immanuel Kant, the most influential modern critic of the proofs for God's existence, found "the starry heavens above" (together with "the moral law within") to be a remarkable testimony to the reality of God. Yes, indeed:

creation

When I consider your heavens,
    the work of your fingers,
the moon and the stars,
    which you have set in place,
what is man that you are mindful of him,
    the son of man that you care for him?
                    (Ps. 8:3–4)

---

[21]In my view, there is no logical difference between presuppositions and conclusions. In a logical argument, belief in the premises commits (obligates!) you to belief in the conclusion; it also obligates you to believe in what the premises presuppose. Logically, then, presuppositions are one kind of conclusion. Psychologically, however, there is a greater difference. We believe the presuppositions of a premise more firmly than we believe the premises themselves, and the presuppositions serve as criteria for evaluating the premises. These facts are not true of nonpresuppositional conclusions. To tell the difference between someone's presuppositions and his nonpresuppositional conclusions, we must either hear that person's own testimony or else have a divine insight into his heart. So, for the most part we don't have this information. But we can still exhort one another to presuppose what we ought to presuppose. Once again, we see that a legitimate presuppositionalism is essentially "presuppositionalism of the heart."

The psalmist probably had only a small bit of our modern understanding of the size and complexity of the universe. We today have so much more reason to admire God's work in the cosmos and to wonder why he should give attention to tiny beings like ourselves!

We also cannot help but be impressed by the intricacy of the microcreation. The amazing programming of the DNA code, the intricacy and precise balance of the many tiny parts needed to produce sight through the eye—this too boggles the mind. The wisdom of it goes far beyond the most sophisticated human technology, and when we see that this kind of wisdom is spread through all the molecules and atoms in the billions of stars throughout this immense universe, we begin to get a sense (albeit a very inadequate sense) of the Creator-creature distinction. Evolution? Well, as I noted earlier, many are critical of evolution today, and the Word of God denies in decisive terms the evolution at least of man (Gen. 2:7).[22] The fact that the ability to see requires the independent development of all sorts of organs and powers and their eventual cooperation toward the production of sight makes it difficult indeed to suppose that the process happened "naturally," either by natural selection or random mutation. Indeed, many evolutionists, recognizing the great complexity and remarkable achievement of evolution itself (assuming it to be true), have posited a divine origin for it.

All of this is teleological reasoning. As Thomas Aquinas put it, when we see unintelligent things (atoms, matter, energy) working together for a purpose, we generally attribute that to an intelligent designer. *Teleological* means "pertaining to purpose or goal."

---

[22]I also take Genesis 1 to indicate that there are certain divisions among living things, called "kinds" in the text (which are not necessarily equivalent to the "species" identified in modern biology), which can never be transgressed by the process of natural selection: each creature reproduces only "after its kind." And even Darwin recognized that the evidence from geology and biology is consistent with this picture. Far from there being a continuum of creatures between one general type and another, as one would expect on the evolutionary hypothesis, there are distinct types which reproduce within clear genetic limits.

Intuitively, we feel the power of such thinking. But how do we formulate it into an argument?[23] Historically, most such attempts have been unsuccessful. There is, for one thing, counterevidence for design, sometimes called "dysteleology." The existence of evil is the strongest piece of counterevidence (we shall discuss that in a later chapter). For another thing, David Hume proposed alternative explanations for the order of the world: polytheism and organism (i.e., the world is like a giant vegetable rather than a designed piece of machinery). And Hume also objected that to posit a designer of the world is to go beyond our experience: we have seen watches designed and manufactured, but we have never seen a world designed and made.[24]

Even on Christian presuppositions (Hume's, of course, were not Christian), one may object to the teleological argument. For to say that the world looks like something "designed" is to state an analogy between the world and objects designed by human beings. But we are not interested in showing that the world was made by human beings! We want to show that it was made by someone who radically transcends human beings. A perfect analogy between the world and objects of human design would actually be counterproductive to Christian apologetics; if anything, it would prove that man, rather than God, created the world.

A naive teleological argument may in this way be counterproductive to the Christian's case, but some of Hume's ob-

---

[23]Notice again (as I emphasized in the previous chapter) the important difference between evidence and argument. The evidence is powerful, the arguments not necessarily so. In this case, the distinction is especially plausible. For the intuition lying behind the teleological argument incorporates a vast amount of data. The macrocreation, the microcreation, and the world in which we normally function are all huge. Intuitively, the mind is impressed with the sheer vastness of the design, the myriads of details we observe. We could never begin to formulate all of these details in a formal argument or group of formal arguments. This is one reason, at least, why the intuitive teleological argument has been far more admired than the formal, logical version of it. As Pascal said, "The heart has its reasons that the reason cannot know."

[24]See Hume, *Dialogues Concerning Natural Religion* (various editions).

jections are actually productive. If the world is designed and made by God, then we would expect both analogy and disanalogy between the world and the products of human design. On a Christian view, the world is something like an object of human design, because it is designed; but it is also unlike such objects, because it is a product of divine design. Thus, dysteleology[25] actually favors the Christian conclusion; even the existence of evil can be listed among the evidences for Christianity! The evidence—both apparent teleology and apparent dysteleology—is what we would expect if the world was planned and made by a transcendent God. The same thing is true for the disproportion between the making of watches and the making of the world. Of course we did not see the world made; if we had, we would have been God. That disproportion is precisely what we would expect on the theistic hypothesis.

But once we grant all this, do we still have an argument? Granting that teleology and apparent dysteleology are both compatible with Christian theism, can we then argue: "Both teleology and apparent dysteleology exist; therefore, God exists"? I do not find that argument persuasive! And then Hume reminds us of his alternative explanations of the world order, and it becomes hard to show that the evidence points exclusively to God. Is there, then, any way to capture the powerful intuitive force of teleological reasoning in the form of an argument that is not subject to such objections?

In my view, we can do this simply by making the teleological argument equivalent to the epistemological argument that we considered earlier. The two arguments share the teleological intuition. Like the teleological argument, the epistemological argument begins with the observation that the universe is a rational order, accessible to the human mind. When presenting the epistemological argument, I stated this point in general terms, while in presenting the teleological, I followed the usual procedure of including some specific illustrations.

---

[25]I prefer to call it "apparent dysteleology," because ultimately everything does exist for God's purposes (Rom. 8:28).

But in both cases, the fundamental point is the same. Still, there is one advantage in the epistemological formulation: it is built on the premise that truth and rationality are moral values. Thus, the epistemological argument was reduced, in turn, to the moral argument, and the two arguments yielded the same theistic conclusion.

In the teleological argument as well, it makes a difference when we are able to see truth and rationality as moral virtues. Our ability to distinguish between apparent teleology and apparent dysteleology, and our ability to speak intelligibly about the limits of our knowledge and about alternative explanations for data, imply that we have (or think we have) access to criteria by which to resolve questions of this sort. Ultimately, then, we have access to the values of rationality and truth. And if these are indeed moral values, where does their authority come from? Once again we must answer: from the absolute personality, the biblical God.

The essential antithesis discussed earlier between the two worldviews, absolute personality versus ultimate impersonality, eliminate consideration of Hume's alternative explanations. They all boil down to the impersonalist alternative. Even Hume's polytheistic suggestion boils down to impersonalism, unless the plural deities are themselves products of the absolutely personal God. For only one being can be the ultimate warrant for moral and epistemological values.

Cause: The Cosmological Argument

The cosmological argument is somewhat broader than the teleological. For while the teleological focuses on one phenomenon within the world (that of purpose or design), the cosmological asserts that *every* finite reality, whether it appears to be designed or not, must be dependent on an infinite God, simply because of its finitude. There are many kinds of cosmological arguments. Thomas Aquinas's *Summa Theologica* lists five proofs, three of which are generally regarded as cosmological.[26] The first is an argument from motion: every motion is caused by a previous motion, a process which ultimately requires an "unmoved mover." The second is an argument from cause: every effect is caused by something else; the whole process requires a "first cause" or "uncaused cause." The third is an argument based on necessity and contingency: not everything can be contingent; somewhere there must be something which exists necessarily.[27]

I shall consider here only the argument from cause, which is the clearest and the most intuitively cogent. The Kalam form, from Muslim sources, seeks to prove that the world was caused to exist at the beginning of time. The Thomistic-Aristotelian form seeks to prove that there is a present (or perhaps supratemporal) reality whose existence is necessary to explain the present phenomenon of causality.[28] My remarks will pertain equally to both forms.

Belief in causes is an aspect of a commitment to reason. Roughly speaking, causes are reasons and reasons are causes.[29] To say that event A has a cause is to say that there is some reason why event A took place.

Those who believe that reason is essentially reliable, and therefore that the universe is susceptible to rational analysis,

---

[26]The fifth is teleological; the fourth hard to classify. I think it is based on the notion that the criterion for x must be maximally x. My epistemological and moral arguments also make the case that values require criteria and that the only adequate criterion is the absolute personal God.

[27]Something "exists necessarily" if it cannot fail to exist. Something "exists contingently" if it can fail to exist. Whether or not something contingent exists depends on factors outside itself. Therefore, "contingent existence" (such as ours) is "dependent existence." Necessary existence is aseity or self-existence.

[28]Thomas's proof, therefore, is compatible with the assertion that the world has no beginning in time. However, he also maintains a temporal origin of the world on the basis of faith, apart from "reason."

[29]I say "roughly," because there are many different kinds of reasons and many different kinds of causes, and they do not all correlate neatly. For example, I am comfortable with saying that God's actions have reasons (reasons lying within his own wisdom), but not that God's actions have causes, because a cause would normally be understood as something outside of God (although it does not necessarily mean that).

are attracted to the proposition that all events in the world have causes.[30] To deny that is to claim that some events are irrational happenings. But the rational quest can never remain content with such a claim. If some event took place without a reason, how could reason know it? For example, how could reason prove such a negative as "This event has no cause at all"? To prove that, one would have to assure oneself that all possible causes have been ruled out, and to reach that conclusion would require omniscience.

Further, the nature of reason is to inquire after causes. And if reason does not find a cause, it does not conclude that there is no cause; rather, it looks further—or else it sets the problem aside for future investigation.[31] Of course, there must be one exception to this rule. Once reason finds what it regards as the complete cause, the final and ultimate explanation for the phenomenon under consideration, then it must cease its inquiry. I will later claim that such completeness can be found in God. But rational people do not find such completeness in the creation as such. Not stop inquiry.

Those who claim that some events in the world are uncaused are to that extent irrationalists. Like all irrationalists, they run into problems when they try to argue their case rationally! For there is no way to prove rationally (apart, of course, from divine revelation) that any particular event in the world is causeless. And if some event was causeless, how could it have happened? From nothing, nothing comes, as the saying goes. Furthermore, if one event in the world lacks a cause, then the world as a whole lacks a cause. And if the world as a whole is without reason, then irrationalism triumphs.

---

[30]I have stated this proposition, which is in effect the first premise of the argument, with some care. I would, of course, deny that God's existence has a cause, and I exclude that claim by adding the phrase "in the world" to my opening formulation.

[31]Occasionally, scientists will claim that some event is causeless: e.g., movements of some subatomic particles, the "Big Bang." But in my view, this claim can only be temporary. Eventually, either these theories will be abandoned, or else some tireless scientist will renew the search for causes in these areas.

The irrationalism that denies causation at some point in the world process is not so much a reasoned position as a failure of nerve. The irrationalist fails to find a cause here, there, or somewhere else, so he despairs and says there is none. But what gives him the right to make such a dogmatic assumption? Paradoxically, an element of rationalism enters here, for the irrationalist at this stage is so impressed with the authority of his own autonomous thought that he thinks if he and others haven't found a cause of the event in question, there can be no cause.

Of course, as we saw earlier, an irrationalist can always justify himself by saying that to him rationality, logic, and moral value do not matter. To such a view, our reply is the same as before.

Nevertheless, granted the extent to which irrationalism has penetrated the thinking of our time, it is not surprising that the cosmological argument has often been disparaged. Indeed, the concept of cause itself has been revamped (e.g., by Hume and Kant),[32] so that while it may be said that everything has a cause, those causes cannot imply any conclusions about what was, is, or will be the case. Such concepts, however, fail to do justice to our basic intuition about cause, namely, that cause gives a reason why things happen.

Once that intuition is honored and irrationalism is excluded, the cosmological argument can make some progress. That every event in the world has a cause means that everything in the world happens for some reason. But suppose that there is no first cause, no uncaused cause at the beginning of the process. In that case, there is no complete explanation, no complete reason why any event takes place. If there is no first cause, the process of explanation keeps going on and on—an infinite regression in which there is no ending point. But if there is no end, then there is no "cognitive rest" (as I described it in *Doctrine of the Knowledge of God*). You just keep

---

[32]For Hume, causality is the frequent (but coincidental) accompaniment of one event by another. For Kant, it is a structure that the mind imposes upon events.

going on and on, from one partial reason to another, and your quest never ends. You never reach the complete reason you set out to find. Thus, in the end irrationalism wins out. There is no final explanation for anything.

The non-Christian rationalist is here in a quandary, for his motivations press him in two directions simultaneously. On the one hand, he wants to affirm that there *are* complete explanations of events; therefore, he wants to honor a first cause. On the other hand, if the rationalist honors the first cause, he will have to cease his rational quest and submit his mind to the conclusion implicit in the first cause. But he does not want to cease his rational quest. He wants always to have the privilege of asking why. But if he denies the possibility of a first cause, he becomes indistinguishable from the irrationalists.[33]

So, in the end we are forced to choose between belief in a first cause and irrationalism. Irrationalism, as I pointed out earlier, is self-contradictory ("It is objectively true that there are no objective truths"). That leaves the cosmological argument in a strong position indeed.

Nevertheless, one might well ask, if it is possible for God to be self-existent and self-explanatory, causeless, and an ultimate reason, why can't the world be too? If we may end our causal inquiry with God, why not stop with the world and be done with it? Well, the answer is that the world is not self-existent and self-explanatory; it is not causeless; it is not an ultimate reason. We know this by the reasoning of our moral and epistemological arguments. The ultimate source of moral norms, of the norms of thought and logic, is personal, not impersonal. But if God is the ultimate source of these norms, then he is also the ultimate source of the world. The material world is not something separate from the rational and moral order. That order is the order of the material world. The ultimate source of rationality is the ultimate reason for every-

---

[33]Recall that we earlier found rationalism in the irrationalists; here we find rationalism reverting to irrationalism. From this we can observe that the two positions are not substantially opposed; they are only two emphases, two "perspectives" within the "conventional wisdom."

thing, as we saw earlier. And "everything" includes the material aspect, as much as the moral and rational aspects, of the universe.

Notice, however, that in the final analysis the cosmological argument is epistemological in character. The question about rational causes is really the same as the question about rational order. It shows how, if we assume that the world is rational, we must assume that God is the author of reason. The point, as in our earlier epistemological argument, is that reason is covenantal. The search for causes and reasons will be self-defeating unless it is willing to rest ultimately in God.

Being: The Ontological Argument

The ontological argument is in some ways the most fascinating—and exasperating—of all the classical arguments. It can be presented as a sort of "find the fallacy" parlor game,[34] or it can be presented, as Anselm of Canterbury did, in a prayer of profound Christian devotion. To some it is a joke, to others the very foundation of reason and faith.

Of the greatest philosophical and theological minds down to the present, some have despised it, others have honored it. Parmenides, Plato, and Augustine used reasoning that prefigures the ontological argument in some ways. Anselm of Canterbury provided the most influential formulation of the argument itself. Aquinas rejected it, but Descartes, Spinoza, and Leibniz all accepted various versions of it. Jonathan Edwards (followed by *Classical Apologetics*) used a Parmenidean form of it that verges on a pantheistic conclusion. Kant developed an influential refutation, but that did not stop Hegel and his disciples from, some would say, building their whole philosophies around it. Most twentieth-century philosophers, such as G. E. Moore, Bertrand Russell, Jean-Paul Sartre, Antony Flew, Kai Nielsen, and J. L. Mackie reject the proof, but many highly

---

[34]I recall a party in my high school days where someone brought in a mathematical proof that $1 = 2$ and dared us all to find the error in it. The error turned out to be a concealed division by zero. But the fallacy in the ontological argument, if such there be, is not at all easy to locate.

competent and distinguished philosophers have accepted versions of it, such as Norman Malcolm, Alvin Plantinga, and Nicholas Rescher. Process philosophers like Charles Hartshorne place great weight upon the ontological proof, but their version of it concludes with a process god, one very different from the orthodox God of Anselm.

Simplifying a few matters, we can formulate the ontological argument as follows:

Premise 1: God has all perfections.[35]
Premise 2: Existence is a perfection.[36]
Conclusion: Therefore, God exists.[37]

The earliest critic of this proof was the monk Gaunilo, whose remarks Anselm graciously included in his own book, with a response by Anselm himself. Gaunilo said that this argument could prove not only a perfect being such as God, but a perfect anything. For example, one could argue that a perfect island would have all perfections, and since existence is a perfection, the perfect island must exist. Anselm, however, replied in effect that a perfect island does not have all perfections. It is, after all, only an island, and therefore has only those perfections proper to islands. The ontological argument will, therefore, work in only one case, the case of a perfect being who has all perfections in limitless measure.

Others have objected that this proof makes a (quasi-Platonic) jump from "concept" to "reality." It says that since our concept of God includes his existence, he must exist in reality; but that does not follow. Plato, to be sure, thought that our concepts are recollections of the ultimate forms of things and therefore that all of our concepts, especially those of ultimates, have correlates in the "world of forms." We know that Augustine and Anselm were both heavily influenced by Plato, and perhaps Plato is the ultimate source of their argument.

---

[35]Anselm: God is "that than which no greater can be conceived."
[36]Or, as in some formulations, "Necessary existence is a perfection."
[37]Or, "God exists necessarily."

But modern thinkers do not find Plato's speculations about forms to be cogent, and therefore we should not suppose that our ideas have correlates in reality.

But, on the other hand, is it possible that none of our concepts correlates with objective reality? Such a view would be skepticism. To avoid that (and we have given reasons why skepticism, or irrationalism, is not an acceptable option) we must accept the fact that at least some of our mental concepts correspond to realities in the world. But which ones? Surely at least those which conceptualize ultimate criteria. For, as we have seen, all thinking presupposes such criteria. And surely we must also presuppose the objective reality corresponding to our concept of the ultimate source of such criteria. Christians believe that source is God. Others may believe that that source is something else.

Despite Plato's rather mythological presentation of his view, I think that the above paragraph represents his actual rationale for the "world of forms." Human thought presupposes criteria, he thought, which cannot be simply derived from sense experience. Our idea of a perfect triangle is not derived from any specific object of the senses, but it must correspond to *something* real; else it would not be useful as a criterion. The same is true for the forms of blue, red, courage, wisdom, humanity, and that "highest form," goodness. Plato's reasoning here is a kind of moral argument, like the one I proposed earlier. He concludes not to God, but to a plurality of impersonal forms, but we have seen that the source of moral values must be both one and personal.

So Anselm says that our concept of the source of all perfection, the being who has all perfections, must be objective, not merely a figment of our own thinking. Even if Anselm is under the influence of Plato here, I cannot deny the cogency of his basic reasoning. But this argument, like the others, is reducible to my earlier argument from moral values.

However, there is one major problem with this argument. The term "perfection," as used in the argument, is fairly slippery. It presupposes an already known system of values. What is perfect to a Christian might not be perfect, e.g., to a philo-sophical naturalist. Is existence a perfection, as the argument implies?[38] Well, it is not a perfection in Buddhism, where Nir-vana is explained as a form of "nothingness" and life is dis-paraged as "suffering." It is a perfection in Christianity, where God saw all he had made and declared everything to be "good" (Gen. 1:31; cf. 1 Tim. 4:4).

In other words, the ontological argument proves the bib-lical God only if it presupposes distinctively Christian values and a Christian view of existence. Substitute other values and you change the conclusion. This is why the ontological argu-ment has been used to defend so many different kinds of God: polytheistic (Plato), pantheistic (Parmenides, Spinoza, Hegel), process (Hartshorne), monadic (Leibniz), and Christian (Anselm, Plantinga).

Remarkably, the prayer in which Anselm formulates his ar-gument identifies him as a sort of Christian presuppositionalist. He indicates that he is not really in doubt as to God's existence, but that he is seeking a simple way to prove the God whom his heart "believes and loves." He seeks "not to understand, that I may believe, but to believe, that I might understand" *(credo ut intelligam)*. Faith here is the basis for understanding, rather than the product of it. Indeed, even Anselm's reply to Gaunilo is an attempt to address not the unbeliever whom Gaunilo represents, but the Catholic whom Gaunilo is. And it is essentially an ap-peal to Gaunilo's "faith and conscience." Have we not found here another "presuppositionalist of the heart"?

---

[38]A number of people, including Kant, have argued that existence is not even a "real predicate," since it "adds nothing to the concept of a thing." True, when one defines a cocker spaniel, the fact that cocker spaniels ex-ist is not usually part of the definition. And when I describe the Taj Ma-hal, I would probably not go out of my way to state that it exists. But that is because existence is not usually in question when one defines or describes something. But sometimes it is. Clearly one would not adequately define a "phoenix" (to people who know nothing of it) without a predicate like "fic-tional" or "mythical," predicates which imply nonexistence. Certainly, ex-istence or nonexistence is in one sense often part of our concepts (even when, understandably, it is not part of our images of things). I know the difference, e.g., between Secretariat and Black Beauty.

My conclusion is that either the ontological argument is a Christian presuppositional argument (and thus is reducible to our earlier moral argument) or it is worth nothing.

FIVE

▼

Apologetics as Proof
Proving the Gospel

Proving the truth of a historical narrative (such as the gospel, as presented in 1 Cor. 15:1–11) is rather different from proving the truth of a general worldview. In the latter case, we can deal with common features of our experience, such as values, truth, cause, and purpose. But in the former, we are pretty much restricted to evidence relating to a historical period in the distant past. The primary sources are the Scriptures themselves. Extrabiblical sources confirm what the early Christians believed, but they do not add much to the biblical testimony concerning the events themselves.

While the existence and many attributes of God are "clearly seen" in the creation (Rom. 1:18–20), the gospel message is not visible in the world as such. A preacher is needed to communicate the gospel (Rom. 10:14–15).

This does not mean, of course, that we must simply accept the biblical account on blind faith. Scripture itself argues for its contentions; it presents what we have earlier called a "rationale." It presents evidence for the truth of its message.

So, our main task is to isolate the Bible's own argument

for the truth of the gospel message. That argument is both explicit (as when Paul says the risen Christ was witnessed by some five hundred people at once [1 Cor. 15:6]) and implicit (as when scholars trace the textual history of 1 Corinthians 15:1ff. back to an account written or presented orally only a few years after the Resurrection). That is to say, sometimes Scripture provides an actual verbal argument for elements of the gospel; sometimes it simply states these elements, but in such a way and under such conditions that the reader finds the statement persuasive.

Our starting point must be the Christian worldview itself, as we have discussed it in previous chapters. We have seen that God exists as an absolute person, and, to quote the Westminster Shorter Catechism (Answer 4), as "a Spirit, infinite, eternal, and unchangeable, in his being, wisdom, power, holiness, justice, goodness, and truth." I argued in chapter 2 that this conception presupposes a distinction, not a continuum, between God and the world, with God as absolute sovereign. Although I have perhaps not argued the doctrine of the Trinity,[1] I have tried to show that that doctrine reinforces the other elements of the Christian doctrine of God, while denial of the Trinity leads to the distortion and compromise of those elements.

I have also argued that absolute-personality theism is found mainly in the biblical tradition. Certainly, of all the major religious movements, only those influenced by Scripture conceive of God as absolute personality. Now if our previous

---

[1]It is common for theologians to say that the doctrine of the Trinity is known only through special, not natural, revelation. I don't know, however, of any scriptural reason to exclude the Trinity from natural revelation, and I have presented some reasons to suppose that a study of nature itself favors a Trinitarian conception of God. I would not, of course, claim to have presented absolutely certain proof! But if a proof for the existence of God allows for the possibility of a unitarian God, the question arises as to the sense in which it proves distinctively *Christian* theism. Interestingly, even Thomas Aquinas, who insists that the Trinity is known only from special revelation, nevertheless produces proofs from the nature of knowledge and love which, if sound, would have to be described as natural-theology proofs of the Trinity.

arguments are correct, and the world is created and governed by an absolute personality, this fact creates an immense presumption in favor of the biblical tradition. If the absolute personality cares about human behavior (and our moral argument implies that he does), we would expect him somewhere to present his case to man. Further, since God speaks clearly and expects us to hear and obey, we would not expect the location of that case to be obscure or to be debatable among God's people. But the Bible is the only major religious book which claims to fulfill that expectation, which claims to be the place where God presents his case to man. If God's speech has an obvious location, that location must be the Holy Scriptures. There simply is no other candidate.[2]

Inquirers, then, may be glad to know that the real issue is between biblical religion and "conventional wisdom." One does not need to study every world religion and philosophy thoroughly. Only two are of any importance. As Scripture puts it, we are faced with a choice between the wisdom of God and the wisdom of the world (1 Cor. 1:18–2:16).

In that sense, then, our theistic arguments have already settled the truth of the gospel, the total message of Scripture. Since there is no other logical candidate for a source of God's words, we must hear and obey that message.

I realize, of course, that the above argument will not carry much weight with some people. It doesn't rule out every possibility that God's message to man might not exist, or that it might be found somewhere else. Therefore, I intend to continue bearing the burden of proof as we consider the claims of Scripture. To people who understand the full implications of my case for theism, the following argumentation is "gravy"—not strictly necessary, but useful. To others, it will be of some importance.

---

[2]Recall that in past chapters we have judged the claims of Islam, modern Judaism, and in effect those of the Roman Catholic hierarchy, the latter-day prophecies of the Mormons, Seventh-day Adventists, Christian Science, etc., as being dependent on the Bible and yet distortions of the biblical message. It would, of course, take a much longer book to debate those issues in detail.

The reader here may profitably review the exposition in chapter 2 of the biblical "good news." To summarize: Scripture tells us of our creation in God's image, our fall (through Adam) into sin, and God's free gift of his only Son to die an atoning death for our sin and to raise us up with him in newness of life.

Scripture's Doctrine of Scripture

Why should we believe this? Essentially, because God has told us so in the Bible! The old song is right:

> Jesus loves me, this I know,
>   For the Bible tells me so.

The Bible presents us with a doctrine of the Bible. The Bible itself is not merely an incidental human record of Jewish history and early Christianity; rather, the Bible is God's self-witness. It is God speaking to us. Therefore, the doctrine of Scripture is part of the good news; Scripture itself is one element in the saving message. And the doctrine of Scripture is not found only in a few texts of the Bible. Rather, it pervades the Scriptures. God is very concerned, not only that we believe in Christ, but also that we believe the Word which tells us about Christ, the very Word of God. God has not only given us salvation in Christ, but also a wonderfully simple way to know about that salvation.

As Scripture describes its own status and presents its self-witness, we come to see an important part of the scriptural rationale for the gospel message. If we find Scripture's self-description to be credible, then, at the same time, we will find the message of Scripture to be credible.

Crass as it may sound to modern religious speculators, it is evident from biblical history that God intends to rule his church through a book. God's church is to have a written constitution.

When God brings Israel out of Egypt and meets them as they are gathered around Mt. Sinai, he adopts them as his people (Ex. 19). There he declares to them the "Mosaic covenant," which promises God's gracious blessings to them and requires their obedience. "Covenant" is a literary form of the ancient Near East, sometimes called the "suzerainty treaty," instances of which have been found outside the Bible. In the suzerainty treaty, a great king imposes on a lesser king the status of a servant-ally. In the literary form of the treaty, the great king speaks as the author. He begins by giving his name. Then, in a historical prologue, he explains how he has helped the servant king in the past. He then sets forth his law, the obligations which the servant must perform. Then come the sanctions: blessings upon the servant if he obeys, and curses if he disobeys. The treaty concludes with procedural details: dynastic succession arrangements, keeping of the treaty documents, provisions for their public reading, etc.[3] We can see this literary form in the Ten Commandments of Exodus 20,[4] and Kline has identified other passages (including the entire book of Deuteronomy) that reflect this form.

The written document is not at all peripheral to the covenant. Indeed, being the very provisions of the covenant, it *is* the covenant. To violate the document is to violate the covenant, and vice versa. The covenant is written by the great king and it is kept in two copies, one in the sanctuary of the great king, the other in the sanctuary of the servant king. The document is suited to the holiest places. As the kings revere their gods, they honor the covenant.

Similarly, in the covenant between God and Israel, the covenant document plays a major role. At first, that document includes only the two tables of the Ten Commandments.[5] In

---

[3]For more details, see Meredith G. Kline, *The Structure of Biblical Authority* (Grand Rapids: Eerdmans, 1972). Kline's work is the most important contribution to the evangelical doctrine of Scripture since Warfield.

[4]"I am the LORD your God" (name of suzerain-author), "who brought you out of Egypt, out of the land of slavery" (historical prologue); "You shall have no other gods before me," etc. (laws), "for I, the LORD your God, am a jealous God . . ." (sanctions).

[5]Kline sees the two tables as two copies of the entire Decalogue rather than as one tablet with some commandments and another tablet with the rest. See *Structure of Biblical Authority*, 113–30.

that document, God speaks as author, giving his own name in the usual location for the name of the great king. The passage strongly emphasizes God's authorship, for the tables are written by God's own finger[6] (Ex. 24:12; 31:18; 32:15–16; 34:1; see also Ex. 34:32; Deut. 4:13; 9:10–11; 10:2–4).

Later, more such words are added. In Deuteronomy 32, God teaches his people a song, by which they are to remember his mercies and remember to obey him. It is God's song, and Moses writes it down (31:22). It is a song of "witness" (31:19). But it is not (as modern theologians often have it) Israel's witness to God; it is God's witness against Israel (31:19). When Israel sins and breaks the covenant, the song will accuse and convict them.

The entire law is placed in the most sacred place of God, the Ark of the Covenant, as a witness against the people (Deut. 31:26). It is holy, because it is God's own word. For that reason, no one may add to or subtract from these words (Deut. 4:2; 12:32; cf. Josh. 1:7; Prov. 30:6; Rev. 22:19–20).

From time to time, until Malachi, God adds new words to the canon of Scripture. Prophets have God's word in their mouth (Deut. 18), and many of their prophecies are written down (see, e.g., Isa. 8:1; 30:8ff.; 34:16–17; Jer. 25:13).

Now if you open the book of Deuteronomy almost at random, you will find passages where God calls the people to heed his "words, commandments, testimonies, ordinances, statutes, laws," and so on (note the eloquent redundancy). What words are these? Evidently, they are the written words of God which Moses has recorded. Psalm 119 and other Old Testament passages speak in reverent terms about God's words. (In Ps. 56:4, 10, the words of God are objects of religious praise.) What words are these? Again, they are God's written words.

Jesus speaks about the written law of the Old Testament in these words:

---

[6]The second pair of tables, however, was written by God (34:1) through Moses (34:27). Here Moses is the "secretary," but God is no less the author.

Do not think that I have come to abolish the Law or the Prophets; I have not come to abolish them but to fulfill them. I tell you the truth, until heaven and earth disappear, not the smallest letter, not the least stroke of a pen, will by any means disappear from the Law until everything is accomplished. Anyone who breaks one of the least of these commandments and teaches others to do the same will be called least in the kingdom of heaven, but whoever practices and teaches these commands will be called great in the kingdom of heaven. (Matt. 5:17–19)

When Jesus makes belief in Moses the prerequisite to belief in his own word (John 5:45), and when he denies that Scripture should ever be broken (John 10:33–36), he is adding his witness to the teaching of the written Old Covenant. When Paul speaks of Scripture as "God-breathed" (2 Tim. 3:16),[7] and when Peter says that the prophets spoke, not by their own will or interpretive faculties, but rather by the Holy Spirit, they are talking about the written word. To Jesus and the apostles, the whole Old Testament is the covenant document of the people of God.

What of the New Testament? In the nature of the case, it could not talk about itself as a completed collection of writings. Yet it leaves no doubt that it is God's purpose to give such a collection to the church.

People sometimes suggest that while the Old Testament presents a religion of authoritative words, the New Testament is more "spiritual" and less focused on verbal revelation. But that is clearly untrue. In the New Testament, Jesus comes teaching God's will. His words are tremendously important, the supreme criterion for discipleship. Meditate on Matthew 7:21–27, 28–29; Mark 8:38; Luke 8:21; 9:26ff.; John 6:63, 68–69; 8:47; 12:27ff.; 14:15, 21, 23–24; 15:7, 10, 14; 17:6, 17; 1 John 2:3–5; 3:22; 5:2–3; 2 John 6; 1 Timothy 6:3; Rev-

---

[7]That is, "spoken by God."

elation 12:17; 14:12. Without the words of Jesus, we are lost; without his words, we have no gospel.

The words of the apostles are also enormously important (see Rom. 1:16–17; 2:16; 1 Thess. 4:2; Jude 17ff.), including their written words (see Col. 4:16; 1 Thess. 5:27; 2 Thess. 3:14 [cf. 2:15]; 1 Cor. 14:37; 2 Peter 3:16).

Like the Old, the New Testament records a covenant, the "new covenant in my blood" (1 Cor. 11:25). Covenants in Scripture, as we have seen, are verbal in character.

Thus it is clear that there are New Covenant words for God's people. Without them, Christianity would be meaningless. We may expect, then, that God would place those words where we could all find them without too much trouble. And indeed he did.

There was, of course, some controversy in the early church about which books belonged in the New Testament canon. But differences over the canon—unlike other disputes—never divided the church. And, when all the books had been thoroughly read throughout the churches of the Roman Empire, and Athanasius of Alexandria had issued in 373 a list of the books accepted in his church as God's Word, there was no dissent. God had made himself known; his sheep had heard his voice; his Spirit had witnessed with the Word to the hearts of his people.

There is a certain prejudice in our time against written words. From some theological writers we get the idea that a written word is less authoritative than the "living voice" of a prophet, and that even the "living voice" of the prophet is of lesser authority than the direct voice of God (e.g., as heard at Mt. Sinai). Certainly the direct voice of God is more terrifying than the written words of God. But the Scriptures do not know of any distinction in authority, whatsoever. The written word has the same authority as the living prophet, the same as the divine voice. Obeying the written word is the same as obeying God himself; and despising the written word is despising God himself. God rules his church by a written constitution, by a book.

Thus it is that God's people gain their assurance of the gospel from the Word of God. How do I know that Jesus died for me? From Scripture. There is no higher authority, no greater ground of certainty—though of course the Holy Spirit enables us to believe, understand, and use the Scriptures rightly. The truth of Scripture is a presupposition for God's people.

Are we back to blind faith or narrow circularity? Not really. Those who have followed my argument so far understand that we have sought to justify an enormous presumption in favor of the biblical religious tradition, the only such tradition to honor a God of absolute personality. I have been emphasizing Scripture in this chapter in order to show the reader two things about that tradition. First, written revelation is not merely a peripheral element in that tradition, but the central constitutional authority. Second, Scripture, as that written constitution, is not merely a product of human thinking, not merely a historical source—rather, it is the Word of God. Therefore, if anyone wishes to follow the tradition of biblical religion, it will not be enough to have a general allegiance to the ideas of that tradition while maintaining the freedom to pick and choose the doctrines one prefers. Rather, faithfulness to that tradition renounces autonomy and listens faithfully to the wisdom which one finds on the pages of God's book. The true disciple hungers and thirsts for more and more of God's Word; he lives by *every* word of God (Matt. 4:4).

In the traditional apologetic, inquirers are told *not* to presuppose the full authority of Scripture as God's Word until after that authority has been proved by the apologist. They are told, rather, to assume only that the Bible is a generally reliable historical text. However, in the first place, even the general reliability of Scripture is contested by many scholars (see the following section). In the second place, we should never tell inquirers to presuppose less than the truth. In the third place, the Bible's own argument for Christianity (which I am seeking to reproduce) presupposes its own authority in the fullest sense. In the fourth place, I recognize that people have to begin where they are. If one does not believe in bib-

127

lical authority, he cannot simultaneously presuppose it. There are ways to communicate with someone in this position (cf. the story of Oscar in chap. 1), but it is a defective point of view,[8] and the apologist should never encourage it.

But What About Biblical Criticism?

For those who are not yet willing to confess Christ on the basis of the above arguments, I do have more to add—more about Scripture's own rationale for its teachings. But before we get to that, I must answer one substantial objection to the argument of the last section.

It is a continual embarrassment to Bible-believing Christians that many professional Bible scholars and theologians, who are (in one respect) in the best position to defend the gospel, are themselves sharply critical of historic Christianity. This was not always the case. Until around 1650, most— including the most famous—theological scholars were staunch defenders of biblical supernaturalism. But then came the Age of Reason, when traditions were jettisoned, human autonomy lauded, and theories honored as much for their newness as for their truth. Rationalists presupposed (without proof) that supernatural events never occur and that the human mind functions best independently of any purported divine revelation. In other words, they adopted the concept of human autonomy. Although some of these people continued to believe in some sort of God, these presuppositions clearly amounted to flat denials of biblical theism. These denials were made, not on the basis of Bible study, but before that study even began. These presuppositions were intended to govern the very method of Bible study itself; they were in no way influenced by the actual teaching of Scripture.

This meant that from this point on, in the view of the scholarly establishment, the Bible would have to be studied

---

[8]Would it be more "politically correct" to say that such a person is "epistemologically challenged"?

under nonbiblical assumptions, assumptions which flatly contradict the teachings of historic Christianity.

Under that presupposition, it was obvious that the Bible had to be treated as any other book—that is, as a book with a merely human origin and merely human authority. Thus developed all sorts of theories about the origins of Bible books and passages, all bereft of any supernatural reference. Jesus was seen not as the Son of God and atoning Savior, but either as a mere teacher of morality or (later) as a misguided apocalyptic visionary. The miracle stories were routinely disbelieved and ascribed to the pious imaginations of the biblical writers.

Similarly, the Old Testament was carved up into various "sources" and "traditions." The first five books were ascribed to various unknown authors designated J, E, D, P, and sometimes J1, J2, and so on. This was called the "documentary hypothesis." The history of Israel was reconstructed. Genesis 1–11 was relegated to the category of myth, legend, or saga; the stories of Abraham, Isaac, and Jacob were also regarded as unhistorical. Some scholars even denied that there was an exodus of God's people from the land of Egypt.

Again, these scholars routinely denied the supernatural. The evolutionary hypothesis was not only accepted as opposed to the biblical account of creation, but also used as a framework to determine the course of biblical history. The critics assumed that Israel's original religion was coarse and primitive, the religion of a local god whose chief concern was judgment and vengeance, and that it developed by an evolutionary pattern into belief in an infinite God of covenant love.

The biblical concept of prophecy, which involves the placing of divine words in the mouth of a human being, and which includes the foretelling of future events, was simply denied as a matter of principle. Passages which appeared to give detailed predictions of future events were dismissed as fraudulent—as actually having been written after the "predicted" events.

This sort of liberal[9] thinking rapidly came to dominate the teaching of the European universities, which had always been overly enthusiastic about newness and which had always manifested an intellectual pride that in turn fostered the spirit of autonomy. Later, it affected the churches as well. Some denominations capitulated entirely to liberalism, others resisted to some degree, and still others were created by orthodox people who could not remain in the older denominations that were dominated by liberal thought.

Liberal dominance continues today in most mainline universities, theological seminaries, and denominations. Today teaching is often based on Marxism ("liberation theology") and "process thought" rather than the Spinozistic rationalism and Kantian criticism of past centuries. But it is still antisupernaturalistic and especially opposed to the inerrant authority of Scripture. It continues to claim intellectual "autonomy." The most famous scholars (e.g., Rudolf Bultmann, John Hick, the "Jesus Seminar") seem to be those who deny the most biblical teaching.

As before, these scholars offer no proof that their methodology is superior to that of historic Christian methods of Bible study. Instead, we are told dogmatically that man cannot believe in miraculous occurrences in the age of radios and airplanes. How the radio and the airplane refute, e.g., Jesus' feeding of the five thousand is rather unclear. The critics' own belief in their methods is not based on proof in any normal sense. It is a presupposition, as Rudolf Bultmann admitted quite candidly in his famous essay "Is Exegesis Without Presuppositions Possible?"[10] And it is a presupposition quite contrary to those of historic Christianity.

---

[9]I use the word "liberal" to include all theology (including so-called neo-orthodoxy) which does not accept the final authority of Scripture. I grant that there are many differences among liberal thinkers, just as there are differences among orthodox thinkers. But we do need some general terms to denote general movements, even though such terms are often disdained as "labels."

[10]Bultmann, *Existence and Faith,* ed. Schubert M. Ogden (New York: Meridian Books, 1960), 289–96.

There does seem to be a tendency in biblical studies (not always mirrored in systematic theology) for liberal scholars to come to more and more conservative conclusions about the dating, authenticity, and historicity of biblical books. Although liberal scholars in the early nineteenth century routinely denied the accuracy of all biblical narratives relating events prior to Moses and insisted that many of the New Testament books came from the mid-second century, archaeological and documentary evidence has forced many scholars to accept the historicity of at least the settings of the patriarchal accounts. And all the New Testament books are now generally admitted to come from the first century. Interestingly, some of the scholars most radical in their theology (Adolf Harnack, John A. T. Robinson) have been most conservative in their historical judgments. Robinson, who propounded a blatantly unbiblical theology in his infamous book *Honest to God*,[11] returned in a later book to claim that the New Testament documents may all have been written before A.D. 70.[12]

Nevertheless, the basic assumptions of liberalism continue to dominate the theological world. A few brave souls have attempted to cry out, "The emperor has no clothes!" Orthodox scholars like C. F. Keil, Theodor Zahn, and Ernst Hengstenberg battled liberalism in nineteenth-century Europe, along with such American scholars as William Henry Green, B. B. Warfield, and Robert Dick Wilson. In the next generation, famous critiques of liberal methodology were put forward by J. Gresham Machen,[13] Oswald T. Allis,[14] and Cyrus Gordon (a Jewish scholar who questioned the docu-

---

[11]Philadelphia: Westminster Press, 1963.

[12]Robinson, *Redating the New Testament* (London: S.C.M. Press, 1976).

[13]Machen, *Christianity and Liberalism* (Grand Rapids: Eerdmans, 1923); *The Virgin Birth of Christ* (New York: Harper, 1930; Grand Rapids: Baker, 1967); *The Origin of Paul's Religion* (New York: Macmillan, 1921; Grand Rapids: Eerdmans, 1965). These are still very powerful works!

[14]Allis, *The Five Books of Moses*, 2d ed. (Philadelphia: Presbyterian and Reformed, 1949); *The Unity of Isaiah* (Philadelphia: Presbyterian and Reformed, 1950); *The Old Testament: Its Claims and Its Critics* (Nutley, N.J.: Presbyterian and Reformed; Grand Rapids: Baker, 1972).

mentary hypothesis). Still later, Eta Linnemann, once a disciple of Bultmann, dramatically renounced her great prestige as a German Bible scholar for the greater honor of being a servant of Christ.[15]

I am confident that as the reader studies books like these with an open mind (and that may require in some a new work of the Spirit!), he will be persuaded that the liberal case has not been made, and, indeed, that it is deeply flawed—intellectually, methodologically, and theologically. I have also been influenced in my own thinking by a couple of other writers who present the issues in a more popular, less technical way, though their professional credentials in these fields cannot be questioned. One is the *Critique of Religion and Philosophy*,[16] by the philosopher Walter Kaufmann. Unlike the people noted above, Kaufmann is not susceptible to the derogatory epithet "fundamentalist." In fact, Kaufmann was a strongly anti-Christian writer, and this book is, on the whole, an impassioned and reasoned attack on everything I hold dear. But one of Kaufmann's targets is also one of mine: the so-called higher biblical criticism.[17] His arguments against the documentary hypothesis (J1, J2, etc.) are powerful and bring out brilliantly the absurdity of the whole effort.

The other popular writer is C. S. Lewis, in his essay, "Modern Theology and Biblical Criticism."[18] Lewis, too, was not a fundamentalist—unfortunately, he renounced biblical inerrancy. But he was a Christian supernaturalist and wrote some very impressive works of apologetics. Being a professor

---

[15]See Linnemann, *Historical Criticism of the Bible: Methodology or Ideology?* trans. Robert W. Yarbrough (Grand Rapids: Baker, 1990).

[16]New York: Harper and Brothers, 1958.

[17]"Lower criticism" is the determination of the proper biblical text by a study of the ancient manuscripts of Scripture. "Higher criticism" seeks to determine, apart from Scripture's own testimony, the truth of what Scripture claims, especially concerning the authorship, date, and origin of the books. Historic Christianity commends lower criticism and denies higher criticism so defined. The two phrases can, of course, be defined in other ways.

[18]Lewis, *Christian Reflections,* ed. Walter Hooper (Grand Rapids: Eerdmans, 1967), 152–66.

of early English literature at Oxford University, he was in the business of interpreting and evaluating ancient texts and therefore was able to look at the work of biblical scholars from a fresh, though sympathetic viewpoint. Of the prominent Bible critics, Lewis says, "They seem to me to lack literary judgment, to be imperceptive about the very quality of the texts they are reading."[19] To Bultmann's claim that the personality of Jesus was unimportant to Paul and John, Lewis replies, "Through what strange process has this learned German gone in order to make himself blind to what all men except him see?"[20] And then he declares:

> These men ask me to believe they can read between the lines of the old texts; the evidence is their obvious inability to read (in any sense worth discussing) the lines themselves. They claim to see fern-seed and can't see an elephant ten yards away in broad daylight.[21]

Here are some of Lewis's other "bleats," as he called them:

> All theology of the liberal type involves at some point . . . the claim that the real behavior and purpose and teaching of Christ came very rapidly to be misunderstood and misrepresented by his followers, and has been recovered or exhumed only by modern scholars.[22]

> Thirdly, I find in these theologians a constant use of the principle that the miraculous does not occur.[23]

> What forearms me against all these [reconstructions of the "original" settings of biblical texts] is that I have seen it from the other end of the stick. I have watched

---

[19]Ibid., 154.
[20]Ibid., 156.
[21]Ibid., 157.
[22]Ibid.
[23]Ibid., 158.

reviewers reconstructing the genesis of my own books in just this way. . . . My impression is that in the whole of my experience not one of these guesses has on any one point been right; that the method shows a record of 100 per cent failure. . . .[24]

But most biblical and theological scholars still more or less toe the party line established by the seventeenth-century rationalists. If one decides whom to follow by counting the number of recognized experts holding the various views, then one must be a liberal. On the other hand, if one can maintain a healthy skepticism toward conventional wisdom (Isn't this what they always told us to do in college?) and a sense of humor about the really absurd nonsense that passes for scholarship in these circles,[25] one might find himself or herself opening up to radically unfashionable approaches.

And if one is a Christian—if his or her ultimate loyalty is to Jesus—cannot one muster from that loyalty the courage to stand against even the frail reed of modern biblical scholarship? Many ancient Christians (and some modern ones) have had to do much more—to be burned alive, crucified, or thrown to lions—rather than renounce Christ. If Christ calls us to love God with all our heart, soul, mind, and strength, and to follow Jesus in all of our activities, how can we deny to him the small favor of adopting unpopular, but Christian, positions on biblical scholarship? He offers us his own wonderful wisdom in his Word (1 Cor. 2:6ff.). How can we renounce that wisdom for the dry husk of modern fashion, that very unbelieving, yet popular, pseudowisdom that the Lord condemns in 1 Corinthians 1:18–2:5?

---

[24]Ibid., 159–60.

[25]My favorite example is the assumption that no saying of Jesus can be accepted as authentic unless it disagrees with the thinking of the early church; otherwise, the church, not Jesus, is assumed to be the author of the saying. How preposterous! Would anyone take such a position concerning any other thinker, such as Luther (and his Lutherans) or Descartes (and his Cartesians)?

And if the reader is still an "inquirer": do not think for a moment that the prevalence of unbelief in the field of biblical scholarship will excuse you from confessing Jesus and the truth of his Word. Unbelief is prevalent in all areas of culture—science, politics, sociology, psychology, etc. It should come as no surprise that unbelief sometimes also inundates religion. Jesus indicted the religionists of his own time in the strongest terms. The arguments for true Christianity militate against unbelief in all areas, even when it bears a Christian label, and you should give heed to those arguments, not to the proud speculations of so-called scholarship.

We have seen the Bible's teaching about itself. I have given reasons to reject the approach of the standard biblical criticism. But is Scripture's teaching about itself credible? Consider: (1) No other doctrine is compatible with absolute-personality theism. If God is a person who speaks with absolute authority, then he reveals himself with nothing less than supremely authoritative speech or writing. If God revealed himself in such a way that we could freely criticize his words and believe something else instead, then he would not be the God revealed in Scripture. One does not talk back to the biblical God. His word has supreme authority. And just as it cannot be disproved by something else of greater authority, so it cannot be proved in such a way. God's Word, like himself, must be supremely authoritative and therefore self-attesting. On the conventional wisdom, the biblical doctrine of Scripture is implausible; but if you presuppose a Christian worldview, no other doctrine of revelation is conceivable. (2) Like all biblical teachings, the doctrine of Scripture will be credible to you if the Holy Spirit opens your mind to it. Otherwise, it will not be. As we might expect, faith in an absolute personality is a supernatural gift. (3) This doctrine was taught by many different biblical authors, from many different times and settings, with many different strengths and weaknesses. None of them found fault with the Bible; all accepted it as their covenant constitution. (4) Above all, this doctrine was taught by Jesus, by the apostles whom he appointed to communicate his teaching, and by the prophets of the Old Testament, who anticipated his coming. Thus, Scripture is a necessary element in the great drama of redemption. The credibility of that redemption validates the Scriptures and vice versa.

Scripture's Rationale for the Gospel Message

The Argument from Prophecy

Scripture does not merely claim to be the Word of God. It also presents us with reasons for believing its claims. It presents its claims in a credible way.

In one sense, such credibility is not necessary. God could have put the words "Scripture is the word of God" in the Bible and then, through the persuasive power of the Holy Spirit, supernaturally convinced elect readers of the truth of that statement. But God's way is not to persuade people "magically" of the truth of his word. The Spirit certainly does persuade, but he persuades us to believe inherently rational content. As in a sermon, it is not enough just to lay the facts before the congregation; one must present those facts winsomely, persuasively, with clarity and order. Otherwise, we have not presented the facts as they really are. So it is with Scripture's own presentation. In other words, the Spirit's work is not to persuade us of something for which there are no rational grounds, but rather to persuade us by illumining the rational grounds which obligate us to believe. Spirit-created faith is not "blind."

Thus, Scripture does not merely give us the bare statement, "Jesus Christ is Lord." Rather, it presents Jesus in the context of a rich, complex historical drama. Jesus is the expectation of God's people over a period of several thousand years before his birth. After man's fall in the Garden of Eden, God announces to the Serpent (Satan),

> I will put enmity
> between you and the woman,
> and between your offspring and hers;

he will crush your head,
    and you will strike his heel.
                        (Gen. 3:15)

And so God's people began to look for a deliverer, one who would save them from the effects of the Fall. He would be human, an "offspring" of the woman (Eve). Yet his victory would be in the supernatural realm: he would crush the head of Satan. And in the process, Satan would wound the deliverer ("strike his heel").

The child of the promise is often threatened. Over and over again, circumstances arise that threaten to prevent his birth, but the woman's offspring is maintained by God's power. Wicked Cain kills righteous Abel (Gen. 4), the only one through whom the promise can be fulfilled. But God defeats Satan by giving to Eve a third son, Seth (Gen. 4:25), and in his time people first gather to worship the Lord (4:26).

God himself endangers the "seed of promise" by demanding that Abraham sacrifice his son Isaac, the only son of Abraham through whom the promise can come. But as Abraham lifts the knife:

The angel of the LORD called out to him from heaven, "Abraham! Abraham!"

"Here I am," he replied.

"Do not lay a hand on the boy," he said. "Do not do anything to him. Now I know that you fear God, because you have not withheld from me your son, your only son."

Abraham looked up and there in a thicket he saw a ram caught by its horns. He went over and took the ram and sacrificed it as a burnt offering instead of his son. So Abraham called that place The Lord Will Provide. And to this day it is said, "On the mountain of the LORD it will be provided." (Gen. 22:11–14)

137

Here God teaches his people (1) that there is no higher test of covenant loyalty than to give up one's beloved son for another; (2) that God will preserve the seed of the promise so that it will certainly be fulfilled; (3) that a substitutionary offering is nevertheless necessary (cf. v. 8); and (4) that God thus provides for his people in all their needs, their greatest being the forgiveness of sins.

In Exodus 12–15, God delivers Israel, his people, from Egypt. In the process, he sends an "angel of death" to kill all the firstborn sons in the land. The families of Israel escape this curse by killing a lamb and placing some of its blood on the doorframes of their homes. When the angel of death sees the blood, he passes over that house and spares it. Here we see that: (1) God again demands a sacrifice. (2) The firstborn son represents his family, taking their fate on himself. Once again the seed of the promise is endangered. (3) Apart from that sacrifice, everyone—even the chosen people of God—deserves death. (4) Only substitutionary blood can avert the wrath of God. (5) That blood must be displayed publicly.

In Exodus 17, after God has delivered Israel from Egypt, the people complain that they have no water. They threaten to stone Moses, the leader, but the real object of their complaint is God himself. The Lord stands before the people (that is, he puts himself in the position of a defendant) by a rock, and at his command, Moses strikes the rock. The Lord symbolically receives the blow, and through the suffering of God, water comes from the rock to bless the people.[26]

It is not only the explicit prophecies of Christ, though there are a great many of them (e.g., Pss. 2; 110:1ff.; Isa. 7:14; 9:6–8; 11:1–16; 35:5ff.; 53; Jer. 31:33ff.; Dan. 9:20–27; Mic. 5:2; Zech. 9:9–12; 12:10; Mal. 3:1–5), that are important. The biblical narratives also lead people to expect a deliverer who can be no one other than Jesus Christ. Narratives fash-

---

[26]For these and other remarkable readings from the Old Testament, see Edmund P. Clowney, *The Unfolding Mystery: Discovering Christ in the Old Testament* (Colorado Springs: NavPress, 1988; Phillipsburg, N.J.: Presbyterian and Reformed, 1991).

ion the values of a people. When they think of salvation, they think of a salvation which includes a perfect sacrifice. They expect (if they understand rightly) that God will somehow sacrifice himself in that perfect sacrifice and through it provide blessing. Otherwise, how can the ultimate salvation be greater than that of Exodus 17? And how can it be greater than that of Genesis 22, unless it exhibits a divine love, measured according to the giving of an only Son? How can it be greater than the salvation of Genesis 4, unless it brings together a people to call on God's name?

And though the deliverer is human, how can his mission be anything less than the coming of God himself (Pss. 2:12; 45:6; 110:1ff.; Isa. 42:6ff.; 43:1ff.; 59:15–20; Jonah 2:9)? How can he be tempted less than Adam was? How can his teaching ministry be any less authoritative and profound than that of Moses? How can his healing ministry be anything less than that described in Isaiah 35:5ff.? How can he provide for his people less abundantly than Moses and Elijah did? And if God is to suffer for his people, how can that suffering be less than that described in Psalm 22? There the King of Israel suffers mocking, scorn, and physical pains—a description which amazingly anticipates aspects of crucifixion.

So Israel learns from the Old Testament the nature of man's plight, the sort of sacrifice needed to deal with sin, the sort of suffering that must be involved, the remarkable combination of divinity and humanity required for the work of salvation, the divine self-giving. One would have expected that when Jesus came on the scene, at least after his crucifixion and resurrection, a lot of "pennies would have dropped." Suddenly all the pieces of the puzzle came together in Jesus. Hundreds of prophecies and narratives were involved, all pointing in various ways, from various perspectives, in only one direction—to Jesus. Alas, even the disciples of Jesus were blind to these extraordinary relationships until Jesus instructed them after his resurrection. What instruction that must have been! Suddenly the Scriptures took on a whole new shape, a form both strange and familiar, for there was always the sense of "surely, at some level, we knew this all along." They realized that that was the way the Scriptures *ought* to be interpreted.

The "argument from prophecy," then, is actually an argument from the whole Old Testament (see Luke 24:27; John 1:45; 5:39) and is in reality an appeal to the extraordinarily rational structure of Scripture itself. Here we have a wide variety of human authors, writing across many centuries, with very different interests, concerns, styles, and levels of intellectual sophistication, saying many different things, and yet, at the same time, saying one thing: Jesus is coming, and this is what he will be and do. Does this not indicate something of God's sovereignty over history? Does it not show that the Old Testament is more than an ordinary book? Does it not show some remarkable things about Jesus? Is this not a powerful witness to the Word of God? If you hesitate to agree, then read it and see. And claim the promise of John 7:17, accepting the responsibility which comes with it: "If anyone chooses to do God's will, he will find out whether my teaching comes from God or whether I speak on my own."

The New Testament Witness to Christ

Continue your reading into the New Testament, and see how the Old Testament expectation is fulfilled in Jesus. Open your heart to the remarkable person portrayed here: one whose ministry is endorsed by God the Father himself, speaking from heaven (Mark 1:11); one who is faithful to God, despite a more stringent temptation than Adam experienced (Matt. 4); a teacher who speaks with amazing authority (Mark 1:22); one whose power to heal is the power of God's word itself (Luke 7:1–10), and yet who declines to save himself from death (Luke 23:35), only to rise again from the dead (Luke 24:1ff.)!

Jesus speaks with amazing authority and wisdom, and he also claims to be God! In John 8:58 he takes upon himself the divine name "I am" (cf. Ex. 3:14), which the Jews consider too sacred to pronounce.[27] His relationship to the Father is unique—a sonship unlike that which all believers have with God. He speaks of God as "his own Father" (John 5:18), plainly distinct from the position of his disciples (20:17). He says that it is only through him that anyone else can become a "son" of God (John 14:6; 17:26). To see him is to see the Father (John 14:9). The Father has given him all things (Matt. 11:27), including a distinctive knowledge (John 5:26; 17:24). That he makes such claims, even claiming the power to forgive sins (Mark 2:7; Matt. 9:3; Luke 5:21), leads the Jews to accuse him of blasphemy. And when the high priest charges him with making such a claim, Jesus affirms it (Matt. 26:64). If Jesus' claims were false, he certainly was a blasphemer, and we can well understand why the strongly monotheistic Jews would be quick to accuse any man who claimed to be God. On this matter, they did understand him rightly.

What is perhaps even more amazing, however, is that many Jewish monotheists believed him. The apostle John begins his gospel by identifying Jesus as the powerful Word of God which created the world (Ps. 33:6; John 1:1–3) and then identifies that Word with God. Old Testament passages which speak of the Lord God are quoted by New Testament writers and applied to Jesus (compare Isa. 45:23ff. to Phil. 2:10–11; Isa. 2:10, 19, 21; 66:15 to 2 Thess. 1:7–9; Ps. 102:25–27 to Heb. 1:10–12). Jesus does everything that only God does in the Old Testament: he creates (John 1:3; Col. 1:16–17; Heb. 1:2), initiates a covenant (1 Cor. 11:25), controls the course of nature and history (Heb. 1:3), forgives sins (Isa. 43:25; 44:22; Mark. 2:7; etc.), and saves his people (Isa. 40:3; 41:14; 43:25ff.; 45:21; 46:13; Titus 2:13). New Testament writers almost "casually" place Jesus on the side of God when they contrast God and man (see Gal. 1:1, 10, 12).

How could these Jews believe such a startling claim, one which apparently contradicted the monotheistic foundation of

---

[27]See also John 18:5–6, where Jesus says "I am" (in the original Greek) and the soldiers coming to arrest him fall to the ground.

their early religious training?[28] Well, when Jesus taught the Scriptures to his disciples, they evidently saw that the day of salvation would be simultaneously a coming of the Lord and the coming of a human Messiah. Mysterious passages of Scripture which equated the Messiah with God (e.g., Pss. 2; 45:5; 110:1ff.) suddenly came to light. When they were compared with Jesus himself—his power, his authority, his saving love, his resurrection glory—the conclusion was inescapable. Jesus was God! In John 1:18 (the reading "only God"); 20:28; Acts 20:28; Romans 9:5; 2 Thessalonians 1:12; Titus 2:13; 2 Peter 1:1; 1 John 5:20 the Greek term *theos*, meaning "God," refers to Christ. Philippians 2:6ff. and Colossians 2:9 are perhaps even clearer in their testimony to Jesus' deity.

The personal impression made by Jesus upon his disciples must have been entirely unique. His words were quite different from those of any other teacher: "The crowds were amazed at his teaching, because he taught as one who had authority, and not as their teachers of the law" (Matt. 7:28, 29). Peter knew he could find no one with words like those of Jesus: "Lord, to whom shall we go? You have the words of eternal life" (John 6:68). And perhaps even more amazingly, people who knew Jesus intimately were convinced that he had never done wrong. Peter referred to him as the one who "committed no sin, and no deceit was found in his mouth" (1 Peter 2:22). John, also a disciple, said, "But you know that he appeared so that he might take away our sins. And in him is no sin" (1 John 3:5).[29] To be a fit sacrifice, the Passover lamb of the Old Testament had to be perfect, without defect (Ex. 12:5). Jesus was the perfect Lamb of God, who takes away the sins of the world (John 1:29).

---

[28]Of course, the doctrine of the Trinity, as we have seen, does not compromise monotheism, but fulfills it. When the New Testament emphasizes monotheism, it also mentions more than one Trinitarian person (1 Cor. 8:5–6; Eph. 4:3–6). But a monotheist looking at this doctrine for the first time is more than likely in for a shock. And in the New Testament, many of those monotheists become avid opponents of Jesus. But, amazingly enough, some of them believe.

[29]Cf. 2 Cor. 5:21; Heb. 4:15; 7:26; Acts 3:14.

This concept of a perfectly sinless man is unique, not only to our experience, but also to biblical history. Scripture does not idealize the great men among God's people. Though recognizing many as heroes of the faith (Heb. 11), Scripture presents their flaws: Abraham's cowardly deception, Moses' disobedience, David's adultery and murder, Solomon's harem, the wretched behavior of most of the kings of Israel and Judah. But of Jesus, the central figure, there is no critique. His sinlessness became proverbial in the early church. Coming from such witnesses, is that testimony not credible?

Miracle and Resurrection

Throughout Scripture, God does wonderful works so that people will know that he is the Lord (Ex. 6:7; 7:5, 17; 8:22; 9:14; 10:2; 11:7; 14:4, 18; 16:12; 29:46; etc.) This is a pervasive theme in the Old Testament. Miracles, therefore, constitute evidence of God's reality and of his nature and will as Lord. Apologists, therefore, have regularly appealed to biblical miracles to confirm the truth of Christianity. However, there are some problems with this approach. In the first place, few of us today would claim to have seen a miracle. What we find in Scripture are not miracles as such, but miracle stories and testimony concerning miracles. Secondly, Scripture warns us against putting too much confidence in miracles to convert unbelieving hearts. In Jesus' story of the rich man and Lazarus, the rich man in hell asks for someone of the dead to be sent back to tell the truth to his five brothers. Abraham replies, "If they do not listen to Moses and the Prophets, they will not be convinced even if someone rises from the dead" (Luke 16:31).

Indeed, that was the experience of Jesus himself. He wrought many miracles, but they rarely led people to faith. Often the enemies of Jesus admitted the miracle, but still refused to believe. And even the Resurrection itself failed to convince many. Jesus had harsh words for those who demanded to see signs (Matt. 12:39; John 4:48).

Yet, as in the Old Testament, the signs were not without value. They were intended, as then, to show who was Lord.

They confirmed the apostles as servants of God (2 Cor. 12:12) and their message as God's (Heb. 2:4). Miracles do have an epistemological function, even though they themselves will not convert an unbeliever. Unbelievers suppress the truth, as we have seen, and the truth of miracles is no exception. If he wants, an unbeliever can write off an apparent miracle by saying, "Well, yes, it happened; but a lot of strange things happen in the world. It doesn't mean anything." Yet a miracle may be the occasion, as in the case of doubting Thomas, for the Spirit to implant faith in the heart. Remember how Jesus tells Thomas to examine the evidence, but also to "stop doubting and believe" (John 20:27). Thomas replies in faith, "My Lord and my God!" (v. 28). All the signs recorded in the gospel of John are there so that the readers may, like Thomas, believe and thereby have life in the name of Christ (20:31).[30] Thus, not only the miracle, but even the report of the miracle, can be a divinely ordained means of knowing Christ as Lord.

But are the reports of miracles in Scripture credible? David Hume argued that one could never accept testimony concerning a miracle, because it will always be outweighed by the evidence that everything behaves naturally and regularly. But is there really such evidence? Certainly, in most all of our experience, things happen in regular patterns, to some extent describable by scientific law. But there is nothing in this experience to persuade us that irregularity is impossible, or that everything always behaves naturally and regularly. Experience tells us what is happening; it does not tell us what is or is not possible, or what "always" happens. We have not seen what everything always does, for we have neither seen everything nor seen things always.

---

[30]I have found it helpful, in trying to assess the efficacy of miracles, to think of them (as the Reformers thought of sacraments) as "visible words." Miracles have the same purpose and efficacy as the Word of God, except that they are more vivid, providing a spectacle to the eye, as well as the ears and brain. Like the Word, they communicate saving truth, but an observer can remain unmoved unless the Spirit creates a proper response.

Evidently, then, we ought to be open to the evidence for miracles. That is to say, we must look at that evidence, not from Hume's presuppositions, but from Christian ones. When we do, we assume the primacy of the divine absolute personality. If he wishes to work "irregularly" in the universe he has made, who will prevent him or find fault?

Is there reason to reject the biblical writers as unfit witnesses? Not if we accept the doctrine of Scripture outlined earlier! Certainly they themselves believed what they wrote—after all, they were willing to die for it. Indeed, we have no record from the first century denying that Jesus worked miracles, even from his enemies. They admitted that he worked the miracles, but accounted for them as coming from Satan (Matt. 12:24ff.). Jesus' reply to this was that in every case his miracles counteracted Satan's power and purposes.

The greatest miracle, of course, is the resurrection of Jesus from the dead. I shall not add much to the voluminous literature showing the credibility of the biblical witness to this great event. More than one writer has sought through research and hard thinking to disprove Christianity, only to be constrained to faith by the evidence for the Resurrection. This is the foundation stone of traditional Christian apologetics, and this is in general an area where I do not differ from that tradition.[31]

However, I would mention again, contrary to the traditional approach, that the chief evidence for the Resurrection is the Word of God itself. Paul's argument in 1 Corinthians 15:1ff. is made chiefly to remind the Corinthians that the res-

---

[31]There seems to be a new book out nearly every week on the evidences for the Resurrection. One of the better accounts, in my view, is that of William Lane Craig, in his *Apologetics: An Introduction* (Chicago: Moody Press, 1984), 167–206, and in his *Knowing the Truth About the Resurrection* (Ann Arbor, Mich.: Servant Books, 1988). Also, take note of Gary R. Habermas and Antony G. N. Flew, *Did Jesus Rise from the Dead?* ed. Terry L. Miethe (San Francisco: Harper & Row, 1987). This is mostly a debate between Habermas, an evangelical, and Flew, a well-known atheistic philosopher, with comments by a number of others. Flew seems quite out of his depth here! In my estimation, Habermas wins the debate hands down.

urrection of Jesus is part of the apostolic preaching, which they believe. But, in the course of his argument, he does also refer to post-Resurrection appearances and witnesses to those appearances who are still living.

It appears that the apostles were able to proclaim the Resurrection largely without fear of contradiction. There was simply no evidence on the other side. The Jews concocted the story that the disciples had removed Jesus' body, thereby conceding the reality of the empty tomb. But in the unlikely event that the disciples had done such a thing (risking their lives in the face of the Roman guards), would they have died to perpetuate the fraud?

The story of the Resurrection was related too soon after the fact to be the product of legendary development. The ornamentation and elaboration characteristic of legends is not there. The story of the women discovering the empty tomb bears remarkable marks of authenticity. No one inventing such a story would have placed women in this role, because they were not acceptable as witnesses in Jewish courts of law.

Attempts to explain the Resurrection as something other than a supernatural event have always fallen flat. Some have said that Jesus did not actually die on the cross, but only fell into a coma, from which he was roused in the tomb. But in such a weakened condition, Jesus could not have rolled away the heavy stone and appeared to the disciples as the triumphant Lord of heaven and earth. Some have said that the disciples engaged in a conspiracy, but that has been dealt with above. Some have explained the post-Resurrection appearances as hallucinations or "visions." But hallucinations do not work that way. They do not produce the same images in many persons, who then report that they have all seen the same thing.

The fact is, then, that the Resurrection is as well established as any fact in history—indeed better than most, for it is attested by the Word of God itself. One cannot deny it, save by a radical skepticism which calls all knowledge into question. Nor can it be written off merely as a "strange event," for the Word of God gives it tremendous significance: the Resur-

146

rection vindicates Jesus' sacrifice for sin and allows us to claim in faith that we have been raised with him from sin to eternal life (Rom. 6).

God's Word makes this gospel "absolutely certain." Jesus—God in the flesh—has died as a sacrifice for the sins of his people and has been raised to glory. All who believe, who trust in this sacrifice for divine forgiveness (John 3:16) and who recognize Jesus as Lord (Rom. 10:9), will be saved from hell and raised to eternal friendship with God. Do you believe in him?

Conclusion

What Scripture teaches, it teaches credibly. It presents an extraordinary spectacle of many authors of different times, social strata, and literary skills, producing a story which is perfectly unified around the person of Jesus. The facts are presented with remarkable credibility (even the kings of Israel are shown "warts and all"), despite the radical uniqueness of Jesus and his message. Indeed, Scripture even presents a credible reason for its being so credible—its divine authorship as the covenant constitution of the people of God. So, biblical religion alone, of all the religions and philosophies of the world, provides an authoritative answer to the question we most need to ask of God: How can my sins be forgiven?

Is its credibility absolutely certain? Ultimately, yes, for it is the Word of God himself and therefore deserves to be presupposed as the highest standard of credibility. How can we be persuaded of that certainty? By the Holy Spirit's witness to us, reinforcing the credibility inherent in the text itself (1 Cor. 2:4; 1 Thess. 1:5).

SIX

▼

Apologetics as Defense:
The Problem of Evil, 1—Questions,
General Principles, and Blind Alleys

Having considered apologetics as proof, we now turn to the second function of apologetics, that of defense. We have seen that the Bible defends itself in an important sense, but God also calls his people to defend his truth (Phil. 1:7, 16; 1 Peter 3:15). In defense, as in proof, Scripture supplies the fundamental standards and criteria which the apologist must employ. We are not, however, restricted to Scripture for the data of our arguments. All facts have apologetic significance, because all facts are created and ordered by God. But Scripture supplies the presuppositions for every phase of Christian apologetics.

Is There a Problem of Evil? Is There an Answer?

In this chapter, we shall consider what is perhaps the most serious and cogent objection that unbelievers have brought against Christian theism: the problem of evil. A typical formulation of it is as follows:

Premise 1: If God were all-powerful, he would be able to prevent evil.
Premise 2: If God were all-good, he would desire to prevent evil.
Conclusion: So, if God were both all-powerful and all-good, there would be no evil.
Premise 3: But there is evil.
Conclusion: Therefore, there is no all-powerful, all-good God.

Such is the philosopher's way of looking at the problem. But the essence of it is a concern to nonphilosophers as well. Who of us has not cried out "Why, Lord?" when beset by tragedies in our experience? We simply feel a terrible discrepancy between our experience and what we believe God to be. That cry from the heart may be simultaneously a cry of pain, a cry for help, a cry for enlightenment, and a cry of doubt which questions our own deepest presuppositions. That "Why, Lord?" says everything that the philosophical argument says and more.

I said that this problem is perhaps the most serious and cogent objection to Christian theism. Professor Walter Kaufmann, mentioned in an earlier chapter, always referred to this as his strongest argument against Christianity—he had lost family members in the Holocaust. To him the reality of evil was a "complete refutation of popular theism." Many people who have experienced the suffering and death of a child, or some other suffering that seems entirely undeserved, will hold a grudge against God, the intellectual content of which can be described in our premises and conclusions. Every Christian, perhaps, has at least wondered about this issue, and many of us have experienced periods of doubt on its account.

Is there an answer to the problem? That depends on what you mean by an answer. If you are seeking an explanation that will vindicate God's providence in every instance of evil, I certainly cannot supply that, and I doubt if anyone else can, either. Nor, I think, can we supply a totally satisfying theoretical reconciliation between divine sovereignty, goodness, and evil. The mystery of God's relation to evil is one that will, I am convinced, never be completely dissolved in this life, and I am not sure whether it will be in the next.

Jay Adams's recent book, *The Grand Demonstration*,[1] is in many ways a fine biblical study of the problem of evil. Dr. Adams is a colleague and friend of mine, a man who has been a great help to the church and to me personally, and I dearly love him in Christ. But there is something about this particular book that, to say the least, rubs me the wrong way. Adams is a problem solver, and he doesn't like to see loose ends flying around—in counseling, in preaching, or in theology. He is very unhappy with wimpish talk that gives up on problems before the best solutions have been tried. And he doesn't seem to like the "maybe this, maybe that" approach that theologians employ when they cannot find something definitive to say. Adams wants to be able to say, "Thus says the Lord! Here is the answer, right here!" And so, his book says, he has found the answer to the "so-called" problem of evil.[2] In his view, all the wimpish theologians who have agonized over the problem down through the centuries (such as Augustine), who have mumbled "mystery" and tiptoed around the issue, have simply failed to see the answer that has been right there in black and white in front of their noses! That answer is Romans 9:17, "For the Scripture says to Pharaoh: 'I raised you up for this very purpose, that I might display my power in you and that my name might be proclaimed in all the earth.'"

God raises up evil people (and, by implication, all evil) so that by prevailing over them he can display his power and his name throughout the earth.

Adams's answer is a good one, certainly. But it does not remove all the mystery from evil. It does not completely answer the question we have posed. For the question then arises, Why should the display of God's power and good name re-

---

[1]Santa Barbara, Calif.: EastGate Publishers, 1991.
[2]The subtitle of his book is "A Biblical Study of the So-called Problem of Evil."

quire the employment of that which is totally opposed to everything that God is? Cannot God display his power without contradicting his goodness? Cannot God display his name without making little babies suffer pain? How can a good God, through his wise foreordination, make someone to be evil, even when that God hates evil with all of his being? How can he do that, even to display himself? Does the God so displayed, then, become something less than our God of love? To answer these sorts of questions, Adams must return to the traditional theodicies and, in the end—I think—return to mystery. *The Grand Demonstration* is a fine contribution to the discussion of the problem, but I do wish the tone of it were a bit less cocksure, a bit more open to the agonies of those who still have problems after they have heard Romans 9:17. The book is a help, but it is not "the" answer, and the "so-called" problem of evil will remain a problem to many sensitive readers of the book.[3]

My own verdict is that we are unlikely to find complete answers to all of these questions—answers, that is, which are not subject to further questions.

But I do think we can provide answers in another sense. If what you want is encouragement to go on believing in the midst of suffering, Scripture provides that, and provides it abundantly. If you want help to go on trusting God despite unexplained evil, yes, we can help. And that is what I will seek to provide in what follows.

Focus on the Bible

In this chapter I'm going to be focusing on what the Bible teaches concerning the problem of evil, following Jay Adams's good example. His book is itself rather unusual in this respect. Most books on the problem of evil deal with logical and experiential matters without much focus on the Bible, perhaps out of the conviction that the Bible cannot help that much.

---

[3]See Adams's reply, reproduced in appendix B in the back of this book.

As I have indicated earlier, I do not object to using extrabiblical data in dealing with this issue, but I do believe that in this case the Bible itself brings us as close to an answer as we are likely to get. The problem of evil is so connected in our minds with the holocausts of Hitler, Stalin, and Pol Pot, with the terrors of modern warfare and modern scenarios for eco-destruction, that we are often tempted to think of it as a modern problem—as though the prevalence of unbelief today were due to mankind's sudden realization that there is too much evil in the world to justify old-fashioned theism. But who in our modern experience has suffered more, with more apparent injustice, than the biblical Job, or meditated upon that suffering more profoundly? Indeed, the Bible is preoccupied with the problem of evil. We shall see it being raised over and over again on the pages of Paul's letter to the Romans. And we might even say that the whole Bible addresses the problem of evil, for the whole story turns on the entrance of sin and evil into the world and on God's plan for dealing with it.

There is another reason why people often object to dealing with the problem of evil from Scripture. And that is, simply, that they don't believe Scripture as God's Word. Liberal theologians of various kinds often claim to have Christian answers to the problem, but those answers consist in revising the theology of the Bible. They—and this is especially true today of the "process theology" school—think they can solve the problem best by revising the biblical doctrine of God. As long as we regard God as the majestic, sovereign absolute personality of the Scriptures, they say, there will always be a problem of evil, for supreme power will always conflict with supreme goodness. But, say the process thinkers, if we deny God's supreme power and total sovereignty, then we can solve the problem of evil: evil exists because God is not fully able to prevent it.

But such revisions of scriptural teaching always lose more than they gain. Perhaps we can solve the problem of evil simply by denying God's sovereignty! Well, let's go all the way back to worshiping birds—then there will be no chance at all that the problem of evil will arise! No, no. Somewhere along this line of reasoning, you end up with a god who is simply not worthy of worship. In my view, a god who is not sovereign—indeed, a god who differs at all from the biblical absolute personality—is an idol, and is to be despised rather than worshiped. A nonsovereign God is an idol of conventional wisdom, not the absolute personality of Christianity.

We need to sharpen our sense of proportion. It would be nice to have a solution to the problem of evil, but not at any price. If the price we must pay is the very sovereignty of God, the faithful Christian must say that that price is too high. After all, it is of little importance whether any of us discovers the answer to the problem of evil. It is possible to live a long and happy and faithful life without an answer. But it is all-important that we worship the true God, the God of Scripture. Without him, human life is worth nothing.

Who do these theologians and philosophers think they are, anyway? Why do they imagine that they are in a position to correct the Bible's teaching concerning God? For the most part, they are known for their scholarship, not, to put it mildly, for their piety. They are not prophets or priests; they are not known for the depth of their personal relationships to God. They are not candidates for sainthood on the Roman Catholic model, people who give their lifeblood for the poor and overwhelm us with their universal, unconditional love. Their only credentials are their academic degrees and academic positions. But such credentials have never qualified anyone as an expert on God. Some of us can at least get by, maintaining our credibility as teachers by sticking close to the Holy Scriptures. But the liberals proudly dismiss the teachings of Scripture as inferior to the brilliance and cogency of their own thoughts, thus exposing themselves as partisans of the wisdom of the world and enemies of the wisdom of God. Why, I ask, should anyone pay any attention to them?

Modern man must get it clear in his own mind once and for all that Christian doctrines are not subject to revision. A novelist may, of course, revise his novel if he doesn't like the way the narrative is turning out. But if one seeks to revise the law of gravity because of its sometimes troublesome consequences, he will not only fail, but look silly trying. Scripture in this respect is like the law of gravity, not like a novel. I may wish that Scripture taught something different from what it teaches, but what it says is so, and I have no control over that. To pick and choose among its teachings, to revise this and modify that, is just as foolish as trying to revise the law of gravity.

And if Scripture were wrong, how would we know what is right? Indeed, the actual truth, which itself will not be subject to revision, might be far harder for modern man to take than the supposed errors of the Bible.

So we shall again look at Scripture. There are other methods, but in my mind, a direct inspection of biblical teaching is often the best way to defend the faith against objections. In that respect, our treatment of the problem of evil will furnish a model for the treatment of other difficulties.

What the Bible Does Not Say

The first thing we can learn from Scripture is what it does not say. Of course, as I have often said before, the apologist is not limited to repeating what is explicitly stated in Scripture. It is instructive, however, to see that many of the devices used by philosophers to solve the problem of evil are not present in Scripture. Very often there is a good reason why they are not present.

We will consider here most of the defenses and theodicies used in the historic discussion. We should note that some thinkers have combined two or more of the following strategies; some of them are compatible with others.

The Unreality-of-Evil Defense
Some Eastern religions and western cults (e.g., Buddhism and Christian Science) maintain that evil is really an illusion. Even some respected Christian thinkers, such as Augustine, have suggested that evil be classified under the category of nonbe-

ing.[4] Augustine does not quite mean to say that evil is an illusion, but rather that it is a "privation," a lack of good being where good being ought to be. Still, he does use this idea to remove responsibility from God. God creates all being, but he is not responsible for nonbeing.

These explanations are quite inadequate. There is no reason for us to think that evil is an illusion. Further, to say that it is, is to play games with words. For if evil is an illusion, it is a terribly troublesome illusion, an illusion that brings misery, pain, suffering, and death. If it is said that the pain also is illusory, I reply that there is no difference between illusory pain and real pain so far as the problem of evil is concerned. The problem just backs up a step and asks, "How could a good God give us all such a terrible illusion of pain?" One great advantage of Scripture's viewpoint is that it doesn't play games with suffering people. In Scripture, evil is treated quite simply as something we must deal with, whatever its metaphysical status may be.

Nor is Augustine's version any more biblical.[5] Whatever we may say about the relative distribution of good (i.e., being) throughout the universe, Scripture is clear that that distribution is in God's hands. God is as responsible for the lacks and privations (if we wish to call them that) as he is for the good being of the universe. God works *all* things after the counsel of his own will (Eph. 1:11), as Augustine later in his life came to recognize. This includes sins and evils (Gen. 50:20; Luke 22:22; Acts 2:23; 4:28; Rom. 9:1–29). It is true that all things are good, but the fallen human heart is evil, and because of that, human actions and attitudes are evil. And because of that, we describe many events in the world as evil because they express God's response to sin (Gen. 3:17–19). There is no point in creating a distinct metaphysical category ("nonbeing," "privation") for evil. The problem is simply that

---

[4]Of being, God says, "It is good" (Gen. 1:31; 1 Tim. 4:4). That would seem to indicate that only nonbeing can be evil.

[5]We should, of course, give Augustine credit for recognizing that evil has no power of its own and is in some sense parasitic on goodness.

God is sovereign over all events, good and evil, and however one analyzes evil metaphysically, it is part of God's plan.

The Divine-Weakness Defense

Many have urged some sort of divine weakness or inability as the solution to the problem: God does not overcome all evil because he cannot do so—although he does do his best. This is the answer of process theology[6] and also of Harold S. Kushner's popular book, *When Bad Things Happen to Good People*.[7] This solution denies the historic Christian doctrines of divine omnipotence, omniscience, and sovereignty, while seeking to preserve God's attribute of goodness. But Scripture itself not only fails to teach this solution, but firmly contradicts it. God's omniscience (Ps. 139; Heb. 4:11–13; Isa. 46:10; 1 John 3:20), omnipotence (Ps. 115:3; Isa. 14:24, 27; 46:10; 55:11; Luke 18:27), and sovereignty (Rom. 11:33–36; 1 Tim. 6:15–16) are central to the biblical doctrine of God.

One may prefer to believe in a weaker god than the absolute personality of the Scriptures, but he should be aware of the cost of such a preference. He may thereby get a solution to the problem of evil, but he loses any sure hope for the overcoming of evil. He gains intellectual satisfaction at the cost of having to face the horrible possibility that evil may triumph after all. Surely there is something ironic about calling this a "solution" to the problem of evil.

The Best-Possible-World Defense

The philosopher G. W. Leibniz and others have argued that this world, for all its evils, is nonetheless the best world which God could have produced. The reason is not the weakness of God, as in the previous defense, but rather the very logic of creation. Certain evils are logically necessary to achieve certain good ends. For example, there must be suffering if there

---

[6]As, for example, in David Ray Griffin, *God, Power, and Evil* (Philadelphia: Westminster, 1976). Cf. his *Evil Revisited* (Albany, N.Y.: State University of New York Press, 1991).
[7]New York: Schocken Books, 1981.

is to be compassion for sufferers. So the best possible world will include some evil. God necessarily, on this view, makes the best world possible, including whatever evils may be required for the best overall result. Because of the very excellence of his standards, he can do nothing less.

Scripture does teach that God observes the laws of logic,[8] not because there are laws "above" him to which he must conform, but because he is by nature a logical person. That God is logical is implied by the scriptural teachings that he is wise, just, faithful, and true—attributes which would be meaningless if God were free to contradict himself.

But does a perfect world logically require the existence of evil? God himself is perfect, but there is no evil in him. And, according to Scripture, the original creation contained no evil (Gen. 1:31). Was it imperfect for that reason? The consummate new heavens and new earth—that is, the ultimate perfection of the created order—will also be without evil (Rev. 21:1–8). As for the earlier example, suffering may be necessary for the exhibition of compassion, but it is not necessary for the existence of compassion in a person. God has always been compassionate, even when there was no one for him to show compassion to.

And is God, because of his perfection, able to create only perfect beings? That may seem logical, but Scripture teaches otherwise. Indeed, in the Bible, God creates beings who lack perfection in many ways. Adam was created good, but not perfect. He was "alone," for one thing, and that was not good (Gen. 2:18). He was also untested; his righteousness had to be confirmed through trial (Gen. 2:17; 3:1–21). Satan himself was most likely created good, but was from the beginning capable of rebellion against God. Thus, even in the good creation there were imperfections. And so it goes throughout the historical providence of God. There is much that is imperfect

---

[8]I am, of course, talking about God's own logic, which may not be identical to any humanly devised logical system. Logic as a human science strives, like all human sciences, to think God's thoughts after him, but it does not always do so perfectly.

that will be perfected (or destroyed) only in the new heavens and new earth.

Of course, Leibniz's view is not that everything God makes is perfect, but that the world as a whole is perfect, granted the logical necessity of some evil. While rejecting the idea of the logical necessity of evil, I would grant the possibility that, taking the whole historical sequence into account, including God's glorious redemption of sinners, this is the best world that God could have made. But that is only a possibility. If God can make imperfect individual beings, if God can make a whole world that is imperfect and requires renovation, surely it is possible that he can determine a whole historical sequence which is imperfect in comparison with other worlds he might have made. So the bottom line is: I don't know whether this world (taken as a complete historical sequence) is the best possible world. So far as I know, God is free to make things that are either imperfect or perfect. So we cannot solve the problem of evil by saying that we know a priori that this is the best possible world and that all evils are logically necessary for its perfection.

The Free-Will Defense

The most common defense among professional philosophers today is based on human free will.[9] The free-will defense says that evil came about by the free choice of rational creatures (Satan or Adam or "everyman"). Since that free choice was in no sense controlled or foreordained or caused by God, he cannot be held accountable for it.[10] Therefore the existence of evil does not compromise God's goodness.[11]

---

[9]One of the most influential formulations is that of Alvin Plantinga, *God, Freedom, and Evil* (Grand Rapids: Eerdmans, 1977).

[10]Strictly speaking, Plantinga's argument is based, not on the actuality of free will in this sense, but in the mere possibility of it. But if we have reason to believe, as I do, that free will in this sense is not actual, I cannot see that Plantinga's argument will be very cogent. In this sense, Plantinga's book is a brief for an Arminian concept of human freedom, though it was published while he taught at Calvin College, a supposedly Calvinistic institution.

[11]Plantinga combines this traditional free-will defense with a form of the greater-good defense, which we will discuss later. Essentially, he claims that

Scripture does teach that man is, or can be, free in certain senses. (1) He does what he wants to do, acting in accord with his desires, whether those are holy or wicked.[12] (2) Adam had the freedom or ability to choose either good or evil. The Fall removed this freedom from us, for fallen creatures can[13] do only what is evil (Gen. 6:5; 8:21; Isa. 64:6; Rom. 3:10ff.). But redemption restores this freedom to those who believe (2 Cor. 5:17). (3) Redemption brings to us an even higher freedom, a freedom from sin and its effects altogether (John 8:32). "Freedom from sin" is the usual meaning of "freedom" in the New Testament. (4) We are free in the sense that we are not the helpless victims of historical determinism. Scripture does not allow us to plead deficiencies in heredity, environment, psychological balance, self-esteem, and so on, as excuses for violating God's commandments. We are, in all our actions (1 Cor. 10:31), responsible to obey the Lord.

Further, Scripture does agree with the defenders of free will in teaching that the blame for sin rests on man, rather than on God. Even when Scripture specifically mentions God's foreordination of an evil event, the blame for the evil rests exclusively with the human perpetrators (see Gen. 50:20; Acts 2:23; 4:27).

---

the divine gift of free will, even with the attendant possibility of evil, makes for a better overall good than there would be in a universe without such freedom. In general, we shall see that the greater-good defense contains some biblical truth, but I doubt that free will in Plantinga's sense actually is a greater good.

[12]This is sometimes called "compatibilist" freedom, since it is compatible with the causal determination of human choices.

[13]The "can" here is a moral-spiritual "can," not a "can" of physical or mental ability. Sinners have the physical and mental capacity to obey God, but they lack the moral-spiritual motivation. Their problem is a heart problem, not a lack of some capacity or other. The problem is that despite their capacities, they *will* not obey; and that *"will* not" is so deeply ingrained, so intensely reiterated, so much a part of their very nature, that in an important (but unique) sense they "cannot." I do think there is some confusion between Calvinists and Arminians on this point. In certain obvious senses, fallen man *can* do right, and his responsibility depends on that "ability." As Van Til emphasized, depravity is ethical, not metaphysical; it does not involve a decline in our physical capacities, skills, or IQs, but a misuse of these. Calvinists need to be clearer in admitting that, while making the proper distinctions.

However, Scripture does not teach—in fact, it denies—free will in the sense that it is used by the free-will defense. For on that view of freedom,[14] man's free choices are not in any way foreordained or caused by God. But Scripture frequently speaks of God determining our free choices (see Gen. 50:20; Acts 2:23; 4:27; also 2 Sam. 24:1, referring specifically to evil choices; also Prov. 16:9; Luke 24:45; John 6:44, 65; Acts 2:47; 11:18; 13:48; 16:14; Rom. 8:28ff.; 9; Eph. 2:8–9; Phil. 1:29). And certainly the free choices of human beings are included among the general statements of Romans 11:36 and Ephesians 1:11.[15]

It is remarkable that in Romans 9, where the problem of evil is raised explicitly, Paul does not resort to the free-will defense; rather, he contradicts the assumptions of that defense. He raises the question of why so few Jews have believed in Christ. This is a matter of some agony for him (vv. 2–5), for these are his people and, historically, the people of God, the heirs of the promise. We should note that this very question presupposes a strong view of the sovereignty of God. For why would the problem of evil arise here at all unless Paul were assuming that faith is a gift of God? The problem is that God has taken Israel to be his people, yet he has largely withheld from them the gift of faith.

Paul's answer is that since the time of Abraham, there has been a division among the "people of God" between those who actually belong to God by faith and those who are only physically descended from Abraham. What causes this division? Here, Paul could easily have said "human choice."[16] But

---

[14]That view was taught by Pelagius, Molina, and Arminius, among others in church history. In secular philosophy, it is called the "incompatibilist" (cf. note 12) or "libertarian" view.

[15]Even Arminians must reluctantly admit that God in some sense controls our free choices. They can escape this conclusion only by moving toward even more unbiblical positions, such as process theology. See the discussion of divine sovereignty in chap. 2.

[16]Had he said this, he would not have been wrong, even on a Calvinistic basis. For Calvinists also accept the importance of human choice. The question is whether that choice is itself a gift of God. Had Paul referred to human choice in this context, he would simply have sidestepped that issue.

he does not say this. Rather, he traces the division back to "God's purpose in election" (v. 11), adding, "not by works but by him who calls" (v. 12). Indeed, God foretold the fate of Esau and Jacob before they were born, indicating that he had foreordained their destiny (vv. 12, 13).

In verse 14, the problem of evil comes to the fore: was God unjust to ordain evil for Esau before he was even born? No, says Paul. Why? The free-will defense would say that God foresaw Esau's autonomous free choices and therefore determined to punish him. But Paul traces the evil to God's own free choice:

> I will have mercy on whom I have mercy,
> and I will have compassion on whom I have compassion.
> (v. 15, quoting Ex. 33:19)

He then reiterates: "It does not, therefore, depend on man's desire or effort, but on God's mercy" (v. 16). Then comes verse 17,[17] which tells us that God's purpose for raising up evil Pharaoh was to declare God's name throughout the earth. "Therefore, God has mercy on whom he wants to have mercy, and he hardens whom he wants to harden" (v. 18).

In verse 19, the problem of evil comes up again: Why does God still blame us? And again, the answer is not "Because God does not control our free choices." Rather, the answer is that he has full rights over us to do whatever he (sovereignly!) chooses to do.

Scripture never uses the free-will defense in any passage where the problem of evil is up for discussion. You will not find it in the book of Job, in Psalm 37, or in Psalm 73. Indeed, all of these passages presuppose the usual strong view of divine sovereignty.

So the free-will defense is unbiblical. There are also problems with its internal coherence. If, as in classical Arminian-

---

[17]Adams's key verse!

ism, our free choices are literally causeless, then they are not caused by our character or our desires any more than they are caused by God. And if this is the case, our "free choices" are totally accidental happenings unconnected with anything in the past. They are surprises, worse than hiccups occurring at awkward times. A person with an upright character and no previous inclination toward theft, would, walking past a bank, suddenly, on some strange impulse, go inside and rob the bank without even wanting to.[18] Surely, this is not what we normally think of as free choice. And such chance happenings can hardly be the ground of moral responsibility, since, as we saw in previous chapters, they are essentially irrational. They are events of which there is no first cause, no origin in an absolute personality.

On the other hand, if the Arminian-libertarian sees free choice as caused by character and desire, then he is introducing factors which themselves have causes[19] in heredity and environment, causes which precede the conscious life of the individual. He is substituting an impersonal cosmic determinism for the personalistic "determinism" of biblical Christianity. I do not see this as any sort of gain for moral responsibility.

The Character-Building Defense

The fifth unbiblical defense we shall consider is sometimes called "Irenaean," after the church father Irenaeus, who employed it. In modern times it has been urged by John Hick,[20] who calls it the "soul-making" theodicy.[21]

---

[18]Of course, libertarians usually do admit that our character and desires "influence" our free choices, but without "determining" them. But what that usually means is that character and desires somewhat limit the alternatives available for free choice and perhaps incline us to choose in one direction or another. But of course we may choose against inclination on this view, and that choice emerges, again, as a sheer accident. Thus, even with these qualifications a person might make a "free choice" that is quite out of character, and simply by chance.

[19]If they do not, then they are evidently accidents, and the argument of the previous paragraph pertains to them.

[20]See Hick, *Evil and the God of Love* (New York: Harper & Row, 1966).

[21]*Theodicy* means literally "justification of God." It is used to describe proposed solutions to the problem of evil.

The argument is that man was created in a state of moral immaturity. For man to come to full maturity, it was necessary for him to undergo various forms of pain and suffering.

It is true that suffering sometimes builds character. Hebrews 12 says that believers experience God's fatherly discipline and chastisement. Just as an earthly father's spankings bring discipline to a child's life, so our heavenly Father puts us through trials so that we will learn habits of godliness.

However, I think that it is unbiblical to turn this principle into a full-scale theodicy. For one thing, Scripture teaches that Adam was not created morally immature with a need to develop character through suffering. He was created good, and had he obeyed God, he would not have needed to experience suffering. Suffering is the result of the Fall (Gen. 3:17).

Furthermore, Scripture teaches that not all suffering builds character. Unbelievers suffer and often learn no lessons from it. And not all character improvement comes through suffering. Believers are created anew in Christ (2 Cor. 5:17). The basic change from sin to righteousness is a gift of God's grace. Moreover, our sanctification will be perfected in heaven—not through a purgatory of suffering, but through God's own action.

The Stable-Environment Defense

C. S. Lewis, in his *Problem of Pain*,[22] argues that a stable environment is necessary for human life. We know one another through regular and stable signs of one another's presence (facial appearance, voice, etc.). To live happily and productively requires a universe of regular law, so that we can make plans and fulfill them. If, when I reached for my comb in the morning, it randomly turned into a tortoise, I would not be able to develop a dependable plan and practice of combing my hair.

But, says Lewis, a stable environment opens up the possibility of evil. It means, for example, that the law of gravity will not be temporarily repealed to save me from falling down the stairs.

---

[22]London: Geoffrey Bles, 1940.

True enough. But does a stable environment necessarily produce evil? Is it a sufficient cause for evil? Certainly not. God created Adam (concerning whose literal existence, I gather, Lewis had some doubts) and placed him in a stable environment, but without evil and pain. I don't know how this worked—did God revoke physical laws now and then to protect Adam, leaving enough regularity for a fairly normal everyday life, or did God simply foreordain that Adam would not run afoul of these laws? However it was, there was no pain and suffering until the Fall. Heaven will, certainly, be another stable environment, but one without evil.[23]

And how does a stable environment bring about evils of the human heart, the spirit of rebellion against God?

So, although some evils may certainly be traced proximately (see below) to natural laws in a stable environment, these are not a sufficient explanation for evil. The Bible never refers evils to such a source. To do so would be to blame creation rather than our own hearts.

The Indirect-Cause Defense
The indirect-cause defense differs from the first six defenses in that it is rather commonly found in Reformed theology. Van Til endorses it in a discussion of Calvin's use of it against Pighius.[24] Gordon Clark also makes use of it, in his *Religion, Reason, and Revelation*.[25] The argument seems to be that since God is the indirect rather than the direct cause of evil, he bears no blame for it.

Clark explains the distinction this way: God is the ultimate cause of my book, but he is not its author; I am. Therefore, I bear responsibility for its contents, not God. The author is the closest cause to the effect, the "proximate" cause.

---

[23]The reader may notice that several of the proposed defenses fail to take into account either the goodness of the original creation or the perfection of heaven or both. An adequate defense or theodicy must be consistent with these biblical teachings.

[24]Van Til, *The Defense of the Faith* (Philadelphia: Presbyterian and Reformed, 1955; 2d ed., 1963), 182–87.

[25]Philadelphia: Presbyterian and Reformed, 1961, 238–41.

If I hit billiard ball A, and it hits B, and B hits C, then I am the ultimate cause of C's movement, but the movement of B is the proximate cause or author.

It is true that in Scripture God's relation to evil is indirect. It was not God who tempted Eve, but the Serpent.[26] James 1:13 persuades us that such is always the case with temptation. And it is also true that in Scripture moral blame attaches only to creatures. It is, therefore, tempting (!) to find a connection between these two facts.

But indirectness of causality does not in itself mitigate responsibility—at least on the human level. If I hire a hit man to kill someone, I am as responsible for the murder as the man who actually pulls the trigger. Scripture warns us that enticing someone else to sin is itself a sin (Deut. 13:6ff., Rom. 14). Is God so different from creatures in this respect that the indirectness of his role in evil insulates him against moral censure? Scripture never says that he is different in that way.

And if that were the only solution we had to the problem of evil, it certainly would be a most inadequate one. For it would picture God as some kind of giant Mafia boss who keeps his hands legally clean by forcing his underlings to carry out his nasty designs. Is that picture a biblical one? Is it compatible with the goodness of God which Scripture teaches us?

The *ex Lex* Defense

In the volume just cited, Gordon Clark also presents another theodicy, which, if sound, would render his indirect-cause defense wholly beside the point. That he includes both defenses may indicate some lack of confidence in one or the other, although you couldn't tell that from reading the text.

His argument is that God is *ex lex*, which means "outside of the law." The idea is that God is outside of or above

---

[26]Even with this statement, however, there are problems. If God in providence "concurs" with second causes, maintaining them and directing them to their effects, then the distinction between indirect and direct causes is not easily made. More of this will appear in my forthcoming *Doctrine of God*.

the laws he prescribes for man. He tells us not to kill, yet he retains for himself the right to take human life. Thus, he is not himself bound to obey the Ten Commandments or any other law given to man in Scripture. Morally, he is on an entirely different level from us. Therefore, he has the right to do many things that seem evil to us, even things which contradict scriptural norms. For a man to cause evil indirectly might very well be wrong, but it would not be wrong for God.[27] Thus Clark neatly finesses any argument against God's justice or goodness.

There is some truth in this approach. As we shall see, Scripture does forbid human criticism of God's actions, and the reason is, as Clark implies, divine transcendence. It is also true that God has some prerogatives that he forbids to us, such as the freedom to take human life.

Clark forgets, however, or perhaps denies, the Reformed and biblical maxim that the law reflects God's own character. To obey the law is to imitate God, to be like him, to image him (Ex. 20:11; Lev. 11:44–45; Matt. 5:45; 1 Peter 1:15–16). There is in biblical ethics also an imitation of Christ, centered on the atonement (John 13:34–35; Eph. 4:32; 5:1; Phil. 2:3ff.; 1 John 3:16; 4:8–10). Obviously, there is much about God that we cannot imitate, including those prerogatives mentioned earlier. Satan tempted Eve into seeking to become "like God" in the sense of coveting his prerogatives (Gen. 3:5).[28] But the overall holiness, justice, and goodness of God is something we can and must imitate on the human level.

So God does honor, in general, the same law that he gives to us. He rules out murder because he hates to see one human being murder another, and he intends to reserve for himself the right to control human death. He prohibits adultery because he hates adultery (which is a mirror of idolatry—

---

[27]But on this basis, it would also not be wrong for God to cause evil directly. That is why I said that this argument makes the indirect-cause argument beside the point.

[28]John Murray said that the difference between the two ways of seeking God's likeness appears to be a razor's edge, while there is actually a deep chasm between them.

see Hosea). We can be assured that God will behave according to the same standards of holiness that he prescribes for us, except insofar as Scripture declares a difference between his responsibilities and ours.[29]

But on this basis, the problem of evil returns. If God prohibits us from tormenting others, how can he allow his creatures to be tormented? If he abides (essentially, with some exceptions) by the standards revealed in Scripture, how can he plan, foreordain, and cause evil to take place? Thus we cannot agree with Clark's *ex lex* defense. It simply is not biblical. The problem remains to be solved.

An ad Hominem Defense

Some Christian apologists have approached the problem of evil on the theory that the best defense is a good offense. Thus, when an unbeliever questions the consistency of God's sovereignty with his goodness in the face of evil, the apologist replies that the unbeliever has no right even to raise the question, for he cannot, on his basis, even distinguish good from evil.

The point is correct, as far as it goes. As I argued earlier, moral values presuppose the absolute personality revealed in Scripture. If there is no such God, then the world is governed either by chance or by impersonal laws, neither of which commands the loyalty required by moral values. If, like the unbeliever, we seek to think and live without God, we have no basis for identifying or describing good and evil.

---

[29]Oddly, Clark, who is usually accused of being a Platonic realist, at this point veers into the opposite of realism, namely, nominalism. The extreme nominalists held that the biblical laws were not reflections of God's nature, but merely arbitrary requirements. God could as easily have commanded adultery as forbidden it. I mentioned this once in a letter to Clark, and he appreciated the irony, but did not provide an answer. Why, I wonder, didn't he deal with moral law the same way he dealt with reason and logic in, e.g., *The Johannine Logos* (Nutley, N.J.: Presbyterian and Reformed, 1972)? There he argued that God's reason/logic was neither above God (Plato) nor below God (nominalism), but God's own rational nature. Why did he not take the same view of God's moral standards?

It is also useful to bring this point to the unbeliever's attention. He, in a way, has a more serious problem than the believer does. If the believer faces the problem of how there can be evil in a theistic world, the unbeliever faces the problem of how there can be either good or evil in a nontheistic world. In terms of the larger apologetic enterprise, this sort of truth needs to be driven home to the unbeliever.

Unbelievers must surely not be allowed to take their own autonomy for granted in defining moral concepts. They must not be allowed to assume that they are the ultimate judges of what is right and wrong. Indeed, they should be warned that that sort of assumption rules out the biblical God from the outset and thus shows its character as a faith-presupposition. The unbeliever must know that we reject his presupposition altogether and insist upon subjecting our moral standards to God's. And if the unbeliever insists on his autonomy, we may get nasty and require him to show how an autonomous self can come to moral conclusions in a godless universe.

However, valuable as this point is in itself, it is not really an answer to the problem of evil. It is an ad hominem argument; that is, it is addressed to the person rather than to the issue. The unbeliever asks how we account for evil, and we reply that he has a worse problem. He may indeed, but we have not thereby answered his question. And he might well reply, "Well, I grant that atheism has its share of problems, but for now let us talk about yours. I am pointing to what looks like a contradiction in your system. Whether or not my system is an adequate alternative is quite irrelevant to the question. Even if I were a Christian,[30] I would still have the same question, and I would like to have an answer to it."

Scripture does, as we shall see, rebuke people who raise the problem of evil in certain ways. And Scripture is not en-

---

[30]In Van Tillian language, "When I consider Christianity on its own presuppositions, for the sake of argument . . ."

tirely averse to some types of ad hominem response. But its typical responses are rather different from the one presently under discussion. We must hasten, then, to discover positively what Scripture does say.

SEVEN

▼

Apologetics as Defense: The Problem of Evil, 2—A Biblical Response

In the previous chapter, we examined several solutions that various philosophers and theologians have put forward to solve the problem of evil, and we found them to be unbiblical or at least inadequate. In this chapter, we will see what the Bible itself says about the problem of evil.

God Is the Standard for His Actions[1]

Scripture never assumes that God owes us an explanation for what he does. In a number of biblical passages, the problem of evil arises for the reader, but the text itself never comments on it. For example, we often wish that God had told us much more in Genesis 3, the story of the entrance of evil into the world. Where did the Serpent (Satan) come from? If he was originally good with the rest of the creation (Gen. 1:31), how

---

[1]Students of the triadic system explained in *DKG* will identify the three sections of this chapter as normative, situational, and existential, respectively.

171

did he become evil? Why was he allowed into the Garden to tempt Eve? Why, indeed, did a good God foreordain this entire event to take place? If he foreordained the response of Adam and Eve, by what right does he punish them? All these questions naturally arise in the context, but the passage does not answer them. Indeed, when Adam in effect raises the problem of evil by blaming God for giving him the wife who tempted him (v. 12), God offers no rationale for what he has done. Rather, he points out Adam's own wickedness, imposes a curse upon him,[2] and then leaves the scene.

The same pattern is present in Genesis 22, where God tells Abraham to sacrifice his beloved son, the child of the promise. The reader naturally wants to know how such a command is compatible with God's goodness. Granting that God prevented it from being carried out, was this not a horrible trifling with a father's love? But God does not explain. Unlike Adam, Abraham never raises the issue, and God commends his quiet, unflinching obedience, his faith that God will provide the lamb (vv. 15–18; cf. Rom. 4:17–25; Heb. 11:8–19).

By his failure to defend himself, God is claiming his sovereign right to be trusted and believed, whatever suspicions his actions may provoke in human minds. In the final analysis, he is sovereign in the granting and withholding of mercy. He makes that clear in Exodus 33:19, which is, in context, an exposition of his very name: "I will have mercy on whom I will have mercy, and I will have compassion on whom I will have compassion." In his decisions, he will not submit to man's judgment. He reserves the right to behave in a way that may offend human values, that may even appear, from a human viewpoint, to contradict his own values. And when that happens, he is not under man's judgment. He is not obligated to explain.

This is one of the main themes of the book of Job. Job believes that he is suffering unjustly, and he demands an interview with God (23:1–7; 31:35ff.). He imagines that he will

---

[2]This is, to be sure, also a blessing, because it permits him to go on living and allows history to continue until the deliverer comes to defeat Satan.

ask questions of God, and that God's answers will in turn vindicate his (Job's) righteousness. Well, God does grant the interview (see chaps. 38–42), but not on Job's terms. God, not Job, asks the questions. The Lord says to him, "Brace yourself like a man; I will question you, and you shall answer me" (38:3). The questions deal with mysteries of the universe, somewhat sarcastically pointing up Job's ignorance:

> Where were you when I laid the earth's foundation?
>   Tell me, if you understand.
> Who marked off its dimensions? Surely you know!
>   Who stretched a measuring line across it?
>   (vv. 4–5)

The point is that if Job is so ignorant concerning God's works in the natural world, how can he expect to understand the workings of God's mind in distributing good and evil (cf. John 3:12)? In this stylized debate, Job confesses utter defeat. He puts his hand over his mouth—a sign of shame and also an admission that this would-be indicter of God has nothing to say (40:4). But God initiates another round (40:6–41:34). There is the same result. No hint is given of any weakness in God! Job admits, "I know that you can do all things; no plan of yours can be thwarted" (42:2). And he confesses his sin in claiming to know more than he really did:

> Surely I spoke of things I did not understand,
>   things too wonderful for me to know. . . .
> My ears had heard of you
>   but now my eyes have seen you.
> Therefore I despise myself
>   and repent in dust and ashes.
>   (42:3–6)

Notice how the charges are reversed. Job, like Adam, intended to bring charges against God. But the result, again as in Adam's case, is that the complainer is convicted of sin.

173

Notice also that Job never learns why he has had to endure suffering. The reader knows a bit more than Job, for he can read the prologue, in which Satan is permitted to tempt Job in order to prove his faithfulness. But that is not a complete explanation of why Job suffered. The reader then wants to know why God allowed Satan to do such a thing. Did God not know that Job was faithful? Who was it that needed additional proof? Why did God have any interest in convincing Satan of anything? (Why should he even assume that Satan's question was sincere?) Why was the bizarre wager made? Indeed, what was Satan doing in heaven anyway? And why was Satan created and permitted to make evil choices in the first place?

The book provides no answers to these questions. In the end, the reader is in the same position as Job himself. But in the end, the reader's questions must be handled in the same way that God handled Job's questions. For, like Job, we were not there when God laid the foundations of the earth. None of us knows who marked off its dimensions or stretched a measuring line across it. We need, too, to be cautious in probing the problem of evil. I don't believe it is sinful merely to pose questions. But when our questions take on the quality of accusations, when they express actual doubt of God's goodness, when we put ourselves in the proud position of demanding an answer, then we can expect a rebuke from God like the rebukes he gave to Job and to Adam.[3]

Let us note the same pattern in a few more passages. In Ezekiel 18:25, there is a brief exchange: "Yet you say, 'The way of the Lord is not just.' Hear, O house of Israel: Is my way unjust? Is it not your ways that are unjust?" Again, a complaint against God's justice is reversed. For details, look at the context.

Another interesting passage in this connection is Matthew 20:1–16, Jesus' parable of the workers in the vineyard. Some work only one hour, others all day, but they all

---

[3]And I expect that some of those rebukes will be visited upon the theologians who are so insistent on a solution to the problem of evil that they are willing to turn their back on the sovereign God revealed in Scripture.

receive the same pay.[4] Some complain about unfairness (i.e., the problem of evil). But the master (God) replies, "Friend, I am not being unfair to you. Didn't you agree to work for a denarius? Take your pay and go. I want to give the man who was hired last the same as I gave you. Don't I have the right to do what I want with my own money? Or are you envious because I am generous?" (vv. 13–15).

Note here some of the same themes that we observed earlier: (1) The charges are reversed: the complainer is accused of envy. (2) The sovereignty of God is underscored ("Don't I have the right . . . ?") in contrast to any weakness-of-God theologies. (3) The reason for the uneven distribution is not given; the master senses no obligation to provide it. To these we may add (4) the reliability of the master's word ("Didn't you agree . . . ?"). The master offered a denarius, and that is what he gave. His revelation is dependable; he is not a liar.[5] Thus, whatever problems may be connected with God's distribution of good and evil, we may not conclude that his Word, in which he promises blessings for his people, is unreliable.[6] And notice also that (5) a true interpretation of the facts actually vindi-

---

[4]This is not to be construed as a biblical model for labor-management relations! In the context of Matthew's gospel, it seems to focus on the fact that Gentiles are soon to share the blessings of God with the Jews, and that the two groups will receive the same blessings, even though the Jews have been God's people for a much longer time. Note a similar point in the parable of the prodigal son (Luke 15:11–32), in which the returning profligate receives a blessing far greater than the older brother thinks is fair (vv. 28–32).

[5]Reformed theology distinguishes between God's decretive will and his preceptive will. The former governs whatever comes to pass; the latter expresses what God wants us to believe and to do. The former is secret until it is carried out in history; we cannot use it to predict the future. Nor can we use it alone to direct our lives; for such direction, God has given us his preceptive will in the Scriptures. (Of course, God's preceptive will must be applied to our circumstances, which in turn arise from his decretive will. To that extent, the decretive will is involved in God's guidance of our lives.) Jesus' parable tells us, then, in these theological terms, that although the structure and motivations of God's decretive will are highly mysterious, that mystery casts no doubt on the reliability of his preceptive will.

[6]Again, this is contrary to the suppositions of many theologians.

cates the master's character. As the master sees it (and he, of course, is right!), the disparity in pay shows, not unfairness to those who worked all day, but generosity to those who worked only an hour. A proper perspective—proper presuppositions—can make a great difference in how we evaluate things!

Finally, let us look at Paul's letter to the Romans, which also has a great concern for theodicy. Indeed, Romans is to the New Testament what Job is to the Old—the book most systematically focused on the problem of evil. Of course, we usually think of Romans as a description of how God justifies sinful people, together with the implications of that justification. That is true enough. But 3:26 indicates that Paul is concerned here not only with the justification of man, but also with the justification of God (theodicy). Specifically, how can God justify sinners without himself being subject to charges of injustice?

Thus, Romans often takes the form of dialogue between Paul and imaginary (or real?) objectors, who raise the problem of evil in various ways. For example, in 3:3 someone asks whether the unbelief of some Jews nullifies the faithfulness of God. Is God unjust to promise blessing to Israel and then to withhold from some the faith that is necessary to receive the blessing? Here is the problem of evil, applied to one aspect of God's plan. Interestingly, Paul, like the previous writers we have considered, does not sense any obligation to answer that question. Rather, he rebukes it, as God rebuked Adam, Job, and the Israel of Ezekiel's time, and as the landowner in Jesus' parable rebuked his complaining workers: "Not at all![7] Let God be true, and every man a liar. As it is written: 'So that you may be proved right when you speak and prevail when you judge,'" (v. 4, quoting Ps. 51:4). Note here again the familiar themes: the complainers have charges directed at them;

---

[7]This exclamation translates the Greek *me genoito*, literally "may it not be" (sometimes translated "certainly not"). It is a strong expression of abhorrence. The King James Version translates it "God forbid." That is misleading, since the word "God" is not found in the Greek; but that added word does help to convey the strength of the expression.

God's word is vindicated; God rejects the supposed obligation to explain himself; God's sovereign rights are honored and his character is vindicated.

But in the very next verse the objector comes back: "But if our unrighteousness brings out God's righteousness more clearly, what shall we say? That God is unjust in bringing his wrath upon us?" (v. 5). Paul quickly reminds us (and God!) that this is not his objection, but one of an opponent: "I am using a human argument" (v. 5). And again, the questioner is strongly rebuked: "Certainly not! If that were so, how could God judge the world?" (v. 6). Paul again upholds God's sovereign right as the supreme judge, without showing how God can avoid a charge of injustice in this connection.

In the next instance, Paul's answer is even more of a rebuke and even less of an explanation:

> Someone might argue, "If my falsehood enhances God's truthfulness and so increases his glory, why am I still condemned as a sinner?" Why not say—as we are being slanderously reported as saying and as some claim that we say—"Let us do evil that good may result"? Their condemnation is deserved. (vv. 7–8)

The last four words are the extent of Paul's answer.[8]

Note also Paul's shortness with questions in 3:31; 6:1–2; 6:15ff.; 7:7. There are some actual answers here, as opposed to those we considered earlier. These questions don't deal with God's own character as directly. But they do indirectly, and to that extent Paul's responses contain at least a touch of rebuke.

The dialogue on the problem of evil resumes in earnest in chapter 9.[9] The question of verse 14, "Is God unjust?" (in

---

[8]One is reminded of the gag line, "'Shut up,' he explained."

[9]Notice, however, that the pattern of rhetorical questions in the book is transformed into a great hymn of divine victory and human redemption in 8:31–39. The questions in the letter begin as unbelieving questions; later they have some measure of sincerity about them; in Rom. 8, they become expressions of mature faith! But chap. 9 brings regression, as we shall see.

hating Esau before his birth), receives Paul's usual answer: "Not at all!" But why must we say that God is just in this connection? Because God has mercy on whom he will have mercy (v. 15, quoting Ex. 33:11). In other words, God has the sovereign right to do what he wishes, and no further explanation is necessary. Anyone who continues to accuse God (as in v. 19) is himself subject to the accusation that he is talking back to God, like a clay pot questioning the purposes of the potter who made it (vv. 20–21). The potter is sovereign over the clay in both control and authority. So much for the weakness-of-God and free-will defenses!

Romans confirms, therefore, what we have seen elsewhere in Scripture. (1) We have no right to complain against God, and when we do, we expose ourselves as disobedient. (2) God is under no obligation to give us an intellectually satisfying answer to the problem of evil. He expects us to trust him in spite of that. (3) God's sovereignty is not to be questioned in connection with the problem of evil; it is rather to be underscored. (4) God's word, his truth, is altogether reliable. (5) As a matter of fact, God is not unjust. He is holy, just, and good.

To summarize: God, as sovereign Lord, is the standard of his own actions. He is not subject to human judgment; on the contrary, our judgment is subject to his word. Once we are thus clear on our epistemological situation, we can be assured, despite our questions, of God's good character, for on that matter the Word of God is clear.

This is not to say with Gordon Clark that God is *ex lex,* although it sounds similar and may indeed meet some of Clark's concerns. God honors essentially the same law that he gives us, for the fundamental law for man is, given the differences between Creator and creature, the law of God's own nature. God's righteousness is the standard for our righteousness. But as sovereign Lord, God may sometimes do things that appear to our finite minds to be contrary to that divine righteousness. When that happens, we must not demand explanations, but rather trust.

This is not to say that we must trust God's goodness with blind faith, although it may sound like that from our discussion so far. We have only seen part of the biblical response to the problem of evil, and when we see the rest, it will not seem to be a blind-faith response that God wants from us. Indeed, we saw earlier in this book that trusting God on the basis of his Word is not blind faith at all. The Word includes its own rationale and points to extrabiblical facts which also rationally confirm its teaching. Nevertheless, although faith is not blind, it is different from sight. The heroes of Hebrews 11 endured terrible sufferings, not seeing the fulfillment of God's promises, the heavenly city. They walked by faith. They had God's word, and that word was reliable. But it did not answer all their questions or tell each one why his or her suffering was necessary. Yet their faith prevailed. The very nature of faith is to persevere despite unanswered questions. Thus does God's word encourage sufferers to hold on tightly to God's promises and not to be overcome with doubt.

Scripture Gives Us a New Historical Perspective

In this section, I intend to go more deeply into Scripture's rationale. Why are the biblical writers so sure of God's justice and goodness? As we have seen, they were not unaware of the problem of evil! Around them were all sorts of voices challenging the goodness and justice of God. One answer, of course—essentially the answer of the last section—is: God says so, and that ought to be enough. That answer is perfectly proper, and it is important, for it keeps our hearts fixed on their proper presuppositions. But that is not the only biblical answer; or, rather, it is not the full biblical answer. Scripture also tells us some things about *how* God reveals, and therefore vindicates, his goodness. We may summarize by saying that God vindicates his justice by giving us a new historical perspective, by helping us to see history through his eyes. Let us consider how the past, the present, and the future look through the eyes of God.

The Past: The Wait and the Dialectic

I have always felt that a great many mysteries in theology boil down to the mystery of time. Why is it that our eternal God loves to draw things out in time?[10] After all, if God's purpose was simply to create a universe and a people to glorify his name (temporal, to be sure), he could have accomplished it in a time barely perceptible to us. Even a drama of sin and redemption might, at least so it seems, have been accomplished in a few moments: a moment of disobedient thinking, a moment of divine-human suffering, a moment of resurrection triumph, and a moment initiating eternal glory.

Certainly a great part of the problem of suffering lies in the fact that our suffering is drawn out in time. We cry out to God, and he does not seem to hear. Or, rather, he in effect tells us to wait and wait and wait.

Scripture tells us a great deal about this waiting process. It shows us how God's people are tested by the passage of time over and over again. But it also shows us, again and again, how God brings the waiting periods to an end, vindicating himself and ending the sufferings of his people.

In the early chapters of Exodus, the people of Israel are in bondage in Egypt. Joseph, who brought the family there, has been dead for generations. During all that time, so far as we know, there has been no message from God. But the people cry out to him in their slavery (2:23ff.). Moses, the eventual deliverer, must also wait. At age forty, he goes into exile for killing an Egyptian; not until age eighty does he meet God and receive his commission to lead Israel to its promised home.

When Moses meets God in the burning bush, God identifies himself as the God of the past—"I am the God of your father, the God of Abraham, the God of Isaac and the God of Jacob" (3:6). The God of the past, however, is also a God of the present. He is here now to deliver his people from

---

[10]In my discussion of Leibniz (chap. 6), I indicated that the question of whether this is the best of all possible worlds looks rather different when you think of the world as a whole historical sequence from creation to consummation.

bondage. The mysterious name "I am" in verse 14 may have some reference to this "temporal problematic": God is not merely the God of the past, but the God who is now, and will always be, present to deliver his chosen people (cf. 3:12). Thus, Yahweh (from "I am" in Hebrew), the Lord, will be his name forever, the name by which he will be remembered from generation to generation (v. 15). Yahweh is the same yesterday, today, and forever (cf. Heb. 13:8)!

This pattern gets repeated over and over. The wilderness journey is a long wait before the people enter their new home—indeed, a long series of waits and new beginnings. Over and over, the people forget about God's great works on their behalf. They complain about their lack of water, of meat, of leeks; they complain about Moses' leadership. Each time, God enters in judgment, but preserves the people in grace. And they continue waiting.

Finally, they (actually the next generation, since the parents were judged unfaithful) enter the Promised Land. The conquest goes relatively smoothly during the days of faithful Joshua, but after his death the people do what is right in their own eyes (cf. Judg. 21:25, KJV) and the cycle repeats itself several times. Israel forgets the Lord; they fall under bondage to foreign powers; they cry out to God; God sends a deliverer. There is some temporary improvement under Samuel and the early kings (especially David), but with the division of the kingdom and the prevalence of wicked kings, the waiting and divine visitations continue.

The whole Old Testament period may be described as a period of waiting. It is evident that Israel's home in Canaan does not in itself fulfill the promise made to Abraham. The bulls and goats offered in sacrifice do not take away the sin of the people. Of all the deliverers, none of them crushes the head of Satan. Indeed, Israel's disobedience—punctuated, to be sure, by periods of revival—becomes worse and worse.

In perspective, the long wait of the Old Testament period accentuates the problem of evil—not just because of its length, but also because it produces a kind of dialectic between justice and mercy. The prophets proclaim justice: Israel will certainly be judged for her disobedience. But they also proclaim grace: God is coming to redeem his people. Judgment is coming, but the promises to Adam and Abraham will nevertheless be fulfilled. But how can this be? Israel's sins are worse than those of the pagan nations of Canaan, even of Sodom and Gomorrah, which God destroyed. How can a just God do anything less than wipe them out entirely? Yet the promise of grace comes again. God will surely redeem his people. But how can he wipe them out and redeem them at the same time? It seems as though God's justice violates his mercy and vice versa. God is, it seems, in a bind. If he redeems, he must wink at sin; if he judges, he must renege on his promise.[11] As to the manner of resolution, there are dark hints—the Messianic passages. But in the Old Testament itself, our question receives scant satisfaction. Indeed, God seems to be wanting precisely to build the tension, and build, and build.

The problem here is not only that evil raises questions about God's justice or goodness. It is that God's justice and goodness raise questions about each other. That is, God's very nature appears to be self-contradictory. If we could prove his justice, we would thereby disprove his goodness, and vice versa. Here the problem of evil becomes even more opaque than it has usually been in history.

And then comes Jesus. The wait is over. We saw in an earlier chapter how Jesus draws together the strands of Old Testament expectation—not only the explicit predictions, but the narratives as well—indeed, the whole religious system of the Hebrew Scriptures. Now let us observe how he solves the problem of evil in its particularly virulent Old Testament form.

Christ is the theodicy of Romans 3:26. When God gave his Son as an atonement for sin, "he did it to demonstrate his

---

[11]Interestingly, the Psalms and the Prophets tend to juxtapose passages on judgment with passages on grace, one after the other, without transition. It is often unclear what motivates the prophet to move from the one topic to the other.

justice at the present time, so as to be just and the one who justifies those who have faith in Jesus."

Notice that the atonement vindicates both God's justice and his mercy. It is just and it justifies the ungodly. In Christ, the just penalty for sin is paid once for all. And because Christ endures that penalty in the place of his people, they receive lavish mercy beyond our power to imagine. God demonstrates both his justice and his love (5:8); neither is compromised, but each is demonstrated in virtually infinite degree. We see this pattern also in Paul's summary statement: "The law was added so that the trespass might increase. But where sin increased, grace increased all the more, so that, just as sin reigned in death, so also grace might reign through righteousness to bring eternal life through Jesus Christ our Lord" (Rom. 5:20–21). Grace reigning through righteousness! The mind boggles!

The Bible revels in this interplay. In the gospel of grace, the righteousness of God is revealed (Rom. 1:17).[12] Psalm 51:14–15 is fulfilled: when God saves us, he does it in such a way as to motivate us to praise his righteousness. And 1 John 1:9 tells us that God is not only faithful, but also just to forgive our sins. The forgiveness of sins is just, because of Christ.

Now let us look at Old Testament history in perspective. As I have mentioned, that history presents the problem of evil both as a wearisome wait through suffering and temptation, and as an exceptionally difficult problem of reconciling divine attributes. Had I been living in the Old Testament period, I would have had very little idea (despite the hints of the coming Messiah) of how God would resolve the problem. Were I of a skeptical bent, I might even have been tempted to say that God could not possibly solve the problem. The problem of waiting could have been solved easily enough by bringing it to an end (but why does God *make* us wait?). But the "dialectic of justice and mercy" seems almost like a problem of logical contradiction: justice, as defined by the prophets, can-

---

[12]One of Luther's great discoveries was that the phrase "righteousness from God" in this passage need not refer to the terror of God's judgment, but may rather refer to God's gracious justification of the ungodly.

not be merciful, or so it seems. But God does solve the problem, in a way that none of us would likely have expected, in a way that amazes us and provokes from us shouts of praise.

And as for the wait, well, in retrospect it almost seems necessary. The tension must be built up to the nth degree so that we can feel to the utmost the liberating power of salvation.

Now I grant that this redemptive history does not solve the problem of evil in every sense. It does not explain genocide or the suffering of little children, nor does it explain our present waiting as we look forward to God's final vindication. But here is the lesson for us: If God could vindicate his justice and mercy in a situation where such vindication seemed impossible, if he could vindicate them in a way that went far beyond our expectations and understanding, can we not trust him to vindicate himself again? If God is able to provide an answer to the exceptionally difficult Old Testament form of the problem of evil, does it not make sense to assume that he can and will answer our remaining difficulties? Does it not make sense to trust and obey, even in the midst of suffering?

We may admire all the more the heroes of the faith listed in Hebrews 11, for they suffered and endured, with faith and trust, not having received the promised Christ. In many ways it was far harder for them than it has been for us. They suffered more than most of us ever will, and they faced more mystery, living before the Incarnation, than we do. Yet they, however sinful in certain ways, trusted in God's promise. Can we, who have experienced the incredible riches of Jesus' redemption, excuse ourselves from doing anything less?

The Present: The Greater-Good Defense

Scripture's new historical perspective enables us to look at our own present experience in a new way. In short, God is even now using evil for his own good purposes. This is sometimes called the greater-good defense, and of all the classical defenses (see chap. 6), it is the only one with scriptural support. It does, however, require some clarification.

As Jay Adams[13] and Doug Erlandson[14] have recently pointed out, Scripture deals with the problem of evil in its typically theocentric, as opposed to anthropocentric, way. So many traditional treatments of the problem assume that God's ultimate purpose is to provide happiness for man, and of course that is not so. God's ultimate purpose is to glorify himself, and indeed man's own chief end "is to glorify God, and enjoy him forever."[15] Greater-good defenses often fail to see this point, and thus they arrive at a doctrine hard to distinguish from pagan hedonism. Erlandson, therefore, rejects this defense. But his point can be made just as well (and other important points can be made more easily) if instead of rejecting the greater-good defense we simply understand it theocentrically. That is, one good is greater than another when it is more conducive to the glory of God.

At the same time, theocentricity does not require us to ignore the happiness of human beings. The biblical God is not Moloch, the pagan deity who demanded human sacrifice. Although we deserve death at his hands, the true God sacrifices his own Son to bring us life, and to bring it abundantly (John 10:10). Obedience to God is a way of life and happiness (Deut. 5:33; 8:3; 11:13–15; 28:1–14; 30:11–20; Pss. 1; 119:7). Self-denial and persecution are, of course, part of the Christian life, but the passages which stress these also emphasize that they lead to the most enduring happiness (Matt. 6:24–34; 10:16–42; Mark 10:29–31). Suffering is for a while; glory is for eternity.[16] Let us not forget that even the Westminster Shorter Catechism adds "and to enjoy him forever" to its theocentric statement of man's chief end. Therefore, when God seeks a "greater good" for himself, he seeks at the

---

[13]In *The Grand Demonstration* (Santa Barbara, Calif.: East Gate Publishers, 1991).

[14]Erlandson, "A New Perspective on the Problem of Evil," *Antithesis* 2, 2 (March/April 1991): 10–16.

[15]Westminster Shorter Catechism, Answer 1.

[16]This is a major theme of the New Testament, especially Rom. 8 and 1 Peter.

same time a greater good for his whole creation, that good described so rapturously in Revelation 21 and 22.

But we need still more clarification. The above paragraph might suggest universalism, the doctrine that all human beings will be saved. Scripture does not teach that; indeed, it teaches that some will endure eternal punishment for their wickedness. For this group, history is not working toward a "greater good," but toward a "greater curse." Obviously, more needs to be said about this than I can say in this particular book.[17] I conclude, then, that God's greater glory does bring with it a "greater good" for creation in general, and for those who love God (Rom. 8:28), but not for every individual person or thing in the universe. So at points the glorification of God does conflict with the happiness of some human beings; when that happens, we must choose the theocentric view.

With those clarifications, it is possible to learn from Scripture some of the ways in which God is using evil to bring about greater good. We must be cautious here. Scripture doesn't give us exhaustive explanations for all evils, as we've seen. It often calls on us to be quiet and accept in faith what providence brings our way. But it does show how God has used some evils to advance his purposes. Those purposes include:

1. Displaying his grace and justice (Rom. 3:26; 5:8, 20–21; 9:17)—the point made so well by Adams and Erlandson.[18]

2. Judgment of evil (Matt. 23:35; John 5:14), now and in the future. Remember, however, that there is not a one-to-one correlation between a person's sins and the evil which befalls him in this life (Job; Luke 13:1–5).

3. Redemption: Christ's sufferings are redemptive in an obvious way (1 Peter 3:18).[19] But Paul claims for his own suf-

---

[17]In general, I agree with the viewpoint of Robert A. Morey in *Death and the Afterlife* (Minneapolis: Bethany House, 1984) and of John H. Gerstner in *Repent or Perish* (Ligonier, Pa.: Soli Deo Gloria Publications, 1990).

[18]This is of course a very general way in which God uses evil; it overlaps other categories mentioned below.

[19]Recall God's use of "wicked men" in this connection (Luke 22:22; Acts 2:23; 4:27–28).

ferings a similar significance (Col. 1:24). He does not claim to atone for the sins of others, but he does see a continuity between Christ's sufferings and his own, because both have suffered to plant the church and to draw individuals into it for their salvation. Many of the sufferings of God's servants today can be accounted for in that way. Those who would witness for Christ will be resisted by Satan, and in that witness, therefore, is suffering (cf. 2 Tim. 3:12).[20]

4. Shock value to unbelievers, intended to gain their attention and promote a change of heart (Zech. 13:7–9; Luke 13:1–5; John 9).

5. Fatherly discipline of believers (Heb. 12).

6. Vindication of God (e.g., Rom. 3:26).

We cannot always understand why God has chosen evil events to accomplish these good purposes. We do know that God never foreordains an evil event without a good purpose (Rom. 8:28). There may be other reasons than the ones we have mentioned, either to be found in Scripture or to remain locked up in God's own mind. We know that God has a reason for everything he does. Everything he does reflects his wisdom. But he is under no obligation to give us his reasons.

Nevertheless, as we see evil used for good again and again in Scripture, can we not accept in faith that those evils which are as yet unexplained also have a purpose in the depths of God's mind?

Again, we do not have a complete theoretical answer to the problem of evil. What we do have is a strong encouragement to trust God even amid unexplained suffering. Indeed, the encouragement is so strong that one would be foolish not to accept it.

The Future: Some Scripture Songs

The third dimension of our new perspective on history has to do with the future. We are, after all, still waiting. We have not seen how all of God's purposes result in good. Thus, the pas-

---

[20]In the Old Testament, I would see Joseph's sufferings in this way (Gen. 50:20)—preserving the seed of the promise until Christ should come.

sage of time still tries our patience. And for those who are suffering, the sheer length of the trial can be an occasion for complaint against God. Still, in Scripture, God promises us that in the future he will be totally vindicated and we will be fully delivered from all evil. As we have indicated, the pattern is that of suffering now and receiving glory later.

When glory comes, the wicked will no longer prosper and the righteous will no longer suffer. From the sanctuary of God (Ps. 73) we see the certainty of God's victory.[21] The valleys will be exalted, and the mountains brought low; the proud will be abased, and the humble raised to greatness (Isa. 40:1ff.; Matt. 25; Luke 1:51).

God tells the prophet Habakkuk, who has complained about the apparent injustice of God's ways, first to wait for God's judgment (2:2–3) and, second, to remember God's past deeds (3:16–17). As we wait for the future, seeking to be patient, it is helpful to remember the ways in which God has vindicated his judgment in the past (see the preceding section).

When the future—the culmination of God's plan—arrives, there will be a great throng of angels and glorified saints singing to God of the righteousness of his deeds:

> Great and marvelous are your deeds,
>   Lord God Almighty.
> Just and true are your ways,
>   King of the ages.
> Who will not fear you, O Lord,
>   and bring glory to your name?
> For you alone are holy.
> All nations will come
>   and worship before you,
> for your righteous acts have been revealed.
>   Rev. 15:3–4 (cf. 16:5–7; 19:1–2)

---

[21]Cf. also Ps. 37. The two psalms which are most sharply focused upon the problem of evil can be remembered easily if we remember that one reverses the digits of the other.

Notice that there is no more doubt among God's servants as to the justice of his ways. The rhetorical question in this quotation has the answer "no one"—no one will fail to fear and glorify God. Why? Because his righteous acts have been revealed. I take it that the consummation of history will somehow reveal enough that remaining doubts concerning God's goodness will be entirely taken away from us. Does this mean that in that day we will finally receive a definitive, exhaustive, theoretical, and practical answer to the problem of evil? Not necessarily. God might simply shut our mouths, as he shut Job's, and reopen them in praise. It may be that when we see God face to face, we shall see a face of such supreme trustworthiness that all our complaints will simply disappear. Or it may be that as we see the one who is greater than Solomon, judging the whole earth in perfect righteousness, we will be far less inclined to bring up the perplexities of past history.

At any rate, we may be assured that in the last day there will be no problem of evil. There will be no more doubt, no more complaint. If there is a residual theoretical problem, it will be one which we will be completely happy to live with. And if we believe now that that day will certainly come, can we not be content in the present?

Again, we find in Scripture not a philosophical solution to the problem, but a great reassurance, a powerful motivation to keep trusting and obeying, despite all the wickedness in the world.

Scripture Gives Us a New Heart

Finally, Scripture gives us faithful hearts. As indicated earlier, the Word of God is powerful to save (Rom. 1:16–17). As the Holy Spirit speaks in the Scriptures, he turns our skepticism into faith. Our hearts are warmed as we hear the gospel (Luke 24:32). In such a mood, we cannot speak from the high horse of proud autonomy. We can only be full of thanks that God has been merciful to us, despite our sin. The marvelous thing, as John Gerstner and others have pointed out, is not that there is evil in the world, but that God has forgiven the evil in our own hearts for the sake of Christ.

Without that new heart of faith, we are blind (1 Cor. 2:14; 2 Cor. 4:4). But Christ opens eyes which were blinded by sin and opens lips to sing his praise (Pss. 51:15; 73:16–17).

Believers, even with their new hearts, do continue to ask about the problem of evil. But there are so many reasons for giving thanks that we can never look at evil with the same passion as the unbeliever. The believer simply looks at the world with values different from those of the unbeliever. And the change in those values is perhaps the closest we can get, at this point in history, to a theodicy.

EIGHT

▼

Apologetics as Offense: Critique of Unbelief

We have already done much by way of apologetic offense. In chapter 2, we indicated that the fundamental choice is between two alternatives: the absolute personality of Christianity and the ultimate impersonalism of every other system (which systems we have described collectively as the "conventional wisdom"). We have seen that the conventional wisdom cannot do justice to values and therefore cannot account for the trustworthiness of reason. This inability corrupts impersonalist ideas in every field of human thought: science, philosophy, psychology, sociology, the arts, economics, business, government, or whatever. But it also corrupts practical living: in a chance universe, what is the point of brushing your teeth in the morning?

In discussing the problem of evil, we mentioned the ad hominem but nevertheless useful point that an impersonalist philosophy cannot distinguish good and evil sufficiently even to raise the problem against Christianity.

As we have mentioned before, it is impossible rigidly to separate offensive from defensive and constructive apologetics. All

191

of our defensive and constructive strategies have depended on offensive premises, namely, that there are only two alternatives, and that the unbelieving alternative is inadequate either to defend its own view or to raise objections against the Christian position. To that extent, surely, "the best defense is a good offense."

But it will be helpful to describe our offensive argument somewhat more systematically. Hence this chapter.

Offense is certainly essential to apologetics in the Bible. We see over and over again how Scripture goes on the attack against doubt and unbelief. Remember how Job wished to have an interview with God, but God surprised him by taking the role of the interviewer, the offensive position, and exposing Job's ignorance (Job 38ff.). This was also important in Jesus' presentation of the gospel. In John 3, when Nicodemus ("the" teacher of Israel, as is suggested by the original Greek of v. 10) comes to Jesus by night, evidently hoping to have a cordial theological discussion, Jesus sweeps away all the pleasantries and tells him that apart from the new birth, he cannot even see the kingdom of God (v. 3). Jesus dismisses Nicodemus's whole way of thinking and demands that it be rebuilt on an entirely different foundation.

The same thing happens in John 4, although Jesus is gentler in his approach.[1] The woman at the well, too, has a theological question: should we worship at Mt. Gerizim or at Jerusalem? Jesus answers quickly, but then proceeds to dismantle her Samaritan orthodoxy by telling her of the coming kingdom in which true worship will not be limited to one location at all—and by telling her that he is the Messiah.

And when the Jewish leaders of various parties try to trap him with trick questions (Matt. 22, esp. vv. 41–46), he first shuts their mouths and then goes on the attack. He does this

---

[1] As I mentioned before, Jesus tended to be tough with those who considered themselves experts in spiritual matters and gentler with those who recognized their ignorance. But Jesus never compromised his message. Reflecting this pattern, Van Til was fond of the saying *suaviter in modo, fortiter in re*—"gentle in our presentation, powerful in the content or substance of what we say."

by asking them how the Messiah could be both David's son and David's Lord, according to Psalm 110.

In his Pentecost sermon, Peter boldly attacks the assembled population as the murderers of the Messiah (Acts 2, esp. vv. 36–41). And Paul even calls Gentiles to account for their ignorant, idolatrous worship and declares that the resurrected Jesus will judge all mankind (Acts 17:22–34).

And let us not forget Paul's militant language in 2 Corinthians 5:1–10; Ephesians 6:10–20; 1 Timothy 6:12; 2 Timothy 2:1–7; 4:1–5.

The Unbeliever's Twin Strategies

If we are to go on the offensive against unbelief, we ought to know more about it. What is unbelief, from a biblical standpoint? What is the structure of what we have called the conventional wisdom?

Remember from previous discussions that the unbeliever, at some level of his consciousness, knows God and knows the truth about God (Rom. 1:21), but suppresses it. Nevertheless, his suppressed knowledge guides him in many of his daily decisions. He usually assumes that there is a point to brushing his teeth, having breakfast, working for a living. He assumes the validity of value judgments when he criticizes politicians or bureaucrats, and even when he attacks the Bible. He may even acknowledge God, as did the Pharisees. As such, he may be an "orthodox" church member, whose fundamental unbelief is known only to God.

Still, the main drift of his thinking, his dominant presuppositions, are unbelieving. He is trying his best to think and live as if the absolute personal God of Scripture did not exist. In most cases, this ambition does not lead to pharisaic orthodoxy, but to ways of thinking that more obviously proclaim unbelief. There are essentially two such ways: atheism and idolatry.[2] These can be mixed together, although that cre-

---

[2]Agnosticism is usually a disguised atheism. See the discussion of this in chap. 4.

ates its own problems (as we shall see), and they can be mixed with that true knowledge that the unbeliever tries unsuccessfully to suppress. Such mixtures create ambiguity; it is not always easy to separate the truth from the error in them. Nevertheless, the basic outlines of idolatry and/or atheism are usually visible behind the overall complexity.

Atheism

Atheism can be either practical or theoretical or both. The theoretical atheist denies God; the practical atheist simply lives as if God did not exist. I include under atheism various forms of deism and theism in which there is some kind of God who, because of his transcendence, modesty, or whatever, has nothing to do with human life.

The natural result of atheism is a loss of standards and values, for we saw earlier that these can be revealed and enforced only by the God of Scripture. Atheists tend to be relativists. Indeed, many find atheism attractive for just this reason. After all, people flee from God (as Adam did) because they don't want to be held responsible before him. Like all forms of unbelief, atheism is essentially an escape from responsibility.

Of course, the natural connection between atheism and relativism is not always made, even by atheists themselves. There are atheists who maintain some value judgments very strongly. In fact, even the most relativistic among them are inconsistent on that score. Some may even wish to defend objective morality. They must be told that they have no basis for making such judgments.

Unbelievers tend to go to extremes, in this case the extreme of denying objective meaning altogether. The unbeliever may resist this extreme, for he knows it is implausible, but there is nothing in his adopted philosophy to guard against it. He rejects the one revelation that would provide a basis for a more balanced assessment of reason and value. The one-and-many God of Scripture makes it plain that there is no such thing as meaningless plurality, plurality not united into order and structure.

Among Christian critics of culture, the late Francis Schaeffer and his disciples have perhaps presented most vividly the implications and dangers of atheistic relativism.[3] They characterize the modern period as dominated by this type of thought, as opposed to the more rationalistic thought of earlier periods. They analyze modern art, music, films, philosophy, and politics along these lines, with fruitful apologetic conclusions.

Idolatry

The other major form of unbelief is idolatry, namely, giving one's ultimate allegiance to some being other than the God of Scripture. This allegiance may be to some primitive god or gods (e.g., Zeus, Baal, Moloch, or Astarte), to some abstract principle (e.g., Plato's Good), to a non-Christian religion (e.g., Islam or Buddhism),[4] to a modern cultural movement like the New Age, to oneself, to human reason, or whatever.

The total loss of meaning implicit in atheism is too much for most people to stand. They need some values, some standard, some ways to orient their lives. Among these people, those who continue to resist belief in the true God become inconsistent in their atheism, or, to that extent, they become idolaters. If they don't want the true God, they must seek some other.

Again, the unbeliever tends toward an extreme. If the idol is to fill the role of God, he must have some divine attributes and fill some divine roles.

Atheism and idolatry are the only alternatives to Christianity. In order to reject Christianity, one must either deny all gods or select some god to worship other than the God of Scripture. In reality, of course, they together form a single alternative, for even the atheist must, practically, allow for some ab-

---

[3]This group includes Schaeffer's wife Edith, his son Frank, his daughter Susan Macaulay, and their present and past associates at L'Abri Fellowship, such as Os Guinness, Donald Drew, Ranald Macaulay, Jerram Barrs, Udo Middelmann, and Jane Stuart Smith.

[4]I realize that I am stretching the traditional definitions a bit to call Islam idolatrous. I am using the term to make a general point which I think is scriptural, however we may want to debate about the terminology.

solute, usually his own reason. To say there is no God is to say that the most ultimate reality in the universe is impersonal—but that in itself is idolatry. Similarly, idolatry relies on atheism and tends to revert back to it. Idolatry depends on would-be autonomous thinking and the rejection of divine revelation. Thus, the line between atheism and idolatry is not sharp.

Like atheism, idolatry can be either theoretical or practical. The "god" can be a theoretical entity like human reason, evolution, dialectical materialism (Marxism), the state, or even the universe (pantheism). Or it can be a practical reality like money (Mammon!), pleasure (Dionysius/Bacchus), family, self, or a non-Christian religion.[5]

Like atheism, idolatry is an escape from responsibility to the true God. It seeks freedom and autonomy. Unfortunately, the natural result of it is slavery—bondage to the idol.

Epistemologically, idolatry tends to be less relativistic than atheism. Indeed, idolatry accounts for the rather dogmatic certainty that accompanies much unbelief. Consider the amazing certainty that many people have concerning the theory of evolution, at a time when the theory has been subjected to serious challenges, not only by Christians, but also by secular scientists and logicians. Why are they so certain and so determined to keep out of the schools any discussion of its only significant alternative, creation?[6] The answer is that evolution has become for many a religious presupposition, an idol. To lose that idol would, for many, be to lose their fundamental worldview, the framework upon which they rely for order and rationality.

---

[5]It is sad to think of how often Christians themselves are tempted to betray their Lord in the interest of such idols. How many Christians today keep the fourth of the Ten Commandments, to "remember the Sabbath day by keeping it holy" (Ex. 20:8)? Must the Sabbath be completely forgotten in our pursuit of money and pleasure? If so, will we not one day be ashamed when our Lord returns?

[6]California's chief of education, Bill Honig, sought to deny the Creation Research Institute of San Diego the right to grant degrees because the Institute (which taught both views, but presented evolution with a Christian critique) refused to teach evolution as established fact. In answer to many prayers, God restrained Honig through the court system.

Nobody can prove evolution. Evolution is a hypothesis held by faith, and all supposed facts must be made to fit into its framework. It is a "paradigm" in Thomas Kuhn's sense,[7] a criterion for judging other proposals, itself not subject to judgment. Indeed, evolution is necessary, once one rejects creation. For either the earth was produced supernaturally (i.e., created) or it was produced naturally, apart from God. Any naturalistic origin of the world will involve evolution, for it will be the result of natural laws operating upon primitive matter, producing complexity over time. Thus, the concept of evolution did not begin with Darwin.[8] Rather, it has been characteristic of every non-Christian philosophy since that of Thales in the sixth century B.C.

Many other ideas are often presented today as undoubted fact, even though they do not have any serious justification. For example: corporal punishment of children is wrong; abortion is right; the state has the competence and obligation to provide education and welfare; all races, genders, religions, and sexual preference groups are equal in every way, and the greatest sin is that of disparaging one of these groups (except for Anglo-Saxon Protestant males).

If the Schaeffer group has been the most effective in identifying and criticizing atheistic relativism in modern culture, perhaps the Dutch "Philosophy of the Idea of Law," following the Christian philosophers Herman Dooyeweerd and D. Th. Vollenhoven, has best dealt with idolatry. They distinguish fifteen different spheres of human interest in the world, including the numerical, the mechanical, the biotic, the economic, the linguistic, the aesthetic, the juridical, the ethical, and the pistical (faith). Each of these reflects the others in various ways, so that it is tempting to regard one of them as the absolute, the origin of the rest. Hence there is a tendency in philosophy to reduce everything to number or space or matter or motion or

---

[7]See Kuhn, *The Structure of Scientific Revolutions,* 2d ed. (Chicago: University of Chicago Press, 1970).
[8]Darwin's accomplishment was to suggest a plausible mechanism for evolution.

economics. But to do this is idolatry. God rules over all the spheres and is not limited to any one of them.[9]

The followers of Schaeffer tend to downplay modern idolatry, because they tend to be committed to a historical model in which ancient optimism concerning reason and order degenerates into modern irrationalism (atheistic relativism).[10] They are therefore so committed to seeing modern man in terms of irrationalism that they often miss his idolatry and dogmatism—his rationalism.[11]

On the other hand, the Dooyeweerdians are less adequate on irrationalism and atheism than they are on idolatry. Dooyeweerd himself was a bit unclear on the role of reason in human thought. He insisted that God was not rational, for to say that God was rational would be to limit him to one of the fifteen spheres of creation. I doubt that it would; it seems to me that if we recognize the differences that Van Til does between the divine and the human mind, we can attribute to God an intelligence analogous to, but not identical with, human rationality. That the Dooyeweerdians consider Van Til himself a "rationalist" indicates to me that they have fundamental misunderstandings in this area.[12]

Idolatrous Atheism

As I have indicated, idolatry and atheism are not as distinct from one another (or as opposed to each other) as they might initially appear to be. Atheism needs idolatry: you cannot live consistently as a relativist without some constant, absolute meaning in life. And relativists are always dogmatic about excluding nonrelativist ideas—for example, when they say that

---

[9]I have a lot of questions about the details of the Dooyeweerdian model, but its main thesis is cogent and of great help to the apologist.

[10]It would be interesting to see how much this is related to Schaeffer's original premillennialism.

[11]My contrast between atheism and idolatry is closely equivalent to Van Til's contrast between irrationalism and rationalism.

[12]Gordon Clark and his disciples have considered Van Til an irrationalist. The distribution of critics on either side of him suggests that perhaps Van Til was very close to the truth.

people "should not" impose their values on others. Also, idolatry needs atheism: the choice to worship a false God is ultimately irrational and rebellious.

Thus, most unbelievers combine these motifs in various ways. Plato and Aristotle taught that the universe is divided into one part that is rational and knowable and another part that is wildly irrational and unknowable. But how do you know the unknowable? To that question they failed to offer any cogent answer.

Plotinus began as a rationalistic idolater. He claimed to have discovered a god who could give us a perfect explanation for everything. But it turned out that this god was knowable only in a nonrational experience. Irrationalism triumphed in the end.

Marxism claims scientific status, but preaches ethical relativism. If ethics are relative, why should we value science?

Modern public schools claim religious neutrality. What this means in practice is that they are relativistic in their values, but dogmatic in excluding Christianity from all substantive discussions.

The modern media tend to convey the message that "anything goes," that values are relative, that it is cute to offend society's typical "prejudices" about sex, religion, and politics. On the other hand, they are highly dogmatic (often unwilling to argue at all, or even to acknowledge dissent) in promoting their own values of legal abortion, a centrally planned economy, high taxes and government spending, "rights" for all sorts of special interest groups, and so on. The same is true of the arts and the entertainment field to a large extent.

Big business tends to be more conservative, more supportive of traditional values. But such conservative ethics are mocked by the "anything goes" attitude of advertisers (who, it seems, will say or portray almost anything to make a sale) and by the rush for government subsidies and protection from competition whenever such become available. "Anything goes" is the slogan of the atheistic relativist.[13] "I have a right to a subsidy" is the cry of an idolater to his idol.

---

[13]Recall Dostoyevsky: "If God does not exist, all is permitted."

Since Kant, scientists have recognized that their discipline is not purely objective, but reaches results that are considerably influenced by what scientists want to see. The epistemological barriers between the scientist and the real world are enormous, not least because scientific theories tend to take on a presuppositional status.[14] When a theory becomes a paradigm or presupposition, it comes to govern all future research, so that it is next to impossible to challenge the theory through scientific methods. Such paradigms tend to be held (very much like religious dogmas) with great tenacity, and those who raise fundamental questions risk ostracism from the community. Thus, we have in the scientific community an oscillation between relativism and dogmatism, atheism and idolatry. This is why, in the face of significant modern challenges to the dogma of evolution, secularists cling to it all the more tightly, even to the point of refusing to present any alternatives to school children.[15]

These attitudes are even more obvious in the social sciences. Sociologists insist dogmatically on their cultural relativism. Psychologists fight fierce "denominational" wars over what sort of therapy should be used (when none of the accepted forms has had much success). Educators dogmatically forbid "politically incorrect" speech while insisting that all viewpoints (in practice, all approved viewpoints!) receive equal respect.

The same is true of "mainstream" or liberal theologians. They reprove orthodox Christians for being dogmatic, but they themselves are highly dogmatic in the way they elevate philosophical, political, and social proposals to the level of gospel.

---

[14]Thomas Kuhn calls them "paradigms" in his important book, *The Structure of Scientific Revolutions.*

[15]Recently, Christian members of the Vista, California, school board sought to encourage teachers to present the "weaknesses" of evolutionary theory. The teachers reacted in strong opposition to this suggestion. But don't all theories have weaknesses? And whatever happened to the liberal idea of presenting all sides of issues? That ideal would seem to be dispensable when the ultimate presuppositions of the secularist ideology are at stake.

If the Schaeffer group has been strong in dealing with atheistic relativism, and the Dooyeweerd group has been strong in dealing with idolatry, it is in recognizing combinations of the two that Van Til has excelled.[16] He above all has seen that atheism and idolatry (he calls them irrationalism and rationalism, as I did in *Doctrine of the Knowledge of God*) are really one position—apparently contradictory, but actually dependent on one another. He has seen the nuances, the way these dialectical motifs interweave, supporting one another while challenging one another down through the history of thought.

Christian Apologetic Responses

I cannot reproduce here all the critical insights of Van Til, Schlossberg, Dooyeweerd, Schaeffer, and the others, although I do recommend their writings to anyone interested in studying these matters further. But let me, in a very general way, suggest strategies which cover a great many actual cases.

Against Atheistic Relativism

When you find an unbeliever who stresses the atheistic relativist side of unbelief, be persistent in asking these questions: (1) How can you be sure that relativism is right, when it itself rules out all assurance? (2) How can you live as a relativist? Having no assurance of anything must be a terrible strain, rationally, emotionally, and volitionally. What basis do you have for making decisions? What basis do you have for criticizing the treatment you receive from others? How can you say anything is wrong, unfair, or unjust? What basis do you have for trusting logic—or, for that matter, your own mind?

---

[16]See also Herbert Schlossberg's excellent *Idols for Destruction* (Nashville: Nelson, 1983). And see James B. Jordan, *Through New Eyes* (Brentwood, Tenn.: Wohlgemuth and Hyatt, 1988), also a response to idolatry and promoting a positive reconstruction of the world after Schlossberg's critique.

Against Idolatrous Rationalism

When you meet someone who tends to stress the powers, rather than the limits, of autonomous thought and action, you will likely be dealing with someone in the grip of an idol. Find out what his idol is and take aim by asking these questions: (1) What basis is there for thinking that this idol is absolute? (2) Does your god really do the job of a god? Did it create the world? Is it the ground of logic, mathematics, ethical value, and universal judgments in science? Is it adequate as a final standard of meaning, truth, and right?

We know that an impersonal god can do none of these things. So the unbeliever will be tempted either to lapse into relativism or to grant to his god some elements of personality. Once he does the latter, he is granting part of our case, and we can pursue him further, especially by asking him, "How do you know this person?"

Against Atheistic Idolatry

Press the fundamental contradiction in this rationalistic-irrationalistic combination: a proof that there are no proofs, an absolute statement that there are no absolute statements. Then attack the original rationalistic and irrationalistic elements, as above. It will not be easy. The unbeliever will slide from one position to another, from rationalism to irrationalism and back again. Argument itself will not be enough; God must intervene. Thus, prayer is the ultimate apologetic weapon.

NINE

▼

Talking to a Stranger

Parts of this book have been fairly technical, but I do want to make it clear that the type of apologetics that I recommend can be used in practical situations. I trust that people looking for this sort of practical help will not be put off too much by the earlier discussions. Perhaps they will follow the advice in the Preface and begin with this chapter. I hope this chapter will whet their appetite to see what theory lies behind the apologetic expressed here.

I readily admit that this is not my own natural milieu. I am far better suited to technical discussions than to exchanges with "people on the street." Indeed, I rarely enter into such exchanges, since I think God has equipped me to carry out the Great Commission through the written medium much better than orally. Among other things, my mind is not nearly as quick, at least in unfamiliar surroundings, as is that of "John" in the dialogue below—how I wish it were. Still, I do feel a certain obligation not to leave the reader entirely up in the air. The following should give the reader at least some idea of how this apologetic would work out in real life.

One more thing by way of preface: this is not a realistic dialogue. In most real conversations of this sort, much time

203

is wasted through misunderstandings, impoliteness, digressions, incidental occurrences, failed attempts at humor, etc. To save time, I will keep them out of this dialogue.

Encounter on a Plane

AL (fuming): What a bummer!

JOHN: What's the trouble?

AL: Well, I bought my briefcase because it was just the right size to fit under an airplane seat. You know how they always tell you to stow your carry-on luggage under the seat ahead of you?

JOHN: Oh, yes.

AL: Well, I bought this briefcase specifically to meet their rules, and now I find that they've given me a seat without a seat ahead of me. So it has to be stowed in the overhead bin. And since all the overhead bins here are full, the flight attendant took it to the back of the plane.

JOHN: They'll bring it back to you after takeoff, if you ask.

AL: I shouldn't have to ask. I have a right to have my briefcase here with me, takeoff or no. Besides, it'll take them forever, if they remember at all. I can picture myself trying to get to the back of the plane, squeezing around the lunch wagon, three flight attendants, and everyone trying desperately to get to the bathroom before lunch.

JOHN: I can understand your annoyance.

AL: By the way, I'm Al. What's your name?

JOHN: John. Nice to meet you.

AL: I'm a securities analyst. What's your line?

JOHN: I'm a Presbyterian minister.

AL: Oh! Well, I used to go to church as a boy, but I haven't been back in many years. I guess you'd say I'm an agnostic.

JOHN: Oh, that's interesting. What kind of agnostic are you?

AL: What do you mean, what kind? Are there denominations of agnostics?

JOHN: No, but there are some agnostics who insist that nobody can know God at all, and then there are other agnostics who don't know God themselves, but leave the door open to the possibility that someone else might know him.

AL: I guess I'm in the second group. I really don't know whether God exists, and I really don't know whether it's possible to know him—if he does exist. I guess I'm a superagnostic.

JOHN: Well, let me invite you to attend my church in San Diego . . .

AL: Wait a minute! I said I was an agnostic!

JOHN: You go to church somewhere else?

AL: No; I told you I haven't been to church in years.

JOHN: Well, we'll have to fix that. Every agnostic should be in church once every two weeks.

AL: Every two weeks?

JOHN: Sure. Look, you really don't know whether or not God exists, right?

AL: Right.

JOHN: Then you ought to hedge your bets, right?

AL: Hedge my bets?

JOHN: Sure. If you were an atheist, you would feel confident in living as if God didn't exist. If you were a Christian, you would feel an obligation to live as a Christian: attending church, praying, loving your enemies, and so on. But how do you live as an agnostic? Shouldn't you adopt a lifestyle halfway between these extremes—maybe go to church every *other* week?

AL: Very clever; but, to be honest, I never go to church, and I never intend to. From a practical standpoint, I live just like an atheist.

JOHN: You never go to church, never pray, never test your conduct by the Bible?

AL: Right.

JOHN: Then you're an atheist.

AL: But I don't *know* whether or not . . .

JOHN: I can only tell your beliefs by your actions. If you claimed to believe that hamburgers were poison, but you kept eating them all the time (without any apparent suicidal impulse), I'd say you didn't really believe hamburgers were poison—or perhaps the truth would be that you held conflicting beliefs, with the pro-hamburger belief being dominant.

AL: Well, OK—let's say I'm an atheist. Prove to me that God exists.

JOHN: What would it take to prove that to you?

AL: Oh, I don't know. It would sure help if he would show himself to me.

JOHN: But he's invisible.

AL: But didn't he show himself in visible form to people in the Bible?

JOHN: Well, yes. But sometimes those forms, like the earthly body of Jesus, were quite ordinary in outward appearance. I can't imagine that would impress you.

AL: I want to see the bright shining light surrounded by angels and all that.

JOHN: What do you make of near-death experiences, where people return from clinical death and report a bright light, visitations from departed friends, and so on? These are quite well documented, you know; it seems to be a fairly common occurrence.

AL: It's evidently some sort of dream or other psychological phenomenon. Of course I haven't had such an experience myself.

JOHN: Well, even if you had, you could write it off as a dream, couldn't you?

AL: Sure.

JOHN: Imagine an even stronger case: suppose God appeared to you at night, in a bright light, surrounded by angels, and said, "Al, I am the Lord, the God of Abraham, Isaac, and Jacob." How would you respond?

AL: I might be pretty overwhelmed, but in the end . . .

JOHN: You'd dismiss it as a dream.

AL: I'd dismiss it as a dream.

JOHN: What if the same thing happened to you in broad daylight?

AL: To be honest, I guess I'd dismiss it as a hallucination.

JOHN: But suppose you were driving past the Vice President's mansion in Washington and you saw Al Gore get out of a limousine in the driveway. Would you dismiss that as a hallucination?

AL: No, of course not.

JOHN: Why not?

AL: Well, that's the sort of thing I'd expect to see there. It would fit in with all my other beliefs.

JOHN: So you interpret alleged facts according to what you already believe. In other words, your beliefs control your judgments about facts. Your atheist presuppositions determine how you interpret what you observe, so that other interpretations are out of the question.

AL: I suppose so.

JOHN: You can understand, then, why I (and God) resist the idea of giving you some visible revelation of God. If you won't even *consider* a Christian interpretation of such an experience, why should God bother to give you one?

AL: I hadn't thought of it that way.

JOHN: Is there another kind of proof you would consider?

AL: How about some evidence among the facts of the world that God exists?

JOHN: Well, every fact in the world testifies to God, because God made them all and directs them to his purpose.

AL: Every fact, huh. My house has been overrun with cockroaches. How does that prove God's existence?

JOHN: Hmm . . . Isn't that just the sort of thing you'd expect if the Bible is true? Scripture says that because man fell into sin, the earth produces thorns and thistles to make our work difficult and our existence wearisome. Cockroaches are part of that.

AL: Interesting, but that doesn't prove that God exists. I can interpret the cockroaches as pure accidents of evolution. The universe doesn't care whether they annoy me or not.

JOHN: But notice again that you are using your atheistic commitment to interpret the facts. You're ruling out a Christian interpretation, because you're already committed to a different one. Can you prove your presupposition to me?

AL: I can't prove that God doesn't exist, if that's what you mean. You'd just give my facts a Christian interpretation.

JOHN: That's right, and we're both doing the same thing, up to that point. So, in principle any proof I could give you, you could reject on the basis of your presupposition.

AL: OK. But then there's nothing more to say. You have your presupposition and I have mine. You interpret facts in a Christian way and I don't. You can't prove anything to me, and I can't prove anything to you.

JOHN: Not so fast! At least, you now recognize that the matter of proof is more complicated than you had thought.

AL: I see that. But I'm wondering how you intend to continue this conversation.

JOHN: Can we go back to the cockroaches?

AL: How can that possibly help your case?

JOHN: I suppose you'd say that the overrunning of your house was a bad thing, right?

AL: Well, it sure was bad for me. But, as I said, from the standpoint of the universe as a whole, it doesn't much matter.

JOHN: What about the flight attendant's taking your briefcase?

AL: That was wicked! Seriously, they should have notified me when I picked this seat that I would be deprived of my briefcase for a time. To me, that is a more serious matter than whether I get a window or aisle seat, or even whether I sit in the smoking or nonsmoking area.

JOHN: Would you say, then, that the airline was wrong?

AL: Sure—not that I would make a federal case out of it, though.

JOHN: Now, tell me how an atheist or agnostic decides what is right and what is wrong.

AL: Conscience, I suppose.

JOHN: Conscience is a moral sense; it senses right and wrong as the eye senses light and color. But the eye doesn't *create* light and color. Would you say that your conscience *creates* right and wrong?

AL: Well, some people would. But I'm uncomfortable with that idea; I mean, if right and wrong are my own inventions, why should anyone else care about them?

JOHN: Exactly. And you think that others ought to care; that, too, is a moral judgment. But it's something more than just a feeling of yours. It's something objective that obligates you and them.

AL: Yes, I can see the importance of objective moral values.

JOHN: Then these values bind us; they impose obligations.

AL: Yes.

JOHN: But why? Why are we obligated to accept those values?

AL: I guess it's just part of the way the universe is. In the physical universe, what goes up must come down. So, in the moral universe, he who hurts others incurs guilt.

JOHN: But physical laws don't *obligate* me to do anything. I can't imagine anything merely material that could impose an obligation. Can you?

AL: Well, I do sense that the obligation is there. Where else could it come from?

JOHN: Look at the alternatives: either the universe is ultimately impersonal (i.e., everything reduces to matter, motion, space, time, and chance) or it is personal (an ultimate being creates and uses matter, motion, etc., for his own purposes). Which is the more likely origin of moral obligation?

AL: I don't see that either is likely. Even if a person tells me what to do—say, a policeman—I am not thereby obligated to do what he says.

JOHN: Sure. A policeman can be wrong. He can exceed his authority. And even when he is right, he doesn't create moral obligations any more than you or I do.

AL: I'm confused. I thought you were leading me in the direction of a personalistic account of morals.

JOHN: I am, but of course moral values cannot be entirely explained by finite personalities.

AL: Oh, of course! This is your proof for God!

JOHN: Well, think it through! Moral values are rather like loyalty, aren't they? In fact, loyalty is a moral value, and it obligates us to behave in certain ways. Now how do we get into positions where we find ourselves loyal to someone or something?

AL: I suppose deep personal relationships are the strongest motivation. If you insult my mother, I'll punch your lights out, for she is the most loving, gentle, kind person on the face of the earth. I'll be loyal to her as long as I live.

JOHN: Sure. Loyalty to one's country is a bit different, but again it probably has much to do with the blessings a person experiences through fellowship with other people of that country.

AL: I suppose so. Loyalty to the people, even generally considered, seems more important than loyalty to a particular system of government; and when we are loyal to a system, it is largely based on our perceptions of what the people running that system are doing for the other people in the nation.

JOHN: Well, to make a long story short: moral values depend on personal relationships. Absolute and objective moral standards presuppose loyalty to an absolute person.

AL: Absolute person? Hold on a minute.

JOHN: What's the worst evil you can think of?

AL: Genocide.

JOHN: Is that always wrong?

AL: Always.

JOHN: What if there were a minority living in the U.S. that you just couldn't stand. Suppose they spent all their time robbing, mugging, raping, and molesting children, all the while sponging off the taxpayers by living on welfare. Wouldn't it make sense to do away with them?

AL: We might be tempted to do so, but it would be wrong. We should prosecute criminals, change the welfare laws, and so on; but we should never destroy a whole race of people.

JOHN: But you use terms like "always" and "never." What kind of personal relationship is it that justifies that kind of consistency?

AL: I guess it's loyalty to the human race as such.

JOHN: But when has the "human race as such" ever voted against genocide? In the cases of Hitler, Stalin, and Pol Pot, the human race itself sat idly by.

AL: What I meant was that if I value people as people, as ends and not merely as means, I could never support genocide.

JOHN: But who taught you to value people as ends rather than means? That sort of ethic has actually been rather rare among the peoples of the world.

AL: Well, this ethic seems bound up with real love for one's fellow man. We ought to try to do what's best for everybody, right?

JOHN: But how do you know that an occasional genocide might not be good for the human race as a whole?

AL: It certainly wouldn't be best for the victims! And, again, it wouldn't be treating people as ends.

JOHN: Your ethic is very lofty. But what makes you think that "humanity in general" deserves this kind of unconditional love? As you say, there is plenty of wickedness out there.

AL: I know what you're saying. I sure spend enough time complaining about nincompoops and moral idiots. People are so thoughtless, like the bureaucrats that make up the airline travel rules.

JOHN: How, then, can a world of idiots and nincompoops motivate unconditional love?

AL: When you put it that way, I guess I have to concede that it doesn't. But I still maintain my convictions against genocide.

JOHN: Fine! But can you honestly find any cogent basis for those convictions other than the God of the Bible? After all, here is a God who is perfectly holy, righteous, and loving. Is there anyone else who deserves that loyalty, with no exceptions?

AL: I can see there's much to be said for theism if you confine yourself to talk of moral values. But morals are so slippery. Who, really, knows where they come from? I find it safer

211

.ny life on human reason than to entrust myself to
.upernatural being.

JOHN: Reason is a great faculty. But why follow its dictates?

AL: Because living irrationally brings failure, pain, and
.ffering.

JOHN: Not always. Don't you know some irrational politicians who are living high on the hog? Don't you know some
rational people who are suffering miserably because of their
commitment to the truth?

AL: Are you advocating irrationalism?

JOHN: No; I am asking *why* I should live according to
reason.

AL: Well, you're committed to moral justice; you ought
to be committed to truth as well, for that is also a moral value.
When your reason shows you a truth, you *ought* to recognize
it and confess it.

JOHN: Exactly! Reasoning itself presupposes the objective
moral standard of truth.

AL: And . . .

JOHN: And that moral standard in turn presupposes loyalty to an absolute person.

AL: To God.

JOHN: To God.

AL: You're going too fast. Maybe there's a person up
there who serves as a criterion of morality. But why call him
God? How can you show that he is all-powerful, all-knowing,
and all the rest?

JOHN: That's where the "absolute" part comes in. If God
has weaknesses, then he cannot be the absolute final judge of
good and evil. If he is ignorant in any measure, then he cannot
rightly judge the good and evil that we do. If he has a beginning or an end, then it is possible to give a rational account of
a world without God. But we have seen that that is impossible.

AL: But what God are you talking about? Allah? Zeus?
Jehovah? Jesus? Buddha? Brahma?

JOHN: I'm talking about the biblical God, who is Jehovah and Jesus and the Holy Spirit as well.

AL: Why not the others?

JOHN: Well, to make a very long story short: Zeus is not an absolute being; he's finite, though a bit larger and more powerful than we are. Certainly he is not a moral paragon. Buddha never claimed to be god, and his original teaching is arguably atheistic. Brahma approaches the idea of absoluteness, but "he" is essentially impersonal, one of many gods in Hinduism, and "beyond good and evil," thus not capable of serving as a moral standard.

AL: What about Allah?

JOHN: Allah is a kind of revised version of the biblical God. Mohammed, the founder of Islam, regarded the Bible as the Word of God; but with some inconsistency he revised its more difficult teachings, like the Trinity, and produced his own religious book, the Koran. Indeed, he turned the biblical God into an arbitrary source of fate, seriously compromising biblical personalism. The chief argument between Christians and Muslims is over whether the Bible itself permits this sort of tinkering. The Muslims say that the Bible predicts the coming of Mohammed to fulfill God's purposes. Christians deny it.

AL: So you're telling me that only the Bible advocates a God with absolute personality?

JOHN: Exactly.

AL: But what of the Mormons and the Jehovah's Witnesses?

JOHN: The Mormons are polytheists. And the Jehovah's Witnesses deny the Trinity.

AL: What's so important about the Trinity?

JOHN: Well, the Bible teaches it, and the Bible is God's Holy Book. Scripture says there is one God, but then it points us to three beings who have divine status. They are not just one person playing three roles: Jesus prays to the Father; the Father and Son send the Spirit into the world. The Father speaks from heaven, while the Son is being baptized in the Jordan River and the Spirit is falling on him in the shape of a dove.

AL: How do we know that the Bible is God's Holy Book?

JOHN: Well, as we've seen, the biblical tradition alone teaches that God is an absolute personality. That same tradition makes it clear that God intends to rule his people in the very personal way of using language. And that language is to be written down in book form. The Ten Commandments were written by the finger of God, and the apostle Paul said that Scripture was "breathed out by God." Throughout the book—see especially Psalm 119—there are praises and superlatives directed to the written words of God.

AL: But you're using the Bible to prove the Bible.

JOHN: Yes, but just as you used reason to prove reason, or just as you earlier used your atheistic presuppositions to prove atheistic conclusions. We all have our presuppositions!

AL: But can't one believe in a God of absolute personality without accepting any single religious tradition?

JOHN: I suppose we could, if it weren't for Jesus.

AL: What difference does Jesus make?

JOHN: Al, how do you think the absolute person looks at you? Since he is a person, and he is the very standard of morality, he must have an opinion. What does he think of your moral behavior?

AL: Well, on a curve, I guess I'm better than a lot of people; of course, I'm no plaster saint.

JOHN: How would you feel if you were called right now to stand before a holy, absolutely righteous God?

AL: Terrified.

JOHN: But what if God loved you so much that he wanted, not to destroy you for your sins, but to save you? Wouldn't it be worth your while to find out about that?

AL: Sure! But where do I go to find out?

JOHN: Again, there is only one alternative—Jesus. All the other religions, even the "theistic" ones, claim that you can win favor with God by your good behavior. That claim produces pride in those who think they measure up to the standard, but despair in those who think they can never measure up to perfection.

AL: To be honest, I'd have to say that I belong to the second category.

JOHN: Me too.

AL: But how is Jesus different?

JOHN: The Scriptures tell us that Jesus is the eternal Son of God, who came to earth to pay the penalty for our sins and thus to provide salvation as a free gift to anyone who believes. Read especially John 3:16; Romans 5:8; 6:23; Ephesians 2:8–9; 2 Timothy 1:9; Titus 3:5–6; and 1 Peter 3:18.

AL: Then he wasn't just a human religious teacher.

JOHN: If he were, you would be doomed to a life of despair.

AL: But look, granted all the evil in the world—and, I must admit, in my own heart—how could this world have come from a good God?

JOHN: The best answer to that question is, I don't know.

AL: I thought you knew everything.

JOHN: In spiritual matters, I know only what Scripture tells me; and it doesn't fully answer that question.

AL: I noticed you said "fully." What *does* it tell us?

JOHN: Well, it does say that God works everything together for good (Rom. 8:28), and it says that everything God does follows a wise plan (Ps. 104:24; Jer. 10:12; 51:15). This implies that God has a good purpose for all the evil that he admits into the world. But what those good purposes are, he has not chosen to tell us fully, and he has no obligation to explain it all to us.

AL: But how can I trust him if I don't have such an explanation? Maybe he is a wicked being, rather than a good one. In that case, I can't allow him to be my moral criterion.

JOHN: Well, what you allow has very little to do with what is the case. He *is* the moral criterion, whether you like it or not. But to answer your question, there are many reasons to trust him, despite unresolved problems.

AL: What reasons?

JOHN: Chiefly, Jesus.

AL: Jesus again?

JOHN: Yes. He shows us that God will not compromise one inch on justice. God requires death for sin, even if his own Son must be the victim. And Jesus also shows that God

215

is willing to give his Son (in an important sense, to give himself) to save us from that awful death. That is not a God of moral wickedness or indifference. We may be sure that a God like that must have had some very good reasons for including evil within his eternal plan, even if we do not know what those reasons are.

AL: I know what I'll do. I'll promise to become a Christian if he reveals himself to me and tells me why evil came into the world.

JOHN: Be careful! Job made that same request, and he got his interview with God.

AL: Good! There is precedent, then.

JOHN: Remember, though, a while ago, how you said you would feel face-to-face with a holy and righteous God?

AL: Hmm, yes. I forgot about that. I guess I didn't think the question of my own sin would come up in the interview. I was hoping God would follow my agenda.

JOHN: Ha! But that's not how he does things. When God met Job, *God* asked the questions, reminding Job of his finitude and his moral inferiority. The outcome was that Job hung his head in shame.

AL: Maybe asking for an interview was not such a good idea.

JOHN: Actually, the best remedy for your concern about the problem of evil is to get to know Jesus better. Jesus is a mirror of God's goodness and righteousness. Indeed, in all of Scripture we learn about the truly good things God has done. So those who know the Bible best tend to be less troubled by the problem of evil, though, to be sure, even Christians go through agony over it at times.

AL: Maybe so.

JOHN: John 17:6–8 promises that if you desire to do the will of God, you can know whether Jesus' claims are true. Are you willing to spend some time studying those claims?

AL: I think I would like to.

JOHN: Just read through, say, the Gospels. Maybe Mark first (it's the shortest), then John (it answers our questions most simply and clearly). Pay special attention to the story of the Resurrection. Ask what could account for that story other than the reality of the supernatural event.

AL: And if Jesus is risen?

JOHN: If Jesus is risen, then God has vindicated his teaching and work, and we—his people—are raised with him to newness of life. If Jesus is risen, then he really is God. And if Jesus is risen, then he is right in saying that "Scripture cannot be broken" (John 10:35; cf. Matt. 5:17ff.).

AL: Where can I go to get help in understanding the Bible?

JOHN: My invitation to come to church still stands.

AL: I'll take you up on it. But what about when I get home?

JOHN: Let's stay in touch. I'll try to recommend a church near your home. It is important that you find a fellowship where you can learn more about Christ. That is God's purpose for the church and for you.

AL: Hey, we're about to land! I didn't even need my briefcase.

JOHN: Perhaps God had a good purpose in removing it from you.

AL: Perhaps so.

Appendix A: Van Til and the Ligonier Apologetic

(Note: This review was originally published in the *Westminster Theological Journal* [47, 2 (Fall 1985), 279–99]. It is reprinted here in the belief that it will help the reader to better understand the differences between presuppositional or Van Tillian apologetics on the one hand and traditional or classical apologetics on the other. Since writing this review, I have become a bit more favorable to the use of probability in apologetics [thus differing both with Van Til and with the Ligonier version of the tradition], and I have become a bit more guarded in my defense of circularity. In general, however, the review continues to speak for me as I interact with the rival approach to apologetics.—J.M.F.)

Introduction

Classical Apologetics, by R. C. Sproul, John Gerstner, and Arthur Lindsley (Grand Rapids: Zondervan, 1984), has been eagerly awaited. This book puts into systematic (and at least somewhat technical) form an apologetic approach of considerable interest, which up until now has been expressed primarily in popular writings and taped lectures. It is also notable for its critique of "presuppositionalism" (mainly in its Van Tillian form). This book is one of the most extensive critiques of Van Til to date,[1] and I think of all the critiques of Van Til this one shows the most thorough research and the most accurate interpretation.[2] In saying this, I should acknowledge a possible conflict of interest: the authors express indebtedness to me for correspondence between myself and Gerstner which "significantly sharpened our understanding of Vantillian apologetics."[3] However, in commending these authors for their understanding of Van Til, I am not intending to commend myself. My contribution to their formulations was relatively small (and, as it turns out, not always understood and/or accepted). But Gerstner himself is a former student of Van Til and has (as I know from personal discussions) been mulling over Van Til's position for many years, with an intense interest and scholarly care not matched, in my view, by other critics of Van Til.[4] Thus the credit for the book's high critical standards must go to the authors themselves.

I shall not discuss the details of the book's historical studies, though these are interesting and are among the book's best features. Gerstner was a professor of church history for many years, and this is his chief area of expertise. In general, the historical sections argue that a kind of "evidentialism" similar

---

[1] Its only rival in this respect is James Daane, A *Theology of Grace* (Grand Rapids: Eerdmans, 1954); but that book is limited in its focus to Van Til's doctrine of common grace, and it shows much less understanding of Van Til's thought than the volume under review.

[2] I will indicate that in this book also there is much, and serious, misunderstanding of Van Til; but these authors are much closer to the truth about him than his earlier critics, such as the *Calvin Forum* group (see Van Til, *The Defense of the Faith* [Philadelphia: Presbyterian and Reformed, 1955], 4ff.) or the critics in *Jerusalem and Athens,* ed. E. Geehan (Philadelphia: Presbyterian and Reformed, 1967).

[3] P. x of the book's preface. Cf. also the slightly extravagant comment on 299.

[4] The book is *dedicated* to Van Til, "who has taught a generation that Christ is the Alpha and Omega of thought and life" (p. v). I do not doubt the genuineness of the authors' admiration and affection for Van Til: see pp. 183f.

to the Ligonier type[5] has been the common view of orthodox Christians through most of church history; hence it deserves to be called the "classical" or "traditional" view. This argument is supported by studies of Augustine, Luther, Calvin, seventeenth-century orthodoxy, Eastern and Roman orthodoxy.[6] However, the authors believe that classical apologetics today is "sick and ailing," though not dead.[7] "Presuppositionalism," they tell us, "has become the majority report today among Reformed theologians, although it cannot even be called a minority report of church history."[8] Other reviewers more historically inclined than I will doubtless seek to evaluate this thesis. Substantial arguments, I think, can be presented on either side. Of course, the issue is not terribly important in evaluating the relative validity of the two approaches. If Van Til's view is relatively new, it is not on that account false; Protestants are not traditionalists.[9] In general, it seems to me that the history of apologetics before our century is ambiguous on these questions. Orthodox Christian apologists have always believed in the supreme authority of Scripture over all human reasoning—the essence of the Van Tillian position. On the other hand, they have also spoken of various kinds of reasoning that in some sense legitimately "precede" faith.[10] The apparent contradiction here was, in general, not perceived as a problem until after Kant's "Copernican revolution," which greatly increased the epistemological sophistication of theologians and philosophers. Only after Kant could the logic of presuppositions be systematically in-

---

[5]"Ligonier" is a convenient shorthand for "Sproul-Gerstner-Lindsley," since all three authors have been associated with the Ligonier Valley Study Center in western Pennsylvania.

[6]Pp. 89–211.

[7]P. 34.

[8]P. 183.

[9]Van Til himself finds relatively little of value in his apologetic predecessors. See his *A Christian Theory of Knowledge* (Nutley, N.J.: Presbyterian and Reformed, 1969) and his syllabus, *Christianity in Conflict* (mimeographed, 1962).

[10]"Precede" adds to the ambiguity. Few concepts in theology are as unclear as that of "priority." More comments on this issue will follow.

vestigated (as it was, even before Van Til, by thinkers like Hegel, Marx, Kierkegaard, Wittgenstein, and by Christian apologists like James Orr). Thus to ask whether Calvin was a "presuppositionalist" or an "evidentialist"[11] is a bit like asking whether Augustine was a Protestant or a Catholic.[12]

As to the modern situation, many of us will be surprised to hear that presuppositionalism is the "majority report" among current apologists. It all depends, of course, on how you define presuppositionalism. I suppose that a case can be made, that, in this age, following Kant, Hegel, Marx, Einstein, pragmatism, phenomenology, existentialism, Wittgenstein, Kuhn, Polanyi, Hanson, Dooyeweerd, and many others, most apologists have taken seriously the issue of presuppositions. In our time, it is exceedingly difficult to deny that human thought (whether scientific, logical, historical, philosophical, religious, or whatever) is influenced by our "pretheoretical" attitudes and commitments.[13] Perhaps this fact is what suggests to our authors that presuppositionalism is ascendant presently; they do not document their assertion, so it is hard to say. In my view, this openness to considering the influence of pretheoretical commitments on thought is a long way from a full-fledged presuppositionalism. Still, it is a positive development in the dialogue. One of my great disappointments about the current volume is its failure to deal in any serious way with these powerful philosophical currents which create, for many, considerable presumption against the Ligonier type of apologetic.

---

[11]I use these terms to accommodate the authors under review, but really I think they are quite misleading, suggesting that Van Til is opposed to the use of evidence and/or that the traditionalists have no presuppositions to examine. On the contrary: all parties to the discussion must deal with both presuppositions and evidences, and they differ only on the *roles* to be played by these.

[12]I am not saying that such questions are unanswerable, but rather that they are subtler than often supposed, and difficult to answer in any useful way.

[13]Contra Dooyeweerd, however, I maintain that the reverse is also true and that no *sharp* distinction can be drawn between "pretheoretical" and "theoretical." See J. Frame, *The Amsterdam Philosophy* (Phillipsburg, N.J.: Harmony Press, 1972).

I. Ligonier and Van Til

I shall now try to analyze the authors' critique of Van Til, before discussing their positive apologetic. In the book itself this order is reversed, but I feel that in this review questions of methodology and epistemology ought to precede discussion of the authors' arguments for Christianity; and the former questions are inseparably bound up with the critique of "presuppositionalism."

Van Til's apologetics is essentially simple, however complicated its elaborations. It makes two basic assertions: (1) that human beings are obligated to presuppose God in all of their thinking, and (2) that unbelievers resist this obligation in every aspect of thought and life. The first assertion leads Van Til to criticize the notion of intellectual autonomy; the second leads him to discuss the noetic effects of sin. The Ligonier group criticizes Van Til in both areas, which we shall consider in that order.

A. Autonomy, Reason, and Circularity

The initial description of presuppositionalism shows insight in the prominent place given to Van Til's critique of autonomy:[14] this is, I think, the foundation of Van Til's system and its most persuasive principle.[15] We must not do apologetics as if we were a law unto ourselves, as if we were the measure of all things. Christian thinking, like all of the Christian life, is subject to God's lordship.

However, the book's *analysis* of the autonomy question reveals unclarity and/or misunderstanding. The authors deduce from Van Til's statements about autonomy that he wants

---

[14]P. 185.

[15]In my view, this point is both more important and more cogent than, e.g., Van Til's view of the noetic effects of sin. The latter is often singled out as being central to Van Til's thought, but it is one doctrine which Van Til himself admitted to have difficulty formulating: see *An Introduction to Systematic Theology* (unpublished class syllabus, 1961), 26f. Autonomy is the more crucial issue, for Van Til's analysis of it indicates that *even if man had not fallen,* he would still have been obligated to reason presuppositionally.

223

us to "start with" God, rather than with ourselves.[16] Now "start with" is (like "precede" and "priority") an extremely slippery phrase in theology and apologetics. It can indicate a pedagogical order of topics, an emphasis, a method of study, a conviction about prominence or importance, a relation of necessary or sufficient conditionality, or a criterion of truth. I believe that Van Til almost always has the last alternative in mind, though there is occasionally some ambiguity. At any rate, one would expect the Ligonier authors to offer some analysis of this concept, to make some attempt to define it (both for Van Til and for their own system). But no such analysis is forthcoming. The authors write as if the meaning of the idea were perfectly self-evident.

So they insist that we must, in coming to know God, "begin with ourselves," and therefore reason autonomously in some sense. "One simply cannot start outside himself. To begin outside oneself, one would first have to depart from himself."[17] Now certainly in one sense this is true, and Van Til quite readily admits it. Our authors even quote him to this effect,[18] but they claim that it represents an inconsistency in his thought, a kind of embarrassing admission.[19] Anyhow, on Van Til's view, the self is the "proximate," but not the "ultimate" starting point.[20] What this means, I think, is that it is the self which makes its decisions both in thought and practical life: every judgment we make, we make because we, ourselves, think it is right. But this fact does not entail that the self is its own ultimate criterion of truth. We are regularly faced with the decision as to whether we should trust our own unaided judgment, or rely on someone else. There is nothing odd or

[16]Pp. 185, 212ff.

[17]P. 212.

[18]Pp. 214f.; cf. pp. 316f.

[19]Unfortunately, this is rather typical of the volume. The authors make statements about Van Til which can be contradicted from his writings; but instead of reconsidering the accuracy of their interpretation in these cases, they simply accuse Van Til of inconsistency. Thus their accounts of Van Til's positions are almost always oversimplified at best.

[20]Van Til, *An Introduction to Systematic Theology*, 203.

strange (let alone logically impossible) about such a question; it is entirely normal.

Therefore, there are two questions to be resolved: (1) the metaphysical (actually tautological!) question of whether all decisions are decisions of the self, and (2) the epistemological-ethical question of what standard the self ought to use in coming to its decisions.[21] Van Til and the Ligonier group agree, I think, on the first question, though it is not of much interest to Van Til; but that agreement does not prejudice the answer to the second question. That one still needs to be posed and resolved. And it is the second question that Van Til—and Scripture—are concerned about. Scripture regularly calls God's creatures to submit their judgment to that of their creator. If someone objects that even a choice to serve God is a choice made by the self and therefore "starting with" the self in one sense, Van Til can simply grant the point, while reminding his questioner that in another sense, in a far more important sense, this choice does *not* "start with" the self.[22]

The same sorts of distinctions need to be made in the discussion of human reason, another topic prominent in this book. *Classical Apologetics* is rationalistic with a vengeance. The authors attack the anti-intellectual trends of our time,[23] laud signs of a "retreat from this anti-intellectual binge,"[24] show at length from Scripture our obligation to reason with unbelievers.[25] "Fideism" is the great enemy.[26] Van Til, however, they

---

[21] Our authors charge Van Til with confusing the order of being with the order of knowing (p. 229). At this point, however, it is they who confuse metaphysics with epistemology.

[22] If "autonomy" in the first sense necessitates autonomy in the second sense, then, of course, it necessitates autonomy for Christians and non-Christians alike. Therefore, if our authors' argument were sound, it would prove too much. It would legislate autonomy for everyone, not just for those who are "beginning" their path toward Christianity, as on the Ligonier view (pp. 231f.). Human reason, then, would be the "ultimate" criterion, not merely the "penultimate" or "provisionally ultimate" as our authors would have it (pp. 301, 331).

[23] Pp. 12ff.

[24] P. 15.

[25] Pp. 18ff.

[26] Pp. 24ff.

say, abandons apologetics,[27] refusing to reason with unbelievers. He doesn't believe in proofs[28] or evidences.[29] He denies that you can find God at the end of a syllogism.[30] The present reviewer, that notorious Van Tillian, cannot engage in rational argument with anyone:

> [The Arminian] can argue with Frame, but Frame will not argue with him. Frame can only tell him that he is in error and that he must change his mind because he, Frame, has been illumined by God to see otherwise.[31]

On the contrary, say our authors: Just as we cannot avoid "starting with ourselves," so we cannot avoid the use of reason (in any area of life, particularly apologetics). Any attempt to persuade an unbeliever of Christian truth requires reasoning; indeed, rational argument is necessary if we are going to show the "rational necessity of presupposing God".[32] And, in fact, presuppositionalists *do* give reasons.[33] In practice, "there is no real difference on the matter of autonomy."[34]

Buttressing all of this is the familiar argument that some basic principles of reason (such as the law of noncontradiction) must be presupposed in any intelligible discourse; indeed, *The Law of Noncontradiction [is] a Universal Prerequisite for Life.*"[35] You can't question logic without presupposing it; you can't argue against the primacy of logic without presupposing it as primary.

So our authors support the "principle of the primacy of the intellect." This does not mean that the intellect is more excellent than the God whom the intellect discovers; rather,

---

[27]P. 188.
[28]Pp. 253ff.
[29]Pp. 276ff.
[30]P. 287.
[31]P. 301.
[32]P. 224.
[33]Pp. 238f.
[34]P. 239; cf. pp. 324f.
[35]P. 80, emphasis theirs; see pp. 72–82.

Proximate starting point

"primacy of intellect means that we must think about God before we can actually know him."[36] Thus, when Van Til speaks of a "primacy of the intellect based on the creator-creature distinction," he seems to be talking nonsense. If the intellect is primary, its primacy is not "based on" anything. And if God is somehow known prior to intellectual activity, then how do we know him at all?

But here, as with "starting point," some distinctions must be made. "Intellect" or "reason" can mean various things: laws of logic, the psychological faculty by which we make judgments and draw inferences, the judgments and inferences themselves, systems of thought.[37] It is certainly true that reason as a psychological faculty is involved in any rational activity. Thus putting it tautologically emphasizes the obviousness of the point. It is the same sort of obviousness we saw earlier in the proposition that one must "start with the self." But just as "starting with the self" leaves open the question of what criterion of truth the self should acknowledge, so "starting with reason" leaves open the question of what criterion of truth human reason ought to recognize. As a psychological faculty, reason has the choice of operating according to a number of different principles: different systems of logic, different philosophical schemes, different religious commitments. Van Til, therefore, may (and does!) grant that reason is involved in all human thought and life. But for him the important question is, What criteria of truth ought our reason to acknowledge?

Our authors would answer this question by saying, first of all, that reason ought to acknowledge the law of noncontradiction. (Perhaps they even define reason in terms of the laws of logic, so that for them the "primacy of reason" means, not the primacy of a psychological faculty, but the primacy of logic; that, again, isn't clear.) Again, however, the main point is true in a sense. The law of noncontradiction denies that p

---

[36]P. 227.
[37]Philosophers, such as Hegel, have sometimes defined rationality in terms of their systems so that, e.g., rationality = Hegelianism.

God & Not God.

and not-p can both be true at the same time and in the same respect. That is a Christian principle, presupposed by Scripture itself. But it is, of course, also highly abstract. Nothing more concrete can be derived from the law of noncontradiction alone. To derive concrete conclusions we need additional principles, principles which are religiously, as well as philosophically, problematic.[38] Hence the tendency for various philosophers to define rationality in terms of their particular systems. It is at this point that Van Til enters the discussion and demands that God's voice be heard in the selection of rational principles. It is at this level, with this sort of concern, that he talks about "a primacy of the intellect based on the creator-creature distinction." He refers here to a reasoning process which recognizes God's standards as supreme. Perhaps for clarity's sake he would have been wiser not to speak of the "primacy of the intellect" at all;[39] but it isn't difficult to understand what he means. Reason is always involved in the human search for knowledge; but reason must always choose its standards, and that choice is fundamentally a religious one.

Our authors reply, however, that we must, after all, "think about God before we can know him."[40] And if we are trying to think about God *before* we know him, then, obviously, at that stage of our inquiry, we cannot presuppose God. We cannot make God our supreme standard until we know that he exists. Therefore we must adopt some other standard, at least "provisionally."[41] But this analysis (1) denies the clear teaching of Romans 1 that everyone knows God already (verses 20, 21), (2) posits an exception to 1 Cor. 10:31, that

---

[38]Cf. V. Poythress, "A Biblical View of Mathematics," in *Foundations of Christian Scholarship*, ed. G. North (Vallecito, Calif.: Ross House, 1976), 159–88; J. Frame, "Rationality and Scripture," in *Rationality in the Calvinian Tradition*, ed. H. Hart, et al. (Lanham, Md.: University Press of America, 1983), 293–317.

[39]There are several other reasons why this phrase is misleading. See my *Doctrine of the Knowledge of God*, forthcoming.

[40]P. 227.

[41]Pp. 301, 331.

[handwritten annotations in top margin: "1? Cannot start an argument by saying → OK; Defras Ro C. we can assume God doesn't exist" "2.) Contradicts Law Contradict"]

when you are just beginning your quest for knowledge, you do not need to think "to the glory of God"; you can justifiably think to the glory of something/someone else. Such notions fall by their own weight. They are intolerable to the Bible-believer.

Our authors, therefore, have failed to show that Van Til abandons rational argument, proofs, evidences. He does abandon neutral, or autonomous reasoning; that is all. And nothing in *Classical Apologetics* shows that he is wrong in rejecting these. For the record, let me emphasize that Van Til does *not* reject proofs, arguments, evidences; on the contrary, he endorses them in the strongest terms.[42] The Ligonier authors are quite aware of this, but they dismiss it as inconsistency or insist that Van Til's arguments aren't really arguments at all.

However, it is quite impossible to argue for Christianity, or anything else for that matter, without making a presuppositional choice. One cannot reason without criteria of truth. And criteria of truth come from a wide variety of sources, ultimately religious commitment.[43] Those criteria will either be Christian or non-Christian.[44] If they are non-Christian, they will be self-defeating and subject to divine judgment. *[handwritten: Principles]*

To say this is to say that argument for Christianity will always be in one sense circular. Arguments for Christianity must be based on Christian criteria, which in turn presuppose the truth of Christianity. You can't prove God without presupposing him. This is one of the principles of Van Til's apologetics which most irritates our authors.[45] To them, circular

---

[42]See *The Defense of the Faith*, 120, 196; *An Introduction to Systematic Theology*, 102ff., 114f., 196; *A Christian Theory of Knowledge*, 292; *Common Grace and the Gospel* (Nutley, N.J.: Presbyterian and Reformed, 1969), 179ff., 190ff. See also T. Notaro, *Van Til and the Use of Evidence* (Phillipsburg, N.J.: Presbyterian and Reformed, 1980).

[43]Again, it would have been helpful if the Ligonier authors had offered some response to the rather broad range of philosophical opinion (even outside Christianity) to this effect. *Classical Apologetics* seems to be written in a curiously pre-Kantian, pre-Kuhnian context, and thus it strains our credibility. The authors have not dealt with the most serious criticisms of their position.

[44]Listen to the law of non-contradiction!

[45]See pp. 318ff.; cf. pp. 137ff., 144ff.

reasoning is a logical fallacy, pure and simple.[46] But what is the alternative? Again, the alternative seems to be that an unbeliever begins his quest, either with no criterion at all or with a "provisional" criterion of a non-Christian (or perhaps "neutral") sort; then by linear, non-circular reasoning, he learns that he must adopt the Christian criterion.[47] But, as we noted earlier, this construction violates Rom. 1 and 1 Cor. 10:31. According to Scripture there is no one in this position—no one without a knowledge of God's criteria. Those who seek to adopt non-Christian standards (and there are no "neutral" ones) are simply disobedient to the revelation they have received. If one could proceed from neutrality to truth, then noncircular argument would be possible. But of course it is not possible, because Scripture condemns autonomy.[48]

Does this circularity entail the death of all reasoning, as the Ligonier authors fear? No: (1) All reasoning, Christian, non-Christian, presuppositional, "classical," is in this sense circular. There is no alternative. This is not a challenge to the validity of reason; it is simply the way in which reason works. (2) There are distinctions to be made between "narrow circles" (e.g., "The Bible is God's word because it says it is God's word.") and "broad circles" (e.g.: "Evidence interpreted according to Christian criteria demonstrates the divine authority of Scripture. Here it is: . . ."). Not every circular argument is equally desirable. Some circular arguments, indeed, should rightly be dismissed as fallacious. (3) Reasoning on Christian criteria is persuasive because (a) it is God's approved way to reason, (b) it leads to true conclusions, (c) and everyone, at some level, *already knows* that such reasoning leads to truth (Rom. 1, again).

B. The Noetic Effects of Sin

Why is it necessary to presuppose God, according to Van Til? The Ligonier authors have a theory about that. They attribute to Van Til the notion that "the fundamental fallacy of the

---

[46]P. 322.

[47]P. 325.

[48]Again, even many non-Christian authors (see earlier note) concede this

traditional approach is in not recognizing that without knowing everything one cannot know anything."[49] (Without the
double negatives: what they are saying is that for Van Til we
cannot know anything unless we know everything.) This point
comes up elsewhere in the book,[50] and the authors think it is
important enough to embellish poetically: ". . . one cannot
know the flower in the crannied wall unless he knows the
world and all."[51] On this account, Van Til would be teaching
that we need to presuppose God in order to have, somehow,
that omniscient perspective on reality. However, they never
give any references in Van Til's writings to show that he believes any such thing; and of course they cannot, for this is
not his position. Van Til does sometimes argue, in terms rem-
iniscent of idealism, that true human knowledge presupposes
the existence of a comprehensive system of knowledge; but
unlike the idealist, Van Til finds this comprehensive system in
the God of Scripture. He explicitly denies the similar-sounding proposition that *we human beings* must have comprehensive knowledge in order to know anything:

> One of the points about which there has been much
> confusion when we speak of the objectivity of human
> knowledge is whether human knowledge of the world
> must be comprehensive in order to be true. . . . But
> we believe that just for the reason that we cannot hope
> to obtain comprehensive knowledge of God we cannot
> hope to obtain comprehensive knowledge of anything
> in the world.[52]

Van Til, in fact, explicitly denies the principle that we
must know everything in order to know anything. He at-

---

sort of point about circularity. It simply is not responsible, in the present
intellectual context, to dismiss all circularity as a mere logical fallacy.
[49]P. 186.
[50]Pp. 306, 313.
[51]P. 186.
[52]Van Til, *The Defense of the Faith* (1955 edition), 60.

tributes this principle to "the non-Christian methodology in general, and that of modern phenomenalism in particular."[53]

On the contrary: to Van Til, our need to presuppose God has nothing to do with such idealist epistemological speculations. Rather, we presuppose God because in the nature of the case that is the right way to reason, and because, therefore, we are obligated to reason that way. The necessity is an *ethical* necessity.

Which brings us to the question of the noetic effects of sin. At this point, I find a surprising amount of agreement between the Ligonier authors and Van Til. "The pagan's problem," they say, "is not that he does not know that God is, but that he does not like the God who is."[54] The nature Psalms and Romans 1 tell us that God is clearly revealed in the world, and all human beings know God through this revelation.[55] Thus the unbeliever is without excuse. This "natural theology," they argue, is mediated through the creation.[56] (I agree that this is the teaching of Rom. 1, but I would add that this fact does not preclude other forms of revelation in addition to the mediate form described in Rom. 1.) Why, then, do people need complex arguments in order to believe? The answer is that they repress the truth revealed in creation.[57] They are not morons, but foolish.[58] Their problem is not intellectual weakness, but moral refusal to accept what is clearly revealed. Or, to put it more precisely, they do have intellectual problems, but "The intellectual problem is produced by the moral problem, not the moral problem by an intellectual one."[59] They know God, but they do not know

---

[53]Ibid., 136 (1963 ed., 119). In the immediate context he discusses idealist epistemology, from which this notion comes.

[54]P. 39.

[55]When our authors say that for presuppositionalists God "reveals Himself exclusively in Holy Scripture"(p. 287) (presumably in contrast with natural revelation), they are evidently getting carried away with themselves. Van Til's belief in natural revelation needs no documentation.

[56]Pp. 43ff.

[57]P. 47.

[58]P. 52.

[59]Ibid.

him savingly. Honestly, in all of this (and in their summary[60]), I have not found anything that I or Van Til would disagree with! The Ligonier men seem to think that Van Til holds a very different position—that he thinks sin destroyed the unbeliever's reasoning power,[61] but as usual they fail to document adequately their interpretation and they ignore statements in Van Til to the contrary.

I will surprise them even more by saying that I agree, in general, with their account of the testimony of the Holy Spirit.[62] The utterly fideistic view which they attribute to me[63] is their own creation, made up out of thin air. They present no documentation of it from my writings. Apparently they believe that my other positions necessitate such a view. I find that hard to believe! They say that for me "the internal testimony of the Holy Spirit must be utterly apart from and prior to speculative knowledge and evidence of the inspiration of the word."[64] Nonsense. I quite agree with them that the Spirit witnesses to the word through witnessing to evidences (along with other ways, to be sure). As for the Spirit being "prior to speculative knowledge," I think I have expounded sufficiently the ambiguities of "priority" language in theology. In any case, I grant what I think they want me to, that people sometimes reach true conclusions about God without the witness of the Spirit.

Van Til's writings do pose some difficulty here. He does clearly recognize that unbelievers know the truth (Rom. 1:21) and that they sometimes reach true conclusions "in spite of themselves," i.e., in spite of their unbelieving presuppositions. However, there are points at which he seems to say that unbelief always leads to intellectual error and that no propositional truth is possible apart from the Spirit's witness. His rep-

---

[60]P. 62.

[61]Pp. 241ff., esp. p. 245.

[62]Pp. 137ff., 162ff. See my article, "The Spirit and the Scriptures," forthcoming in *Scripture and Truth, II* ed. D. Carson and J. Woodbridge (Grand Rapids: Zondervan, 1986).

[63]Pp. 299ff.

[64]P. 299.

resentations, I think, are not fully consistent. What's more, he has admitted some difficulty in this area.[65] The problems stem from Van Til's realization that even though unbelievers do know the truth, their rebellion often infests their intellectual activity. Much pagan philosophy can be explained precisely as attempts to evade the truth of God's revelation. Therefore, it is not sufficient to say (as the Ligonier writers seem to *want* to say; but see below) that the unbeliever's problems are moral rather than intellectual. Morality influences intellectual judgments.[66] At times, indeed, the authors of our volume recognize this fact: they write, "The intellectual problem is caused by the moral problem, not the moral problem by the intellectual one."[67] I agree, and I note that here they at least recognize that there *is* an intellectual problem as well as a moral one, though they don't stress that fact very much in their discussion.

The interesting net result is that *on paper* there is very little difference between the Ligonier group and Van Til on the noetic effects of sin and the testimony of the Spirit. Both maintain that depravity is total, that it causes repression of the truth, that the unbeliever has intellectual difficulties because of his moral rebellion, that he has knowledge of God but not saving knowledge. To both, the testimony of the Spirit works with and through our apologetic arguments to break down that rebellion and lead the unbeliever to acknowledge the truth which he already knows. Part of the reason for this agreement is that the Ligonier form of the traditional apologetic (as opposed, e.g., to that of Clark Pinnock) is self-consciously Calvinistic.

But the Ligonier authors are not very consistent in their confession of total depravity. Note here what they say about people who are not yet Christians, but seeking the truth:

---

[65]*An Introduction to Systematic Theology*, 26f.

[66]More than that, all intellectual judgments are morally determined. A right judgment is a judgment which we *ought* to make (the ought being a moral ought).

[67]P. 52.

[Van Til] always assumes that the person who begins to examine the universe without presupposing the existence of the divine Lawgiver necessarily presupposes his own status as a lawgiver. That is by no means a necessary assumption of the person who begins by examining the data which he has at hand. . . . They do not necessarily deny the divine being as Van Til insists that they do. People do not assert their autonomy against an initially known God as Van Til insists that they do. They simply operate according to human nature.[68]

Here, note that they deny what they earlier affirmed on the basis of Romans 1, that the unbeliever knows God. Further, they deny that all unbelievers are hostile to God, repressors of the truth. At least some unbelievers, in their opinion, are sincere seekers after truth, operating merely according to the necessities of created human nature. Seriously, now: is this a doctrine of depravity worthy of Calvinists?

So, though on paper the differences in this area are not great, there is in the Ligonier authors a lack of seriousness in the application of the doctrine of depravity to apologetics. Similarly, on the question of "common ground," our authors state a position which is precisely identical with Van Til's:

If we consider common ground to mean a common perception and perspective of reality, then obviously no such common ground for discussion exists between believer and unbeliever. From the believer's vantage point every aspect of life, every bit of experience, every dimension of reality, is understood and interpreted from a theological perspective. . . . It would appear that both [believer and unbeliever] enjoy a univocal understanding of the daffodil. . . . [but] The believer acknowledges the *significance* of that daffodil, not as a cosmic accident, but as something that in itself bears

---

[68]Pp. 232f.

235

witness to the majesty and beauty of the Creator God. This the unbeliever does not acknowledge, positing, instead, a completely opposite and antithetical understanding of the daffodil's significance.

From a different perspective, however, there is common ground, namely the whole of creation. Believer and unbeliever live in the same universe. Each sees the same phenomena. The unbeliever and the believer can agree that two and two are four, and that certain principles of deduction are valid while others are invalid. Thus a kind of common ground is established.[69]

In my opinion, Van Til himself could have written this formulation, except for the bit about a "univocal" understanding which raises a few (in my view minor) problems.[70] In fact, paragraphs nearly identical to these might be pasted together from Van Til's writings. But both Van Til and the Ligonier authors have had trouble maintaining consistency here, Van Til tending to forget the areas of agreement between believer and unbeliever ("in spite of themselves"), and the Ligoniers tending (as we have seen) to compromise their concept of "a completely opposite and antithetical understanding" between believer and unbeliever.[71]

One last comment in this area: It is unfortunate that a demonstrable misreading of Van Til at one point leads the authors to a serious misrepresentation of Van Til's position. On page 214 they quote Van Til as saying that the Christian "has no *point of contact* with the non-Christian."[72] They take this as a statement of Van Til's own view, but in context it is actually a paraphrase of Stuart Hackett's critique of Calvinism. I could

---

[69]Pp. 70f.

[70]Van Til seems to resist any positive use of the term "univocal" in regard to our knowledge of God. But if as in this context it simply means "literal," I know of no principle in Van Til's thought that would be violated by such a "univocal" knowledge of God. See my "The Problem of Theological Paradox," in *Foundations of Christian Scholarship*, 310f.

[71]Is some of this inconsistency related to the book's triple authorship?

[72]P. 214, quoting Van Til in *Jerusalem and Athens*, 16.

write this off as a minor mistake, except that it shows, in its way, an extraordinary ignorance of Van Til's position. Van Til would *never* say that the Christian has no point of contact with the non-Christian; in fact he has said the opposite innumerable times. Mistakes like this make one wonder how seriously these authors have tried to understand Van Til. Could they have simply dismissed as inconsistencies the countless positive references in Van Til to "point of contact," focusing upon this one reference as his definitive formulation, without even trying to explain the others? Or did the author of this section have such a poor knowledge of Van Til that he actually thought this was a representative formulation? It is hard to account for this sort of blunder except as a serious lapse of scholarship stemming from ignorance and intense prejudice, a desire to make Van Til say something he does not actually say, in order to make him more vulnerable to criticism.

II. The Ligonier Apologetic

I must needs be briefer in dealing with the book's positive argument for Christianity, because of the demands of time and space, and because the argument itself is not as novel or interesting (to me!) as the critique of Van Til. Still, there are a few new wrinkles.

The Ligonier authors believe, as we have seen, that traditionalist apologetics is sick and ailing, though not dead. One of the reasons for the malaise, in their view, is that other modern classicists have abandoned the traditional claim that the truth of Christianity can be demonstrated, settling for arguments which merely claim probability.[73] Here, interestingly, is another point of agreement between the Ligonier group and Van Til. Our authors here frequently sound Van Tillian notes: that if Christianity is not *certainly* true, then we have, to some extent, an excuse for unbelief.

---

[73]Pp. 100f., 125, 148, 276.

But how can we reach the level of demonstrative certainty? On the Ligonier view, decisive appeal to special revelation is excluded; that would be "presuppositionalism." But that means the argument must be wholly based on human sensation and reason, unaided by special revelation. Everyone agrees that human reason and sensation are fallible. So whence the desired certainty?

The Ligonier authors believe such certainty can be attained by appeal to certain "universal and necessary assumptions." These are assumptions which, though sometimes challenged, cannot be regularly and consistently denied. As such, they are prerequisites of science and, indeed, of all human life.[74] These are the law of noncontradiction, the "law of causality," and "the basic reliability of sense perception." Since these principles cannot be regularly and consistently denied, the book argues, they must be regarded as certain, along with any of their implications. Thus the authors try to show that Christianity is one of those implications: to deny Christianity is to deny one or more of those "universal and necessary assumptions." Since we cannot deny those, Christianity also must be regarded as certain.

The argument is "transcendental,"[75] even presuppositional in a sense. The authors are asking, "What are the assumptions necessary for life and knowledge to be possible?"[76] Van Til asks the same question and concludes that the whole content of God's revelation is such a necessary assumption! In one sense, the Ligonier authors are saying the same thing, but less directly. To deny Christianity, they say, is indeed to deny truths which we cannot consistently and regularly deny. Van Til, similarly, says that unbelievers cannot consistently and regularly deny Christianity, that they can exist only on "borrowed capital," inconsistently making use of Christian ideas which they wish to reject. I am tempted, therefore, to read the Ligonier argument as a kind of "indirect presuppo-

---

[74]Pp. 71f.
[75]P. 71.
[76]Ibid.

sitionalism," an attempt to show (more concretely than Van Til) the *ways* in which Christian assumptions are unavoidable. On such an approach, the authors would be asking the non-Christian to presuppose Christian concepts (concepts compatible with Scripture) of logic, cause, sense-experience, since denying these concepts leads to chaos. Van Til and the Ligonier group, on that interpretation, would again be very close. In my view, the cogency of the Ligonier argument arises from the fact that something like this is going on. But, on the other hand, we have to remember all the talk in this book about autonomy, the inconsistencies on depravity, and so on. Whatever may actually be the case, these authors at least *think* that they are reasoning on a neutral basis, with concepts of cause, etc., which are not distinctively Christian, even though they imply a distinctively Christian worldview.[77]

A brief look now at the authors' theistic proofs. Their ontological argument, following Jonathan Edwards, is virtually Parmenidean: We have an idea of being; in fact, we can think of nothing else than being. Nonbeing is unthinkable. Thus being must be eternal, omnipresent, limitless in all perfections—in other words, God. There is an obvious objection to this, however, which the book doesn't even mention. However infinite being may be, our idea of being extends to finite being as well. Therefore, if "being" is divine, then finite beings are part of that divine being. In other words, without some modifications, the argument proves pantheism. And the argument fails to draw any distinction between the kind of "infinity," "eternity," "omnipresence," etc., attributable to a pantheistic god, and the very different (but similar-sounding) attributes revealed concerning the God of Scripture.[78]

The cosmological argument: Our authors state the "law of causality" first in what they admit to be tautological fashion: "Every effect has a cause."[79] Since the world is contin-

---

[77]How is it possible for a concept logically to imply a Christian worldview if that concept is not itself in an important sense distinctively Christian?

[78]Pp. 93ff.

[79]Pp. 82f., 111.

gent, they argue, it must be an effect. What, then, is its cause? The world is not a mere illusion (nonbeing—see above), nor is it self-created, which is nonsense. If it is self-existent, then it is in effect transcendent and divine, so God's existence is proved. If it is created by a self-existent being, then again, God is proved. An infinite number of contingent beings cannot be the world-cause: if no one of them is sufficient to cause the world, then the whole series will not be sufficient either. Much could be said (and has been said) about this sort of argument. What is most notable to me is that, as in the Ligonier version of the ontological argument, the authors fail clearly to rule out the pantheistic alternative, namely that the universe is its own god. About all I can find in the book responding to this objection is one sentence: "[God] is personal because He is the pervasive cause of all things including the purpose and the personal."[80] But it is by no means obvious that a being must itself be personal in order to be the cause of personality.

The ontological and cosmological arguments together suggest that on the Ligonier view, being is unlimited and therefore possesses all excellencies in infinite degree.[81] These excellencies include all the traditional attributes of the Christian God including personality. Therefore God exists. However, the concept of an "excellency," a perfection, is religiously problematic. What is excellent to one person is a defect in the eyes of another. Personality is a perfection to a Westerner imbued with Christian teaching. To a Buddhist, that would not necessarily be the case. Therefore, the sort of proof offered in our book presupposes a particular set of values, or else it is simply invalid. It is, in other words, either a presuppositional argument or else it is a failure.

I shall pass over the teleological argument to look at the authors' presentation of Christian evidences. Here the authors follow the pattern of other books of this kind. They begin with

---

[80]P. 123.
[81]Ibid.

the premise that the Gospels are "reliable historical sources."[82] (It would not do, of course, to presuppose more than this, that these books are the Word of God. That would be circular and presuppositional.) In these reliable historical sources, we learn about Jesus: that he worked miracles and that he claimed to be God.[83] Jesus' miracles prove divine attestation of his claim; therefore he is God, and his testimony that Scripture is God's Word is to be believed. At that point, we conclude that Scripture is our ultimate standard. Thenceforth, we argue on the basis of biblical authority—i.e., like presuppositionalists![84]

A few comments on this argument: (1) The authors overestimate, I think, the current scholarly consensus on the reliability of the Gospels. They assume that most every New Testament scholar will concede that the Gospels are "generally reliable." I doubt it. (2) Even if we grant that some very unusual events took place in the ministry of Jesus,[85] how can we be sure that these can be explained *only* as a divine attestation to Jesus' authority? It is extremely difficult to prove (apart from Christian presuppositions) the negative proposition that no other cause could have produced these events. The authors need to prove this proposition in order to make their case, but nothing in the book amounts to such a proof. (3) Recall that these authors boasted earlier that they were offering, not just a probable argument, but a demonstration, warranting certainty. Now I can understand how they can make this claim for the earlier part of their argument: the "universal and necessary assumptions," the theistic proofs. (I do not think they

---

[82]P. 141.

[83]Interestingly, at this point, our authors sound another Van Tillian note: miracles are of no evidential value without a theistic presupposition (pp. 146ff.).They believe that they have established the existence of God by means of theistic proof, and therefore have refuted decisively any notion that miracles are impossible. Of course, Van Til would go beyond this and say that the cogency of miracle requires, not a barely theistic, but a full-blown Christian worldview.

[84]Except, presumably, when we are doing apologetics. But why should that be an exception?

[85]And of course the question must be raised as to *how* unusual an event must be before we call it a miracle.

succeed in making good this claim, but I can understand why they *think* they have made it good.) But when they get to the historical evidences, I do not find even the slightest plausibility in their claim to demonstration. The assumption of the Gospels' reliability is highly debatable; the argument that miracles always testify to a divinely appointed messenger is also weak. And some have questioned whether Jesus did warrant belief in the Scriptures. Of course, on these matters I think the Ligonier authors are right and the liberal critics wrong. But if they look at these questions without the full range of Christian presuppositions, I do not see how they can responsibly claim anything more for their argument than a high degree of probability.

Some Formal Matters

At the risk of losing the reader's attention, I think I should point out some editorial problems in the book which ought to be corrected in future editions. There are a great many of these, possibly in part because of the triple authorship. (1) I do not understand the need, in context, for three pages dealing with theological creativity (pp. 64ff.). (2) The excursus on probabilism in theology (pp. 125ff.) seems also to belong somewhere else. It breaks up the discussion of dysteleology. (3) On p. 185, the third point does not make much sense to me; at least it does not seem clearly distinguishable from the second point. (4) Note the typographical error on p. 187— the "poetic influence of sin" (!). (5) On p. 220, the authors give the impression that Van Til's *Survey of Christian Epistemology* is a different book from his *Metaphysics of Apologetics*. Actually, the two books are one and the same, the former being a more recent printing of the latter.[86] (6) Recall our ear-

---

[86] I must say that I am also somewhat disturbed by the large number of references to this title and the relatively small number of references to Van Til's more recent writings. It hardly seems fair to judge Van Til to such a large extent on the basis of his first, relatively unnuanced, class syllabus, dating back to 1929.

lier point about the misreading of the Van Til reference on page 214. (7) I agree with the authors' assessment of Runner's concept of "republication" (pp. 251f.), but it fits rather awkwardly into the context. (8) On page 254, second paragraph, who is speaking? Van Til, Sullivan, or the Ligoniers? (9) The material on Duns Scotus (p. 260) also seems out of place.

Conclusions

There is much here to make us think. I was surprised at how close these authors were to Van Til at various places. There are, I think, some areas here for further dialogue between Van Tillian and Ligonier apologists. There is much similarity in regard to general revelation and the noetic effects of sin. There is recognition of the need for more than mere probability in grounding our faith. The authors also recognize that evidential arguments presuppose some elements of a Christian worldview. The chief difference is in the evaluation of autonomy. There is also room for further debates as to who is the most consistent with the shared Calvinistic premises.

Surely, there is plenty of room for mutual support and encouragement in the Lord. Speaking personally, I owe a great deal to John Gerstner, who for several decades was the most cogent and tireless defender of the Reformed faith in western Pennsylvania. Sproul and Lindsley, through the Ligonier Valley Study Center, continue Gerstner's ministry, sending this Reformed message all over the world by lectures and tapes: excellent communications, on the whole, of the gospel of Christ. We Van Tillians have much to learn from these valiant men; and I dare say they have much to learn from us as well.

Appendix B: Jay E. Adams's Reply to Frame

(Note: Jay Adams was gracious to reply to my critique of him in chapter 6. I'm happy to thank him for this contribution and to announce that we are still friends! As for me, I'm sticking by what I wrote in the text. The reader may decide who is closer to the truth. In any case, I am quite willing to let him have the last word; in that respect I am hoping to set an example to other theological controversialists.—J.M.F.)

What John Frame, in his kindly, somewhat jocular fashion, is saying is that Adams can't stand loose ends and must always try to find an answer to problems; he is a problem solver. That's why he wants to find an answer to what he calls the "so-called problem of evil." Now this inclination to find solutions to everything might be a good thing in counseling, but in theology it doesn't always work. Indeed, in the issue before us, it is clear that Adams has gone too far. There is no solution to the problem of evil (not the "so-called" problem, as Adams puts it), perhaps even in eternity. After all, if Augustine couldn't solve it, who does Adams think he is to do so?

Well, let's look at those thoughts for a moment. First, let me dispose of the Augustine argument. While I must applaud

Augustine for his rigorously biblical theological formulations in some areas, I cannot go along with him in others. For instance, he believed that baptism washes away sin. Augustine is not the final answer—Scripture is!

But enough of that. What of Frame's real objections? Well, on one score he certainly is right: I do like to tie up loose ends. On the wall of my study is an inscription that reads, "Problems are for Solving." I have no difficulty in confessing that I am anxious to tie up as many loose ends as I can—that is to say, as many as can be tied up biblically. But I want you to know that I understand and try to follow the admonition of Deuteronomy 29:29. And I hope you understand that I want to speculate about nothing that that verse prohibits. I am convinced that in my book, *The Grand Demonstration*, I have set forth nothing about the so-called problem of evil that the Scripture has not first revealed. That, then, is the issue: have I or haven't I?

Romans 9 is clear. It gives a reason why evil exists. God says that he wanted to demonstrate his nature. He wanted to demonstrate his wrath and power, and so he endured with long-suffering the vessels of wrath that he designed for that purpose. Unless evil existed, it would be impossible for a good God to exhibit wrath, judgment, and power. The same is true for the other side of his nature. Wishing to exhibit his mercy and grace, God designed the vessels of mercy for that purpose. There would be no need for mercy if evil did not exist. And, of course, God determined to bring this about, not through automatons, but through responsible creatures.

Now I maintain that that is a solution and answer to the problem raised by the so-called problem of evil. The problem may be stated as follows: How can there be evil in a good God's world? The answer? God decreed it in order to demonstrate his nature.

Of course, Frame can play the child's game of asking why, if he wishes. You know how that goes, don't you? The child asks his mommy why in response to every answer she gives. If Frame does not think that the answer revealed in Romans 9 is sufficient, he can go on asking why. "Why did God want to demonstrate his nature?" is the next in line, I suppose. But God has not revealed that to us.

Yet, God has told us why evil men exist. And that should be enough. Indeed, it is far more than most will admit. In my opinion, in Romans 9 God provides the ultimate answer that we need: he determined to demonstrate his nature in this way according to his own good reasons for his glory.

If that is not a solution to the problem, then there is none—at least with revelation as it stands at the moment. Perhaps God, in eternity, will reveal more of his mind to us, but for now he has not. But there is no mystery in all of this; God tells you why he has raised up and fitted men for wrath: for the purpose of demonstrating his nature. Come on, John, what more do you want? Do you want to get into God's mind and ask why?

Scripture Index

General Index

259

Image of God, 83
Indirect-cause defense, 165
Indirect proof. *See*
    Negative/positive arguments
Intellect, primacy of, 226–27
Irenaeus, 163
Irrationalism, 10, 102, 111,
    113, 116, 146, 163, 194,
    201. *See also* Atheism
Islam, 38n, 48, 54, 97, 110,
    121n, 195n, 213

Jehovah's Witnesses, 54, 213
Jesus Seminar, 130
Johnson, Dennis, 29n–30n
Jordan, James, xiii, 24n, 201n
Josephus, 20–21
Judaism, 38n, 54, 121n
Justin Martyr, 5, 28

Kalam cosmological argument, 110
Kant, Immanuel, 42, 51,
    69–70, 72, 75n, 105,
    112, 114, 117n, 130,
    200, 221, 222
Kaufmann, Walter, 132, 150
Keil, C. F., 131
Kierkegaard, Soren, 222
Kline, Meredith, 24n, 123
Kuhn, Thomas, 197n, 200n,
    222
Kushner, Harold, 157
Kuyper, Abraham, 7n

Leibniz, G. W., 49n, 114,
    117, 157, 159, 180n
Lewis, C. S., 69, 84, 132–34,
    164–65

Liberalism, 42n, 43, 51, 53,
    130, 153, 200, 242
Liberation theology, 42–43, 130
Libertarian freedom, 160–61
Lindsley, Arthur, 5n, 219–43
Linnemann, Eta, 132
Living with one's beliefs,
    102n–3n
Logic, 101, 104, 105n, 158,
    226, 227–28
Lordship of Christ, 4n, 6, 44,
    74
Lower/higher criticism, 132n
Luther, Martin, 183n

Macaulay, Ranald, 195n
Macaulay, Susan, 195n
Machen, J. Gresham, 131
Mackie, J. L., 114
Malcolm, Norman, 115
Marx, Karl, 222
Marxism, 130, 196, 199
Metaphysical arguments,
    105–18
Metaphysics, 32, 34
Middelmann, Udo, 195n
Miethe, Terry, 145n
Miracle, 143–47, 241
Moloch, 185
Moore, G. E., 114
Moral values, argument, 71,
    89–104, 109, 168,
    208–11
Morey, Robert, 186n
Mormonism, 42n, 54, 121n,
    213
Murray, John, 167n

Natural revelation, 5n, 22–26,
    60n, 65, 232n